HAVE YOU
BEEN GOOD?

HAVE YOU BEEN GOOD?

A Memoir

VANESSA NICOLSON

GRANTA

Some names have been changed

Granta Publications, 12 Addison Avenue, London W11 4QR

First published in Great Britain by Granta Books, 2015

A CIP catalogue record for this book
is available from the British Library.

1 3 5 7 9 10 8 6 4 2

ISBN 978 1 78378 076 1
eISBN 978 1 78378 077 8

Typeset by M Rules
Printed and bound in Great Britain by T J International, Padstow

To Ellie and Rosa,
always together in my heart

'*Ben and Luisa are going to have a baby at the end of August, what a funny little mongrel it will be.*'

Vita Sackville-West writing to her cousin Eddy,
May 1956

PROLOGUE

Nine months after Rosa's death Andrew and I are on holiday with friends. It is a sunny day and we are on a bus somewhere in Palermo. I am sitting opposite the door, daydreaming, when the bus stops. With a noisy 'whoosh' the door opens and a bright ball of light illuminates the entrance. And there she is – she has come back! She is climbing up the step, luminous and smiling, dressed in a summery frock and ballet pumps, with the sunlight catching the highlights in her hair. Of course she has found us – how could we have thought of going away without her?

I sit up in my seat, a surge of joy expanding my chest. I'm about to speak, to get up and embrace our beautiful daughter. And then suddenly the door closes and the light has dimmed again. With shocked embarrassment I realize that it was simply a trick of my sad, deranged mind.

I lean back, defeated. I have become insane, *I think.* With the loss of her I have lost part of myself.

1985

Horserace, October 1985.

One Sunday morning in autumn I showed Horserace to Andrew for
the first time. We walked up the muddy bridle path until we found the
old house sitting quite on its own, surrounded by overgrown trees and
chestnut coppice. Victorian and steeply gabled, 'The Horserace' was
built in the days when a gamekeeper would breed pheasants and run
a forge, as well as oversee shoots. So there were weathered outhouses
and rusty-railed kennels and all manner of ironwork junk spread
around a wild garden hemmed in by bluebell woods. Once the place
would have bustled with industry but now the house looked forlorn,
its blackhead bricks wearing through a pre-war coat of pink paint, its
peg-tiled roof pitted with holes, the clapperboard sheds keeling over
with persistent ivy. This was the place where my grandmother Vita
Sackville-West occasionally courted female lovers, discreetly set down

the track from her home at Sissinghurst Castle. Over decades, friends and 'secretaries' had been secluded here.

My father Ben had inherited it. He never lived there, but never sold it. He never talked about it either. I only discovered its existence when I saw him open an envelope in London containing a rental cheque from the land agent who managed it. 'Did you know I own a property near Sissinghurst?' he had asked me. He said it like one would announce an old object rediscovered from earlier years, a keepsake unkept.

No, I hadn't known. I was twenty then.

When my father died a year later, I walked the bridle path from the Castle to Horserace with my uncle Nigel, to meet the tenant I had inherited with the house. Mr Gilbert was a retired postmaster, a man of tidiness and organization, known locally as something of a hermit since becoming a widower. Dapper, timid and courteous, he called me 'Miss Nicolson' and spoke with lowered eyes. I was embarrassed by his deference, when I was the intruder. We toured the house, and in his pin-neat bedroom he caught me looking at the nests of hair trapped within a set of old fashioned hairbrushes placed on the dressing table. They belonged to his wife, he said. He hadn't moved a thing since the day she died.

Then in 1985, seven years after that first meeting, Mr Gilbert wrote informing me politely that after many happy years at Horserace he had decided to move in with his sister, as he felt they could care for each other better by joining forces. The following weeks we talked on the telephone several times, discussing his departure – the keys, the meter readings, the furniture removals. One day I called from work to check that everything was going to plan.

'Mr Gilbert?'

A strangulated croak answered, then an anguished 'Yes?'

I was anxious, and everyone in the office could hear me. 'Are you unwell?'

'I'm ... I'm *dying!*' he shouted back.

'*Dying?* What's wrong? Is someone with you?'

'Ambulance coming ...' he spluttered and then slammed down the receiver.

I tried his number again – no luck. And several more times throughout the day. Finally, that evening, I answered a call from a woman in Sissinghurst village. She told me that Mr Gilbert had died in Maidstone hospital that afternoon. He had managed to summon help by telephone.

'It turns out he had some sort of ulcer. They tried to operate but it was too late.'

'I am so sorry ...'

Poor Mr Gilbert, so suddenly gone. But with his loss, everything changed.

Horserace, so named after the field opposite where Victorian blades raced their horses, had been emptied of Mr Gilbert's presence by the time Andrew and I arrived. All his possessions had been removed, the floorboards were bare and the house felt unloved and musty. We noted all the things that needed doing: new plumbing, wiring, decorating. Like the exterior, the interior had been untouched by modernization – not my father's fault, I liked to think, more an un- spoken agreement between his land agent and the tenant that the rent would remain tiny while upkeep was minimal. The basic ele- ments were still in place; the old brick floors, the brown Bakelite light switches, the large yellow trough sink and a wood-fuelled Rayburn in the kitchen. Each of the four bedrooms contained an Edwardian basin and a small wrought-iron fireplace. Nothing had been changed for decades but that was its charm, and despite the amount of work to be done, we were optimistic. The prospect of taking on a cottage in the country felt like a godsend. It was somewhere we could make our own.

We began to use Horserace for weekends and holidays, driving down from London. It took a while to make it comfortable, but we enjoyed going on long walks to the pub and filling the house with friends, some of whom we roped into helping with decorating and weeding. One day in spring I watched Andrew play with a friend's

Andrew at Horserace, 1985.

small son in the wheat field opposite the house, carrying him on his shoulders, throwing him up in the air and catching him again to squeals of excitement.

The longing hit me, unexpectedly.

I want children. And I want this man to be their father.

But how to tell him this?

Andrew, a journalist, was twenty-six years old, while I was almost thirty. I plucked up courage over dinner in a restaurant a few months later.

'Andrew, I've got to talk to you about something. It's important,' I said tentatively. He gave me a questioning look.

'I'd really like to have a child.'

There, I had said it. I stared down at my plate. There was a pause, like a long heartbeat.

'I'd like to have children too, you know, one day,' he replied finally.

'The thing is, I'd really like to have one soon.'

As soon as possible.

'Well, that's good, I just don't want to get married.'

'Neither do I,' I said with relief.

Marriage had actually been a subject Andrew and I had discussed freely. Neither of us believed in it as an institution. My parents' marriage had been difficult and my Italian mother had fled back to Florence with me after seven years. Andrew's parents had divorced acrimoniously when he was twelve. We had commiserated with each other on our parents' difficult relationships and the effect their separations had on our childhoods and agreed that we would never have need of a document to confirm our commitment.

After the death of Mr Gilbert, Uncle Nigel invited me to stay at Sissinghurst. In the 1960s he had given the Castle and much of the estate to the National Trust, along with an endowment from my father, but retained the right to live there. He tended to invite me once a year during his season of summer house parties, or when there was something we needed to speak about. This time he added, almost as an afterthought, 'Do bring a friend if you like.'

Nigel in the Library at Sissinghurst.

9

'Thank you, I may bring my boyfriend,' I answered, struck by my own impetuousness – I had never brought a friend with me to Sissinghurst before, but then Nigel had never previously asked.

'Boyfriend?' Nigel chuckled. 'So is this the man you are going to marry?'

'Oh no! We haven't been together long. So please don't say anything about that,' I laughed.

When we arrived at Sissinghurst, Nigel showed us to a bedroom overlooking the extraordinary gardens, kept by the National Trust according to my grandparents' design. He opened a second door along the corridor – a smaller bedroom in which I used to stay when visiting as a child.

'And this ... hmm ...' he coughed, 'is where Andrew can sleep.'

He noticed my quizzical look.

'Well, for form's sake ...' He smiled, tall and patrician.

Form's sake? 'Nigel,' I wanted to say, 'no one else is here.' But I kept silent and before leaving the following day I turned down the covers in that room. For form's sake.

Andrew made a good impression that autumnal weekend. He was attentive to Nigel and questioned him about his long career in politics and publishing. They discussed current affairs. I was pleased that they got on, not least because it reflected well on me. Obtaining Nigel's approval had always made me feel acceptable. As if I had passed a test.

After I took Andrew to see Horserace that autumnal Sunday morning, I found myself alone with Nigel in his sitting room.

'Andrew seems a nice young man. Charming and intelligent. I like him very much,' he said.

From the corner of my eye I could see Andrew coming into the room. He was about to join us when Nigel, unaware of his presence, continued, 'But oh dear, Vanessa, I'm so sorry he won't marry you.'

I was mortified. 'I don't want him to marry me, neither of us want to get married,' I snapped back, anxious that Andrew might misinterpret the conversation. But on the train home he denied having heard anything at all.

*

I grew fonder of Nigel towards the end of his life. With the written word he could be benign, even affectionate. ('Bless you,' he ended a brief note about a lunch date, 'and love your uncle as much as he loves you.') But I could never reconcile the kindly uncle in his letters with the distant, artificial man he could be in person. I never got close to finding out who the real Nigel was. But then maybe no one did.

Our disagreements and rapprochements were – in the family tradition – forged through letters. When I decided to have children and live with Andrew without marrying, Nigel wrote to me: 'Non-marriage implies a parental reservation about the future. Nobody will be impressed by your audacity or modern outlook.'

I answered that 'nowadays' (we were in the mid-1980s) a third of couples chose not to be married when starting a family.

He replied: 'There is indeed a change of mood if over thirty per cent of babies born in England are born illegitimate! And that marriage is now considered a psychological trap. I dread to think what effect this will have on society if this becomes the norm. It will mean that the family ceases to be the basic social unit, and I wonder what, if anything, will be substituted for it.'

I did marry Andrew a few years later, but only after we had moved permanently to Horserace. We got fed up with having to explain that Andrew wasn't Mr Nicolson, nor I Mrs Nicolson. As we had begun referring to each other as 'my husband' and 'my wife' to save on the explanations, we thought we might as well make it real.

Once we were neighbours, I saw Nigel more regularly. Old age had softened him, but he still had the capacity to make me feel belittled and insecure. We had the occasional spats. Once I took him to task for not including Andrew and our children in the Family Tree published in a new edition of *Portrait of a Marriage*, his account of my grand-parents' marriage. The spouses of Nigel's own children and their children were all listed there, so I wanted to know why mine were not. He attempted an explanation in a letter:

About the pedigree in *Portrait*. I must say that it is very feminine of you to pick upon this one item from so traumatic and richly

illustrated a book! I cannot quite remember how it was compiled.
I must have had a hand in it because it mentions all three of
Adam's boys, and Clemmie and Flora [my cousin Juliet's
daughters]. The reason why I didn't mention your marriage to
Andrew or your two adorable girls was that you weren't married
to Andrew when this edition was published ['But I was!' I wanted
to shout] and I couldn't lie about that, or stigmatize your children
as illegitimates, though that didn't stop your great-grandmother
Lady Sackville boasting of her own illegitimacy, in fact going to
court to prove it! There is no device in typographical trees that
expresses non-marriage or bastardy, so one has to spell it out, as I
did in the case of Pepita and her children. But surely you wouldn't
have liked that?

I do like Andrew so much, and I'm so glad that you did marry
him, as I begged you to right at the start.

I always suspected that Andrew found my family exotic, probably
more so than his own. His father was a genial doctor, his mother a
beauty. Andrew and I had first met in 1984, at the Pollo, a restaurant
I frequented in London's Soho. Back then, you could get a large plate
of pasta and a glass of wine cheaply, and the place was always packed
with the young and hip.

One weekday lunchtime, my then boyfriend Steve, my second
cousin Mary and I met outside the restaurant and made our way to
one of the wine-coloured booths. A young man sat opposite, getting
out his wallet to pay the bill.

Mary seemed to know him. 'Hey, how are you?' she asked.

Andrew was in his mid-twenties, dressed in a sharp dark suit. I was
struck by how fresh-faced he looked, a better-looking version of the
young Orson Welles.

'Would you like to join us?' Mary asked.

'No, I've got to get back to work,' he answered grumpily, stuffing
the change into his wallet. He sounded irritated, as if we were holding
him up.

'See you then.'

'Bye,' he clipped.

He got up and passed us on the way out. He was tall, and walked decisively, as if he had places to go and people to see.

'Who is he?' I asked Mary curiously.

'Ex-boyfriend of my flatmate, Sue. We're friends.'

'He seems a bit tense.'

'Oh, he's all right.'

And then we ordered pasta and I didn't give him a second thought.

A few months later, in early September, I found myself sitting next to him in another Italian restaurant. I had come alone. It was the evening shift, and we were there to celebrate Mary's birthday.

I recognized him immediately. Despite his smile, my heart sank as he sat down next to me.

I'll just ignore him; he won't want to talk to me anyway.

I turned to chat to Martin, another of Mary's friends sitting to my right. But after ten minutes Martin began talking to someone else.

Now I'm going to be left staring at my plate.

I slowly chewed a piece of bread, trying not to look self-conscious.

Andrew was asking me a question. 'So how do you know Mary then?'

'Umm, she's my cousin ...' I answered tentatively, anticipating a sneer. But he was looking at me expectantly as if I was about to say more.

'Well, she's a sort of cousin,' I continued, 'a second cousin.'

Andrew was nodding.

'I mean, her father was my grandmother's first cousin. We sort of missed a generation.'

'Sounds complicated.'

I blushed as he changed the subject. 'Have you been here before?'

He's actually trying to make conversation.

'Yes, I've been here on my own a couple of times.'

'On your own?'

'Well yes, you know, at lunchtime.'

'You come to a restaurant to eat lunch by yourself?' He looked surprised.

'Yes, I do sometimes, I always work better after a proper lunch.'

'That's amazing, I'd never eat alone in a place like this!'

I thought back to the time I had first met him.

'But there wasn't anyone with you at the Pollo . . .'

'*That's* where we met! I couldn't work out where I'd seen you before. No, actually that time I'd just had lunch with my friend Geoff, but he'd had to leave quickly; in fact he left me to pay the bill . . .'

'So that's why you looked so cross?'

'Did I?' he laughed.

'Yup!' I smiled.

I was warming to him. He looked less buttoned-up out of his suit. He filled my glass with wine and my body began to relax, shoulders un-hunching as I turned towards him. I felt myself emerging out of my shyness as he responded with curiosity to what I had to say. What *did* I say? My only memory is a feeling of affinity, a rapport – we sparked off each other. I don't think we were flirting, not consciously anyway, but I can see myself sitting there at that noisy table, laughing, encouraged by his interest.

I was aware of the pretty fair-haired woman opposite, his girlfriend. I experienced a flash of envy when she mentioned that they were getting an early flight to Greece the next day. Steve and I were living together but he had pulled out of our holiday that summer – his work as a production assistant on films had got in the way. I had gone to southern Spain on my own, and felt lonely.

A few months later, Steve and I went to Florence to see my mother Luisa for Christmas. Steve was tense and moody. On Christmas Eve he announced he was going to Turin to visit a (female) friend of his. I was hurt, but part of me was relieved, as we hadn't been getting on. I went through the next few days feeling miserable and wondering what he was up to, because over the previous few years he had been unfaithful to me more than once.

He returned on the 28th, but left for London on New Year's Eve. That evening I drank a large glass of whisky and announced to Luisa that although it was only ten p.m., I was tired and going to bed. I smuggled another glass to my bedroom and drank it down in gulps, to blot out the noise of festivities in the street.

At midnight Luisa was prodding me. I woke to see her crouched close to my face. 'Happy New Year!' she was saying cheerfully.

I decided I needed to live on my own for a while, to take stock. My home, a three-storey terraced house in north London, was part-owned with Luisa – we had pooled resources and bought it after my father died. Steve agreed to move out as soon as he found somewhere else to go to.

The idea of being alone did not worry me. In fact I was looking forward to it. In any case, I wouldn't be completely on my own in the house – I had lodgers who had become friends, living on the top floor. But Steve's search for a new home took longer than expected and we shared a strange, limbo-like existence for a couple of months, like brother and sister living under the same roof.

One day Mary telephoned and said she had tickets to see Desmond Dekker play in Camden, just down the road from me.

'I'm going with my friend Clare, Andrew's coming too. Do you fancy it?'

They arrived for drinks before the concert. Steve was out. Andrew looked boyish in black jeans and a 1950s shirt bought in Kensington Market. I wore a red calf-length skirt, a denim shirt with a lot of buttons, and new, bright blue suede shoes that I was very proud of.

We stood around the sitting room, drinking the bottle of wine I had opened. I was encouraged by the way Andrew laughed at my jokes, but at the back of my mind I felt that surely, being three years older, I couldn't possibly be young or fashionable enough for him.

And then something happened in the dingy, cavernous space at Dingwalls. We were standing very close, joking about the fact that Desmond Dekker seemed to have only one famous song – 'The Israelites' – that he kept singing whenever the crowd got restless.

We were facing each other. Andrew took out a Marlboro and lit it. The flame illuminated a face I hadn't really taken in before. I found myself reaching out towards his hand, indicating that I wanted a drag. We kept our eyes fixed on each other as we shared that cigarette, slowly exhaling, passing it from lips to lips.

At the end of the gig I said goodbye at Camden underground station and walked back by myself to Kentish Town. I let myself into the house as quietly as I could. Steve had returned from seeing his friend Charles and was asleep. I curled up behind him, missing the warmth that was now so absent in our bed.

One day soon after, while I was serving out my notice at the magazine *Apollo*, the arts title that employed me, a secretary from the advertising office came upstairs to see me. It was almost the end of the working day and I was composing my monthly column, 'News from the World of Art'.

'Vanessa, there's a bloke downstairs asking for you ...' Then she whispered, smirking, 'Very dishy!'

'*Dishy?*'

I was taken aback. No one ever visited me in the office, certainly no one 'dishy'. And why was this girl, who had never come upstairs before, looking at me with a conspiratorial grin?

'Who is it?' I whispered.

For a second I thought it might be some contributor I had never met, though most of the art historians who wrote for us tended to have more hair in their noses and ears than on their heads.

'Says he's called Andrew. Shall I send him up?'

I nodded. She went downstairs and as I peered over the banisters I saw Andrew bounding up. I felt a flush of pleasure as well as relief that I was wearing a nice dress that day. And then the double relief of knowing that the editor, Denys Sutton, a curmudgeonly old bully, was out.

'Hi!' said Andrew. 'I was just walking past your office and I wondered if you'd like to come out for a drink, when you've finished what you're doing, of course.'

'Just give me a minute!' I rushed to complete the final sentences of 'News from the World of Art' and walked out to have a drink with him in a bar in Soho.

The first time I invited Andrew in after a night out, we sat on separate sofas self-consciously drinking coffee. Finally he asked,

'Would you mind if I have a bath? There's never any hot water where I live.'

'No, of course not,' I said, thinking this was just a ruse to stay over. Many years later he told me that he really *had* wanted a bath, because there was indeed never enough hot water where he lodged with friends, and he spent his life cadging baths in nice bathrooms – although he was pleased that I had presumed he wanted to stay.

We began meeting after work, going to pubs and bars, eating in candlelit restaurants. It felt like a proper courtship, having dates, waiting for the telephone call that would secure the next arrangement. I had never had a relationship like this before.

Despite being younger, he was mature and ambitious and seemed to lack the insecurity I had always identified with and gravitated towards in previous boyfriends. I no longer wanted that. I didn't want neurosis to be the thing we had in common. I liked the fact that he was a business journalist and I was an art journalist; he could understand about press trips and deadlines and features and printers and layouts. We shared an interest in film and soul music. He was reliable and good company and I got on with his friends. He animated me with his wit and galvanized me into thinking quickly in order to hone my responses. He encouraged the 'strong' part of me, the self that engaged with life and work.

At times, however, he could appear distant, distracted, tetchy, and I felt the pressure to express myself quickly and succinctly in case my slowness irritated him. When I was struggling to convey a thought or find a word, I could sense the beginning of his inattention in the set of his mouth and the restlessness in his eyes, willing me to hurry up and get to the point. He was prone to finish my sentences or ask a question and then suddenly change the subject with an interruption or a different question, as if he wasn't really interested in the answer. His attention darted around, unable or unwilling to remain still for a second before jumping on to something else. But his impatience was also stimulating. My heart beat a little faster whenever I was going to meet him.

When I was introduced to his parents I was nervous, but his

father – a retired anaesthetist – and his stepmother were kind. My first encounter with his mother was less relaxed. She was in her late fifties then, with groomed silver hair and elegant clothes. The day I met her at a family christening, I had a startling new haircut fashioned by a hairdresser in Notting Hill. I had wanted something edgy, and left with shaved sides and a rat-tail down my neck. It looked terrible. When we were introduced I felt scrutinized and very much not 'up to scratch', rather as I had felt with Uncle Nigel as a child. 'So this is Vanessa,' she said with a cold smile as her eyes scanned my body.

Shortly after Andrew and I first got together, he took me to a party at a friend's house. I went with no enthusiasm. I have never felt confident at parties, and I knew this would be no exception. I would be either checked out as Andrew's new girlfriend or simply ignored.

It was as I had anticipated. Andrew and I stood for a while in a sitting room, talking to each other, then moved to the kitchen. Within seconds we were surrounded by a group of bright, blonde, beautiful girls with names like Kiki and Caroline.

'Hi, Andrew!'

Kiss kiss kiss.

I positioned myself next to him, my smile wobbling. The whole kitchen seemed to be full of these gorgeous creatures.

They fit him better, of course they do.

Half an hour later I still hadn't uttered a word. I stuck to Andrew gracelessly, moving only to let someone pass on their way to top up their drinks. I was desperate to leave but where could I go?

I left the kitchen and found a door on to a flat roof. I sat down, leaning against the wall of the house, hoping that eventually Andrew would come and find me. It was getting cold out there, and dark. I could not go back indoors and tell him we needed to leave. That would make me seem possessive and jealous. And then I spotted a fire escape ladder leading from the flat roof to the street. Freedom! I slowly climbed down. A huge sense of relief flooded through me as I ran from the house to the underground station.

Later Andrew phoned me up and said, 'Where the hell did you get to? I looked everywhere for you!'

It was only his puzzled reaction that made me wonder whether it had been a strange thing to do.

After this I became fearful that Andrew would come to realize how flakey I could be, and leave me. So I resolved to keep hidden from him the needy side of my character. When I sensed that I was slipping into old patterns, I made excuses not to see him, claiming pressure of work or the need to do stuff on my own. I made no demands of him and he interpreted this as independence. I think it made me more appealing in his eyes.

A few months into our relationship I was having a difficult weekend. We had been out for the day and I had been quiet and withdrawn, out of kilter with myself, and him, and the world. When we got near his house I told him I was tired and going home. But as I walked to the underground I longed to turn back, to be honest for once. I craved the reassurance that everything was all right between us. I retraced my steps and rang the bell.

'Andrew, I'm sorry, I, I . . .' I was on the verge of tears.

'What's up?' he said, looking baffled. And then I realized I couldn't reveal this weak, vulnerable me. I wanted to be the witty, attractive, professional young woman I presented to him, not the fragile mess I felt myself to be sometimes.

'It's nothing.' I paused, pretending to search for something in my bag. 'I thought I'd forgotten something, but, um, I see I've got it.' I gave him a forced smile. 'See you soon!' I kissed him on the cheek and ran down the steps.

On 8 August 1986, I turned thirty. We decided to celebrate my birthday at Horserace, our new weekend, doing-it-up home, inviting all our friends. I also asked my mother to come as she was staying with me in London on her annual summer visit. We agreed that I would go ahead to set things up and that Andrea and Shaun, the upstairs lodgers, would give her a lift on the day of the party.

But a few days before the event Luisa and I had a terrible row. Andrew had arrived with his birthday present; a concrete birdbath, a scallop dish supported by grey, naked nymphs, bought second-hand in

Luisa in the London garden, early 1980s.

Brixton. Luisa announced that it was not suitable for the garden and that it had to go. She had a right to say this – the ground floor of the house was understood to be for her use. But although we shared the garden, she considered it her domain. There was no place for discussion or negotiation.

'Why can't I keep it here?' I wanted to know.

'There is no appropriate space for it,' she said coldly.

'The garden is not small. It could go near the fig tree or ...'

'It is not staying in this garden, and that's final. If you want it so much, take it to Kent.'

'But I think it would look nice ...' I wailed, blood rising. 'You never let me do anything! Andrew has given me this sweet present ...'

'It's a stupid, stupid present, he understands *nothing* about gardens.'

'Oh, and you understand everything?'

'Don't speak to me like that!'

'I'm sick of you treating me like a child! I'm about to be thirty ...'

'Well, you should act with more maturity and consideration. After everything I've done for you ...'

'All I want to do is to put the birdbath in the garden where I can see it.'

'No, it can't stay here, and it must be removed as soon as possible.'

'But that's *ridiculous* . . . why? Give me a good reason!'

Just a glare.

I stormed upstairs, picked up the telephone and called Andrew in tears. This time I was unable to conceal how I felt.

'Don't worry, we'll take it to Kent,' he said. 'It really doesn't matter.'

'It *does* matter! Why is she like this? What is wrong with her? Why can't I ever do what I want?'

The next day we drove to Kent with the birdbath in the boot of the car. I had avoided Luisa and didn't say goodbye. Usually these things blew over, and I expected to see her the following day, arriving from London with Andrea and Shaun.

The morning of my birthday was sunny and warm. We set up tables with drink and food in the partially cleared garden, and our friends started arriving. Andrew had made everything look festive, with bunting decorating the garden wall, and all the brambles – so prolific in that woodland – chopped back, grass mowed, rabbit droppings swept away. Andrea and Shaun turned up a little late, and Luisa wasn't with them.

'Your mother was in a terrible mood,' said Andrea as we embraced. 'She's so angry you didn't phone her to apologize that she refused to come with us. She asked me to give you this.' She passed me an envelope. 'Maybe you shouldn't look at it till after your party. I'm worried about what she may have written to you. She was so upset.'

I went straight upstairs to my bedroom and opened it.

'Dear Vanessa, Today you become thirty years old. For thirty years you have been "top priority" in my life and I must learn to stop you being so. Maybe a strong character like yours improves with other people's hardness and worsens with success. As a person you were much better when under Denys Sutton's whip. Now you have a kind boss, a lover at your feet, you triumph in society . . .'

'In society?' This made me smile. I carried on. '. . . But you are sharp and selfish and arrogant . . .' Her anger swam in front of my eyes, fogging all. I skipped to the bottom of the page. 'I hope that I am mistaken in my impressions and that this is a temporary phase. However, my present to my thirty-year-old daughter, whom I imagined very different, must be reduced to these admonishing lines.'

I put the letter down on the windowsill. I could hear my friends outside, enjoying the sun in this beautiful, battered place. Laughter and music floated up through the open window. Why were we always so wrong-footed with each other? Why couldn't we just be like an ordinary mother and daughter? Why all these fights? There was no absence of love. But why did I always have to adapt to what she wanted me to be?

I splashed my face with cold water and took a deep breath. I was not going to let this ruin everything. I was going to go downstairs and enjoy being with my friends in the sunshine, and celebrate my birthday as intended.

And Luisa's letter for my thirtieth birthday? Filed away, of course.

1953

I come from a family of archivists and diary keepers: the past remains with us. My grandmother Vita made her name as a writer first, gardener second. My English grandparents wrote reams of diaries and letters which my uncle Nigel published. My father Ben kept a detailed diary and journals intermittently throughout his life. My mother Luisa still keeps just about everything, from academic jottings and offprints of her articles to shopping and 'to do' lists, from old newspapers to every letter she has ever received.

Luisa's talent for archiving is, I think, what made her such a good art historian. It also left me the evidence of her mothering. Throughout her long life she has stored and filed and classified everything from the written word – books, newspaper clippings, letters received, carbon copies of letters sent – to bits of string. Supermarket carrier bags are folded neatly and placed in another bag under the sink; pens and pencils are in the top drawer of her desk; rubber, pencil sharpener and paper clips in the drawer underneath. In another compartment, old pocket diaries are lined up in chronological order, all filled with information, names of people met, appointments made. Her feelings and impressions are only summarized, never analysed: '15 July 1971: Vanessa arrived yesterday. She looks too thin.' '7 September 2010: Vanessa arrived yesterday. She has put on weight.'

Even now, in her nineties, she combs through the newspaper every day, carefully cutting out articles of interest to her. She orders them into piles according to subject: art and culture, politics, international affairs, miscellaneous. Her furniture is buried under mounds of print. She finds it hard to keep up with the task she has set herself and complains about the volume of paper but resists any offers of help. She needs to hold on to this, her main occupation. I think for her it feels like work, even if it has ceased to be a productive exercise. It gives her back her sense of self.

As soon as I learnt to write, she encouraged me to record my thoughts and activities. And when letters arrived, I followed her example and kept them all. It was Luisa who suggested I organize my correspondence into categories: 'Friends from England', 'Friends not from England', 'Cards and Invitations', 'Letters from Daddy', 'Letters from Mummy'. All these I filed in folders covered in pretty Florentine paper, fastened by leather ties. Into my teens and then twenties, letters from boyfriends were stored in a separate box, a big blue thing that I kept unmarked to avoid giving my mother the temptation to peek.

My first diary entry was written in smudgy pencil when I was seven. 'Monday, 25 November 1963. Today I went to the dentist and she put a new tortoise in my mouth.'

There is a lot about going to the dentist and my 'tortoise' retainer in those early journal-writing years. Ten years later I noted every period pain, every headache, every new pair of jeans or record, the weather, who my friends were, who was liked, who was disliked, who was fancied, what I was worried about, what I was looking forward to. As a young teenager I used my diary as a scrapbook as well – the book bulges with receipts and programmes, tickets, cartoons, chocolate wrappers, hair, cigarette ends and strange bits and pieces – 'this used to be part of my tape-recorder' is the caption to a small piece of metal.

It is largely thanks to the family habit of keeping everything that I have been able to piece together the past. Luisa's engagement and marriage and honeymoon are recorded in a large leather-bound scrapbook full of photographs and newspaper cuttings; later, when she set up house, she added wallpaper samples and sketches of how she planned the rooms.

Here are the newly engaged couple, photographed at Sissinghurst

Castle Guest

WEEK-END guest at Sissing-hurst Castle, Kent, was the future Italian daughter-in-law of **Sir Harold Nicolson** and his wife, **Victoria Sackville-West**, the poet and novelist.

She is **Miss Luisa Vertova**, elder daughter of **Professor Avv. Giacomo Vertova** and **Giovanna Vertova Carpena**, of Florence. Her engagement to the Nicolsons' elder son, **Benedict**, was announced to-day.

Met in Florence

The couple first met in Florence, where dark-haired Miss Vertova works for **Bernhard Berenson**, the art critic and writer. That was about nine years ago; since then Miss Vertova has been to England many times.

To-day she was wearing an engagement ring that once belonged to Lady Nicolson's mother. It consists of a green stone surrounded by diamonds.

Mr. Nicolson is 39 and the editor of *The Burlington Magazine*. He was for a time Deputy Surveyor of the King's pictures, holds the M.V.O.

The *Evening Standard* (May 1955) announcing my parents' engagement.
Ben's age is given incorrectly – he was forty. Luisa was thirty-four.

Castle, Ben in badly fitting clothes, stooped next to his pretty Italian fiancée, in her unusual skirt (which still hangs in her wardrobe). Their eyes, downward cast, are fixed on something – one of Vita's dogs, perhaps – just outside the frame.

They married in the Palazzo Vecchio in Florence on 8 August 1955, a year to the day before my birth. A month before the wedding there was a dramatic flurry of letters between Florence and London when a spurned admirer pleaded with Luisa's parents to prevent the marriage, recounting gossip that my father was homosexual. Luisa persuaded her parents that this made no difference to her feelings.

In fact she knew about Ben's past. He had told her everything in a long letter written almost two years earlier. To be quite sure that the letter would not fall into the wrong hands, he had sealed the envelope with wax. It is an extraordinary document, both as a personal confessional and as a piece of social history.

17 November 1953

Dear Luisa

Now you have given me all the encouragement I needed, and I have only to go ahead. As you write so imaginatively, there was a danger that we would be sailing in too calm waters, and that we must brave the ocean. Of course we may get shipwrecked in it, but unless we face the storm, we shall never have a chance of reaching the other shore. Your letters are so sympathetic to me that I have the feeling that whatever I say (provided it is true) you will face with your usual combination of wisdom and sensibility.

My sexual life for fifteen years (it hardly existed before) has been almost exclusively homosexual. I do not know how much you realize of the temperament of the homosexual but I can tell you that those of my type – that is, the congenital type – can never be rid of it, whatever they do. Even very conventional people who hesitate to break the law (of England, that is) and pine for a normal, domestic life, and even achieve outwardly a domestic life with a wife and children, are always to some extent sexually dissatisfied. The urge towards people of their own sex is ineradicable, and is either sublimated, which does not solve the problem, or indulged in, which in nine marriages out of ten ends in distress or disaster. It has to be regarded as a physiological fact, like having too large a nose, or flat feet. It is unfortunate, but there it is, there is nothing to be done about it, except to try and deal with it in the most sensible way.

You may well wonder why it is that, this being the case, I should wish for anything else but a succession of boys throughout my life, until the desire goes. I can give you the answer. As I say, there are two types, the congenital homosexual, and the person who transfers his attachment, from men to women as a young man. The first group to which I belong, can be divided into two subdivisions: the promiscuous and the 'faithful', call it what you like. Of these subdivisions, I belong to the second. Like any heterosexual I am by nature faithful to a lover. I do not 'have casual affairs', I 'fall in love'. I am not in the least interested in stray relationships, only intimate ones of this kind. And during the last six years I have twice fallen a victim to passion. The first as you know, was with David. It ended after eighteen months in disaster, because David belongs to the promiscuous type, and would not stick to me. I blamed him at the time but now that I feel nothing more for him but a vaguely friendly attachment, I do not blame him any more. It was in his nature for him to be like that, and it was foolish of me to wish him, or expect him, to be anything else. The second was with a young man called Michael Rutherston who, as you know, killed himself in my flat in March of this year. Michael was utterly heterosexual and there was never any question with him of a physical relationship. He knew I was in love with him but we managed to sustain an unspoken, mutual affection which was entirely satisfactory to both of us. I know since his death he loved me more than any other man, but this was not enough to prevent his suicide. The question remains, whether if I had spoken of my love for him I could have done anything for him, to save him. But you can imagine, I cannot bring myself to answer in the affirmative. There was a moment when I might have spoken, but it passed. If I blamed myself for

letting that moment pass, my life would not be worth living. So I
don't.

Of course one never quite knows oneself, and I may for all I
know surprise myself again. But at present I feel that I am no
longer capable of the particular kind of passion I had for those
two people – that kind of experience seems to now be a thing of
the past. One may survive that but a third time and we might be
shattered. Besides: I have no further need for the exciting
preliminaries. I could no longer put myself in the correct frame of
mind for it to happen again. For passionate love is not like a fever
in that sense: it does not occur at all unless one is in a suitable
frame of mind for it. So now perhaps you can understand why I
do not relish a life of sexual experiences with young men. I have
more or less worn myself out emotionally for them, and I have
not, what other people of my kind have, the power to take sexual
matters light-heartedly, like getting drunk or going to the cinema.
I think it might be true to say that the promiscuous homosexual
remains a practising homosexual all his life; but the homosexual
who loves and suffers from love, ends by wanting other things
more; things like serenity, companionship, a slower, more
profound and more lasting love, and children. It is, if you like, a
refuge for the suffering he has had.

Of course I can never see myself ceasing to be attracted by
young men, and enjoying their company, but I cannot see myself
ever becoming emotionally involved with them again. And I think
in my particular case I could achieve complete serenity of mind in
marriage. Especially with the binding link of children. And that is
another subject: my passion for children, which is very intense.

So now you see why I hesitated to tell you all this, and waited
for some more encouragement from you before coughing it all
up. I was put in an awkward position: on the one hand, I could not
wait so long that our relationship might have reached such a point
by then that the news would have come to you as an appalling
shock (this would have been cruel); on the other, I did not dare
tell you too soon, in case you would be put off.

With every letter I get from you, Luisa, I warm towards you, as much for the sentiments that you do not express as for those you do. I cannot get over how shrewd you are – a shrewdness which is based on generosity of spirit, never a hint of unkindness. I was especially impressed by your capacity to divine the sad relationship between my mother and myself: and the way you express it, is so absolutely RIGHT. I quote from you: 'I noticed she made a touching effort to find a ground of mutual understanding with you and yet the two of you seemed to me to speak two different languages. I admired her for the good will she put into it and felt sorry for you, who could not help her.' Yes, you have it exactly, except that my own attitude towards her is too selfish. I feel sometimes I do not make enough effort towards her. My defence is that the effort required is superhuman! I suppose because I am so closely involved with her. With a thoroughly unsympathetic stranger, I could have no difficulty whatever in being agreeable.

Your loving Ben

Luisa has often recounted to me the difficult relationship Ben had with his mother Vita, his unease and irritation whenever she was present. But I never heard either of my parents mention the young man who killed himself in Ben's flat. All I know about him now is from a newspaper clipping that does not explain the circumstances of his death.*

Did Luisa have any inkling of Ben's homosexuality before reading Ben's 'confessional'? The one letter I have not come across is her reply, and I can only surmise its contents from the reaction expressed in subsequent letters from Ben. It seems that she responded by revealing her own romantic history; her failed engagement with a Sicilian medical student and her rejection of other admirers. The fact that Ben does not refer to Luisa's 'acceptance' of

---

* *The Times*, March 21, 1953, states: 'The recent death at only 25 of Michael Rutherston deprives the artistic and literary world of the fruition of bright promise.'

his homosexuality indicates that she did not attach too much significance to it.

Having revealed his hand, Ben's letters became more passionate, as
if some barrier had been unblocked, loosening things up between
them. But Luisa was cautious in announcing the engagement. By early
1955 Ben was becoming impatient and began putting pressure on her
to do so. Despite being in his early forties, he had a reckless boyish-
ness about him. Finally unable to contain his excitement any longer,
he announced the marriage to his family and friends before she had
given him permission to do so.

'Oh dear! Oh dear!' he wrote in fear of her disapproval. 'What a
clumsy, gauche, unsubtle, insensitive character I am! I have let the cat
out of the bag, as you will know by now ... if I grovel, kiss your feet,
kiss your big toe, buy you a pair of comfortable shoes, never dare look
at you above the ankle, keep my head bowed permanently, shall I be
forgiven?'

Of course she forgave him.

Ben and Luisa getting married. Vita stands behind.

Just before the marriage Luisa sat down to write to her prospective in-laws:

I always felt in Ben a mine of gold, but hidden under so
many layers that sometimes it was very difficult to get the gold up
to the surface. He keeps his treasure behind a lot of locked doors:
what gives me confidence is that once the door is unlocked, it
stays open. I don't have to worry that it treacherously might close
itself and oblige me to unlock it again. Only I cannot pride myself
of having already opened all the doors. From now on – and in all
the years to come – you can always rely on my wish to make Ben
as happy as it is in my power to make him.

Vita agreed that Ben had 'gold' in his nature. 'I see that you understand him,' she responded, 'and understand also that he is by no
means a simple character; but there is a very deep fund of gentleness,
loyalty, and affection in him, which I am sure you will bring out as few
people could.'

At the same time, Ben was replying to a letter of congratulations
from his old university friend Jeremy Hutchinson: 'I remember writing to you when you got married and sending you my blessings.* I
never knew that our roles would get reversed. I thought I was a bach-
elor for life. But by marrying in middle-age I seem to have the best of
both worlds: freedom behind, security ahead; freedom when I wanted
it, security when that became desirable.'

The London house my parents lived in after their marriage was just
around the corner from the Victoria and Albert Museum. White stucco,
five floors, two columns framing the front door. It was a wreck when
they bought it. The rooms were divided up into cubicles, with pipes and
partitions and peeling paint. Damp and mould had seeped into its fabric.

By the time Luisa embarked on transforming it into an elegant
residence, she was pregnant. She spent much of the next nine months

* In 1940 Jeremy Hutchinson had married the actress Peggy Ashcroft.

A page from Luisa's scrapbook.

in a state of nervous exhaustion, shouting at the builders whom she felt didn't respect her because of her Italian accent. She in turn thought them lazy and incompetent. 'All English workmen ever want to do is drink cups of tea,' she complained from then on.

Once the house was in order, she took it upon herself to become an exemplary wife and expectant mother. As my birth date came closer she turned to her aristocratic relatives (by marriage) for recommendations and on their advice ordered the layette from Harrods and booked a maternity nurse at nine guineas for a six-day week.

Luisa's labour was fast but difficult. Ben, as was the custom in 1956, remained at home, waiting for the doctor to ring. He wrote a letter to his sister-in-law Nori describing his first meeting with me the following morning:

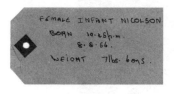

The new human being was brought in for its father to gaze on its exquisite features. It had a little label on its cot inscribed 'Female Infant Nicolson'. It weighed 7½ lbs.

It has everything that a human being should have: eyes, feet, even nails on its feet. And it has a digestion and a heart and small muscles. It is hideous. Its little Chinese eyes play around, but they see nothing. I think they are the hands of a gentleman aged 300 seen through the wrong end of the telescope. Its head looks as though it had been pulled out sideways. It has blotchy patches on its face. But it is an angel. You know, what is so extraordinary, Luisa and I adore this hideous creature! I brought Luisa books to read in hospital but she will not open them. She will gaze on the Female Infant.

What is so strange is that one thinks one can get past the purely instinctive facts of life, by intelligence. But when you are brought up against these facts, you behave as human beings have always behaved. You pace, you shout with pain, you love a hideous creature, like a man and a woman in a goatskin in a cave.

Yours ever,

Ben

35

At Sissinghurst Castle, Vita composed her letter of congratulations.

My darling Luisa,

You may imagine my feelings when Ben suddenly rang last night. How glad I was for you! You have been spared nearly a fortnight, and Vanessa Pepita showed a commendable and most unusual haste in making her appearance. I look forward to seeing my granddaughter as soon as is allowed, which I believe is not until you leave the hospital. Ben will let me know, I hope.

Tanti baci darling, from your very loving,

Vita

Vita and Harold were fond of Luisa but were acutely aware of her foreign-ness. Not in a negative way, but aware of it all the same.

'Feeling so happy about Ben and Luisa,' Vita had written in her diary on their wedding day. 'Not only is she perfectly suited to him, but I like her being a Florentine ...' Eight months later she was writing to her cousin Eddy. 'Ben and Luisa are going to have a baby at the end of August, what a funny little mongrel it will be.'

Vita was herself a 'mongrel'. She was the granddaughter of a Spanish dancer called Pepita, muse to aristocrats, poets and ambassadors, who had a number of illegitimate children with Lord Sackville, but that's another story.* (My parents thought of calling me Pepita as a first, rather than a middle name, but came to the conclusion that I might be teased because of it.)

'Here is Vanessa Pepita,' my grandfather Harold jotted in his diary on the day of my birth, 'a citizen of the world. Ben was so relieved that there was not an inch left for regret that it was not a boy. I was disappointed. But I do not wish to be rude to Vanessa so soon after her arrival.'

Not an inch left, but for Harold there had been. Regret for what? For the absence of a male heir (my older cousin Juliet being female too) who would go to Eton and Oxford and inherit a title and prove worthy of the privileges bestowed on him? As I read those words I feel the loss for what I should have been, and sympathy for this female newborn, already touched by disappointment.

Unable to breastfeed ('I had no milk for you'), Luisa relied on the maternity nurse to feed me. The rigid regime imposed by Miss Richards involved bottle-feeds every four hours and strict sleeping times. This, Luisa told me years later, struck her as 'terribly English and organized and unemotional'. Finally, on coming across the woman attempting to potty train me at a few weeks old, Luisa lost her temper. Miss Richards was sacked and the baby care was taken on by Rosetta, a large and cheerful Neapolitan employed as housekeeper, and a sequence of au pair girls.

With Rosetta's help Luisa gave small dinner parties, writing down everything she had served in a notebook for fear of producing the

---

* See *Pepita* by Vita Sackville-West, 1937, and *The Disinherited* by Robert Sackville-West, 2014.

same menus twice. She had never had to prepare food before her marriage, as both the villa she grew up in, and 'I Tatti', home of the American scholar and collector Bernard Berenson where Luisa had lived and worked, employed a cook.

She taught herself the basics by consulting *Il Talismano della Felicitá* ('The Talisman of Happiness'), an Italian cookery book given to her by her mother as a wedding present. She bought olive oil from the chemist, the only place it could be found in England at that time, and introduced the cut of *osso buco* to the local butcher and to the intellectual elite of London. In her housekeeping notebook she copied down recipes and cooking tips. 'Oxtail stew: make gravy with "Bisto". A "Shepherd's" dish uses remains of a joint – mix with gravy and fried onions. Ribs of pork are good with apple sauce and sprouts.'

Ben and Luisa in front of 11 Thurloe Street.

In the arms of my au pair Giovanna, Sissinghurst Castle, June 1957.

At first, Luisa was content with her life. She was able to leave me with Rosetta and the au pairs to finish a book she was editing for Berenson. When I was six months old she was writing to Harold and Vita: 'I have been very, very busy at the Phaidon Press and next week I go to Florence with the layout of the 1,200 plates of BB's [Bernard Berenson's] book to submit it for the author's approval.'

She followed this with news about various English friends, then, 'I end with the nicest news that I can give you: I am so deeply happy with Ben and Vanessa and I think they are happy with me. And I wish you both endless pleasure out of your interesting and exotic trips.'

But it soon became clear that the decision to abandon her career and her family in Florence had come at a cost. In Italy she had been her own person, a respected art historian, rather than just 'Mrs Benedict Nicolson'. Increasingly, she felt isolated and trapped. She tried to be a 'good wife' but was shocked by the arrogance of some of Ben's male friends, and found it hard to understand their British sense of humour – watching them get drunk and say 'we belong to Herod's club' (i.e. they didn't like children), or being made to leave the men to smoke and drink as soon as dinner was finished, while she was expected to make small talk about home furnishings and fashion with the wives in another room.

There was something else going on. Ben had begun to withdraw. He was spending more time out of the house at his office or in his club, excluding Luisa from the professional and social invitations she would have liked to attend. When at home he disappeared into his study and responded with increasing coldness to her attempts at communication. Little remained of the intimacy they had once been able to share. By 1958, three years into the marriage, Luisa was going back to Italy for long periods of time. Ben was also leaving home as much as he could.

17 June 1958

Dear Luisa,

No tragedies yet, but at breakfast this morning Vanessa came in as usual, glanced at your chair, said 'Mamma' and then shook her head. She then came up to me and again said 'Mamma?' and again shook her head. I could not help meeting her sad eyes with sad ones. It was like a Victorian subject picture in the strong rooms of the Liverpool Museum.

Yours ever,

Ben

At the same time, Harold was writing:

My darling Luisa,

Eileen [the current nanny] tells me Vanessa is well and cheerful. It seems that when she is going to bed she has a passionate desire for conversation, and although most of her sentences are not comprehensible in any language, such words as 'shoe', 'slipper' and 'dog' recur frequently. Evidently, with her powerful literary heritage Vanessa realizes that the basis of style is economy of language.

I gather from Eileen that Ben will be back next week. Meanwhile there is nothing for you to worry about and I hope you are relaxing from the strain of being a housewife, a mother and married to a man of charming character, but difficult temperament.

Yours ever,
Harold

PS Eileen tells me that Vanessa had missed you both very much after you had gone away. She consoled herself for the absence of her mother by the presence of her father, but when the latter also absented himself from her life she started to look around the empty rooms and whimpered slightly. The sorrows of youth are, however, transitory and (although Eileen was too polite to say so) Vanessa has now forgotten that she ever had parents at all.

The light-hearted joke that concludes Harold's letter indicates a darker reality. While Luisa was away, Ben plucked up the courage to express what he could not say to his wife's face.

30 June 1958

My dear Luisa,

I am afraid, owing to my constant silences, that you may not be aware that I am just as much as you fully aware of the difficulties of our marriage, and so often during the last two years it has been on the tip of my tongue to say 'Luisa, we cannot go on, we must separate.' I have not done so, not out of cowardice, but out of feeling that we must go on making the effort, we must go on exploring every possible road to success. But the whole time I knew in my heart of hearts that our problem was not a physical one, it is psychological. We are simply not suited to each other temperamentally, this is a fact we have to face, and we both know it already, although we have not been able to admit it even to ourselves.

Luisa left it a few weeks before replying from Florence:

My darling Ben,

   I suppose I still owe you an answer to your 'nasty' letter asking
for a divorce. I hoped no answer was needed and the subject
would never be brought up again. I shall begin with the practical
side. I cannot divorce. Our Italian marriage does not allow
divorce. You may desert me but we cannot divorce. I hope that
when you wrote the 'divorce letter' you were just in a self-
indulgent mood and did not think at all.

She then wrote to her father-in-law, pleading with him to make Ben
face his responsibility as a husband and father. She confided that Ben's
increasing withdrawal, both physically and emotionally, was causing
her insurmountable suffering. Letters darted backwards and forwards
between London, Florence and Sissinghurst. I have them here, straining the box files they are contained in.

A decade before Ben married Luisa, he had fallen in love with a
clever and ambitious boy called David and they had become lovers.
(This is the liaison Ben referred to in the letter he sent Luisa before
they became engaged.) There is a familiar story to be told about the
affair: an older man excited by the freshness and enthusiasm of a
younger one; a boy attracted by the attention and maturity of an
older man. Their relationship was intense while it lasted, but Ben
was aware from early on that David was less besotted than he. 'I
watch you strutting around the bedroom like a lion tamer and realize you feel nothing for me,' he recorded in his journal shortly
before David left him. 'I shall never recover.' He drank heavily and
for a short time became reckless and self-destructive. It's no wonder
that Harold and Vita had been relieved when he announced his wish
to marry a woman with whom he appeared to have so much in
common. To hear that the marriage had collapsed within three years
was a blow.

'Vita and I will mind dreadfully if this marriage goes wrong,'
Harold wrote back to Luisa. 'It is not only that we have grown

extremely fond of you and hate the idea that you may be rendered miserable. It is also that we have the deepest respect for you and are so grateful for all you have done for Ben. You have by your intelligence and tact been able to improve his whole attitude towards life, to get him away from his untidy surroundings, and to bring out all that is best in his nature and mind. We are profoundly grateful for this human achievement and dread that Ben may relapse into his former life.'

Vita's letter followed close behind. 'We never thought otherwise than how much in harmony you and Ben seemed and what a wonderful change you had worked on him.'

'Poor Luisa. Poor Ben. Poor Vanessa,' she then wrote to Harold (who lived in London during the week), 'my sympathies are torn to rags between the three of them.'

Nothing was resolved, and soon the letters between Luisa and Vita returned to a less perilous subject – that of gardening.

Sissinghurst Castle, Kent
3 September 1958

My dear Luisa,
   It is difficult to tell you what is wrong with your hydrangeas without knowing which kind they are. There are two different kinds and they require different kinds of pruning. I don't know whether you pruned yours at all but if so you are quite likely to have cut off the branches which would have flowered this summer. If I were you I would leave them severely alone and see if they flower next year. I love your expression about whether they needed each other, but the answer is No they don't; even a solitary one ought to flower without encouragement.
   Your loving Vita

My parents continued to cope with their failing marriage by escaping from each other as often as possible. Luisa extended her sojourns in

Vita's desk, photographed in June 1962. The framed picture next to Harold is one of me with Luisa playing the guitar that was used to illustrate an article in the *Tatler* called 'Impact from Italy' on Italian women in London.

MRS. BENEDICT NICOLSON (*Signorina Luisa Vertova, of Florence*) *with Vanessa*

IMPACT ON MARRIAGE: *More Italian women are marrying Englishmen than ever before, perhaps because more Englishmen take Italian holidays and more Italian girls come here to finish, study or work* au pair.

Florence and Ben took every opportunity to go on lecture tours and research trips. When they were back in London they were sweet to me, but they often left me with the nanny and housekeeper for weeks, sometimes months at a time.

This went on for another two years.

The small nursery school I attended was run by the wife of a family friend, Priscilla Gore. Luisa was away a great deal at this point, and Ben was coming and going. The box files and folders from that time are full of letters to Luisa from Rosetta, Mrs Gore, Rosy the Austrian au pair (replacing Eileen, who had become pregnant and left in disgrace). They were keeping her up to date on my well-being and trying to discover when she was intending to return. Rosy sent lists of my food. 'Vanessa is eating well. For supper she had nine biscuits and two glasses of milk. I hope you are coming back soon. Every evening before going to sleep Vanessa says: "Mummy will be coming back tomorrow, won't she?"'

Mrs Gore wrote: 'Vanessa is very mischievous with the other children (which is excellent). But I am sure that she needs you. She is too intelligent and sensitive to be looked after too long by someone else and I don't really think the Rosys of this world are gentle or

With Ben in Thurloe Square gardens, just after my second birthday, August 1958.

understanding enough. I think being an only child is sometimes quite hard.'

From New York Ben made another attempt to persuade Luisa that a separation was the only viable option.

I am very sorry it has got worse and worse during the last two years and will get worse as every year passes. And I even seem to divine that you also are prepared to come to this conclusion. I think that if we were to remain together for the next thirty years or however much we have left of life, we would only be condemning ourselves to perpetual distress. I also think that if the argument were used that we must sacrifice our own feelings for the sake of our child, it can be countered with the argument that it is not good for a child to witness its parents unhappy together. No doubt something of our own distress has already entered Vanessa's spirit. There is no withholding it from her whatever we do; we have got to resign ourselves to the necessity of damaging her.

Trying to hold my parents together. At Sissinghurst, Easter 1960.

I shall make provision for you and Vanessa. I shall try during these next weeks to think of a sensible plan. Luisa, it is all my fault and I do not want you to take any blame for what has happened on yourself. When the news of our separation breaks I shall make it clear to all our friends that it was I who failed as a husband, not you as a wife. I know you also in the end will be happier alone than with me – I have caused you untold distress throughout our married life because you have wanted something I have never been able to give you – the love that a husband should give – and I am conscious of my inadequacy in this respect. All I can say in my defence is: if you haven't got it in you to love your wife properly, you can't simulate it.

Around Christmas 1961, Luisa finally agreed to a divorce. The house in South Kensington was put up for sale. Luisa found a place Ben could rent in Holland Park as well as a flat for herself in Earls Court, but it took a while to divide their property and sort things out. Ben came over every so often to visit me in Luisa's flat. I remember cowering in my bedroom listening to Luisa screaming at him and the sound of things crashing on to the floor as she threw them at him.

Ben never raised his voice. He felt guilty.

My first really vivid memory. I'm five, sitting at the dressing table in my mother's bedroom looking into the mirror straight ahead of me. My legs are dangling off the stool but I can see myself quite clearly. It's a pretty mirror with three sides so that if I position myself right I can see my front and my profile at the same time. Staring intensely back at me is a strange, unsmiling girl wearing a yellow wig. Her dark eyebrows are frowning.

The wig sits awkwardly on my head, like a nest of straw that has landed upside down in the wrong place. It doesn't look or feel right. I can see the black hair underneath. It's hot and itchy. I was so excited when my father arrived. I'd told him I wanted blonde hair like Cinderella and he'd got his pocket diary out and written something in it and then he came back today with the wig all wrapped up. But I don't look like Cinderella. I look like her ugly sister.

I can hear shouting.

Mummy screams at Daddy. That's what happens whenever he comes round. Daddy never shouts back and that makes her even crosser. Either she won't talk to him or she gets really angry and then she shouts and throws something. Usually it's a plate or a vase, and it crashes onto the floor and stays there until he is gone, and I'm not allowed to move before she has cleared it up in case I hurt myself. It's not fair because if I break something by mistake I get into trouble. But she breaks things on purpose.

I'm staring and staring at the little girl in the mirror. Maybe if I stare long enough she'll turn into Cinderella. If I sit very still and I'm very quiet Mummy will stop shouting.

She is still shouting.

The little girl's eyes in the mirror are narrowing with concentration. I peer right in to look at her and she comes towards me. I move backwards and so does she, looking at me sulkily from under the wig. I'm thinking: *That little girl is ME. That is what I would see if I wasn't me but I was someone else looking at me.* Thinking these things makes me feel funny so I pinch myself. Then I look down and see a lipstick lying on the dressing table next to my mother's hairbrush. I pick it up and twist the case until the whole lipstick is exposed. I draw a hard line over my mouth and the lipstick breaks off.

A door is slamming. Something crashes against it as it closes. Daddy has left and Mummy is crying again. I quickly stuff the broken lipstick into my pocket and wipe my mouth with the back of my hand. My eyes glance up at the mirror and I see a mass of red smeared over the bottom half of my face. I can hear my mother walking along the corridor towards the bedroom, the clicking of her heels on the wooden floor. There is a horrible feeling in my tummy. My eyes fix on the round doorknob slowly turning. I rip the wig off and jump behind the floor-length curtains by the windows, my heart beating furiously.

Mummy comes into the room holding one hand over her forehead. She looks around the room. 'Vanessa?'

I'm crouching behind the curtains, biting my lower lip. I can just make out the shape of her. She stands very still, turning her head slowly to look around the room. She leans down to pick up the wig and holds it close to her breast like a baby.

'Vanessa?' Her voice is very quiet.

She kicks off her shoes and sits heavily on the bed. She sighs. I'm frightened that she is going to see that the lipstick is missing. She drops her head onto the pillow, pulls up her legs and lies in a coiled up ball on her bed, staring at the floor. She is still clutching the wig in her arms.

Slowly I come out from behind the curtain, climb onto the bed and curl up behind her. She hasn't noticed the lipstick stains on the pillowcase yet.

London
5 January 1962

Cara Mamma,

I finally went to the divorce lawyer today. I'd been given the name of this man months ago, but I kept hoping that somehow, at the last minute, our marriage could be saved. Unfortunately it's now quite clear that I shall gain nothing if I refuse to agree to comply with Ben's wishes to end the marriage (as I did in 1957/8). I can't cope with being treated like a stranger by my husband, in my own house. He constantly puts me in embarrassing and humiliating situations. I try and maintain some decorum but I am exhausted with trying to keep up appearances. Ben's parents and friends all reassure me that there is nothing to be done: he should never have got married, he will always be unhappy, he is a loner, the only solution is to let him go his own way. Maybe once he is released from any sense of obligation in my regards, he will become kinder and more spontaneous. I think there is already some sign of that, since I agreed to go to the lawyer.

So – this morning I went as far as the City, to the lawyer's

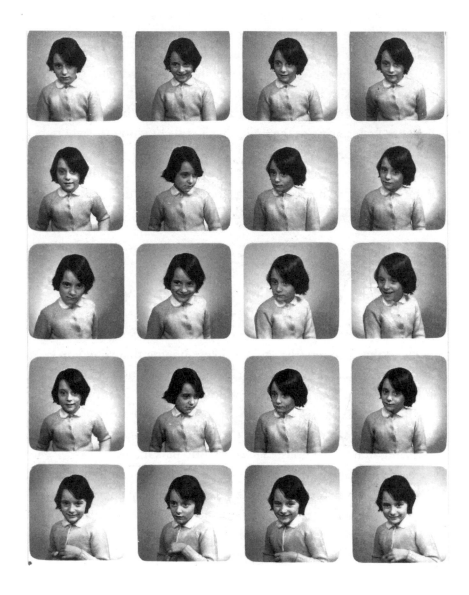

office. It's a strange part of London, so masculine, so unwelcoming: a strange mixture of richness and squalor. From a window in the waiting room I could see the skeleton of a new office building that was coming up – they were already at the seventh floor. The view from the other window revealed the demolition of the enormous walls of Cannon Street station. Crumbling down and demolished, like my poor, doomed marriage.

The lawyer was elderly and very upper class. I am worried that he may be too much the old-fashioned gentleman and not fierce enough. I want to do everything in an amicable way but that requires Ben's lawyer to be equally gentlemanly and I fear he is modern and aggressive. At least my avuncular lawyer made me feel comfortable and I wasn't ashamed to reveal the most intimate details of my marriage. We shall see, we shall see.*

Luisa asked my nanny – it was Hilary now – to take me to a photographic studio and get some pictures taken for my new passport. I was nervous and when the lady asked me to smile at 'Mummy' I was cross. 'She is not my mummy,' I answered. But I liked Hilary and she did eventually get me to smile by making funny faces by the side of the camera.

In August 1962 my suitcase was packed and the day after my sixth birthday I was taken to Heathrow clutching Teddy, and handed over to an air stewardess as an 'unaccompanied minor'. I was proud of that badge pinned to my blouse. It made me feel special. I did not know then that it was the first of many such badges I would collect on trips from Italy to England and back again.

Luisa's cousin Vannozza came to Pisa airport to collect me and took a photograph of the plane I had arrived in. Later on, with a blue cross she marked the spot where the air stewardess was leading me to passport control. She drove me to the house by the sea that she and her family had rented for the holidays. I promptly caught chickenpox

* I have translated Luisa's letter from the Italian.

and spent two weeks in bed. When I recovered Luisa picked me up from the seaside and took me to her parents in Florence. I thought we were staying for an extended holiday, but we were to live there for the next four years.

Pisa airport, 9 August 1962.

1962

With Nonno Giacomo and Luisa, Boboli Gardens, Florence, 1962.

Like many little girls, I loved playing mummy. Teddy, rag doll Sally and Mary were my babies and I spent a lot of my time making sure they were well cared for. Luisa regularly found me asleep on the floor next to my bed where I had tucked them in. 'But they need more room!' I replied when she remonstrated with me.

Nonno and Nonna (Grandpa and Grandma) lived in a ground-floor apartment facing the monumental gates into Florence's Boboli Gardens. I considered Boboli my playground and over the years got to

know every corner. I loved the fat Bacchus sitting on a gigantic turtle in the grotto near the entrance; the elegant pond surrounded by statues; and my favourite: the stone dog at the end of an avenue. I never gave him a name apart from '*mio cane*' (my dog) but whenever possible, I climbed onto his back, stroking his head, whispering secrets into his cold stone ear.

Nonna's bedroom was at one end of the apartment, Nonno's at the other, near the kitchen. Nonna was constantly sewing: making, altering and mending clothes. Luisa worked.

Day after day she sat at the desk behind the closed bedroom door (her bedroom was the largest) engrossed in writing and editing books on Italian painting. I understood that I should only disturb her when I couldn't hear the typewriter clacking. So I spent a great deal of time standing silently with my ear to the closed door, straining to hear, my hand hovering over the brass doorknob. Sometimes I ignored the sound and came into the room anyway, clutching a drawing or story I wanted to show her, unable to wait. I would creep up behind her and linger. And she, in her distracted way, sensed my presence and turned around, her fingers poised over the keys. Occasionally she smiled, but at other times I was dismissed with a 'Not now, Mummy's busy,' accompanied by an irritated wave.

I so wanted to be good, to make her happy. But I sensed the sadness beneath the surface and had to accept that she regularly withdrew, whether for reasons of work or ill health. When she came back to me she often seemed preoccupied by her thoughts, as if looking through me. But she could also be engaged, interested, loving, even playful – recounting myths and stories, teaching me things, drawing pictures, inventing games. And then I adored her, and my confidence grew, only to be squashed with the unreliability of her attention.

Nonno could also be moody. He had the appearance of a Roman emperor, and his manner was imperious. I learnt to keep out of his way as his sympathy towards children could wear thin if they became too boisterous or demanding. His name was Giacomo Vertova but outside the home everyone called him *Professore*, despite the fact he had not taught for many years. His job teaching Philosophy had come to an end with Mussolini, which had made him an extremely angry man.

Around 1930, his disregard for fascist rulings on education, particularly the imposition of enforced religious teaching, had led him to resign from his job. Not only was Giacomo anti-fascist but from an early age he had rebelled against his father's dogmatic Catholicism. He felt that religious sermons would interfere with his efforts to awaken philosophical thought in the young minds of his students.

His decision to give up teaching proved to be a wise one, as Mussolini gradually imposed the *tessera fascista* (fascist party membership) on every working Italian. A citizen who was not a member of the Italian Fascist Party could not officially have employment. The police still kept an eye on him, but fortunately Giacomo's views did not get him into serious trouble with the authorities because he did not publish anything or entertain 'dangerous people' at home.

Nonetheless, his dislike of Mussolini and resentment over the loss of a career he had loved ran deep, and two decades after peace was declared he was still unleashing his fury. As a child, I took his tirades as just a bit of fun.

'*Fai Il Duce, Nonno,*' I would plead and he would indulge me by strutting around impersonating the old leader, head thrown back, pretending to bark orders, insisting that women shouldn't be allowed to wear trousers or go horse riding, that all schoolbooks should be rewritten and that no one should marry anyone who was '*verde o rosa o giallo*' ('green or pink or yellow'). Recently I watched an old newsreel of Mussolini giving a speech from a balcony, hands on hips, chin jutting forward, shouting his imperialistic nonsense in that breathless, staccato style, and there in front of my eyes I saw him turning into my Nonno, playing the buffoon, making me laugh as he got into his stride.

Sometimes he would transfer his mimicking skill to the subject of organized religion, making fun of clerics, pretending to give a sermon in nonsensical Latin in a chanting, whining dirge. The more extreme he became the more I giggled, while my Nonna raised her eyes to the ceiling, having heard it so many times before.

But despite his free-thinking liberalism, Nonno Giacomo could be intolerant and authoritarian. He had been a strict parent to Luisa and her brother Gino, and overly indulgent to their younger sister Nori.

'When we shared a room as children he would come and say goodnight and throw himself on top of her like a lover,' Luisa would later recall, still trying to come to terms with her sense of estrangement. I never heard Nori's side of the story because the sisters did not get on and Luisa cut off all ties once their parents had died.

Very occasionally I spent the day with Nori. She was elegant and glamorous and it made a change to leave the bookish atmosphere of my home for the modern apartment she shared with her doctor husband Ario in a different part of Florence. Nori could be coolly remote, but Luisa would explain, 'She is sad because she cannot have children.'

'Let's play hairdressers,' Nori suggested one day.

I loved having my hair styled. One of my mother's rituals after breakfast was brushing my hair and fashioning it into two plaits fastened with elastic bands. On top of these she tied ribbons – light blue cotton for school, blue velvet at weekends, red velvet at Christmas, pink or gingham check for other special occasions. That day she had brushed my hair into a single plait down my back.

When Nori pointed at the chair in front of her dressing table mirror I went to it enthusiastically. It was a treat to be allowed to look at all the perfumes and potions she had laid out on the dressing table. I picked up a necklace lying in a bowl, savouring the weight of the pearls in my small hand.

Nori was tying a linen towel around my neck.

'So what style would the Signorina like today?' she said cheerfully as she got the scissors out of a drawer.

It was over in a second. One minute my aunt was talking about the latest hairstyles and the next – *snip* – the long plait of hair had fallen to the floor. The horror of that brisk slice through my hair. An intake of breath. I was looking in the mirror at her standing behind me and she was saying, 'That's better, isn't it?' as she arranged my hair into the semblance of a bob.

I was speechless.

'Why are you sulking now?' she asked impatiently.

Luisa arrived to collect me shortly after this had happened and found me still glued to the chair by the dressing table. She spun round to face Nori. 'How *could* you do this?'

'A bob is far more fashionable than long hair. I've done her a favour, can't you see that?' Nori bristled.

'But you had no *right*!' Luisa spat out as she picked up the plait from the floor and led me outside.

Decades later while visiting a now elderly Luisa in Florence I opened a drawer in a desk to look for an envelope. My heart jolted. Nestling in tissue paper amongst the drawings and letters I had sent from boarding school was that thick plait of hair I had been parted from half a century ago, the faded blue velvet ribbon still holding it in place. Back in England I found the self-portrait I had drawn to send to my father, showing him my new haircut.

I'm pleased to see I'm smiling.

Luisa's upbringing was strict, with clearly defined rules. In the 1920s, Italian rural life remained feudal. When she was six her parents left Florence with their children to join the extended family in a large villa owned by Luisa's landowning uncle on the outskirts of the city. He was the *padrone* of a large estate farmed on his behalf by the local *contadini* or farm workers. Rigid routines imposed by her parents and the German governesses they employed meant that Luisa envied the relative freedom enjoyed by the farmworkers' children. She was restless and easily bored.

By the time she left school in 1938 she had decided she wanted to be an artist, but going to art school was deemed highly unsuitable for a girl from a 'good family' as it could severely compromise her and Nori's chances of making a satisfactory marriage.

'An artist? Out of the question!' was her father's reaction.

Whatever his dislike of fascism, he was equally adamant that no daughter of his was going to sit in a room drawing naked men and mix with 'immoral bohemians'. The study of the history of art was acceptable to him, and that is what Luisa chose to do.

Her years at Florence University during the war, however, were not happy. Most of the young men and teachers were absent, and food was scarce.

'Ah, I will never forget the cat lung floating in a grey, watery sauce that was served up in the university canteen,' she recalled years later.

Luisa's life under German occupation as a twenty-two-year-old was grim, dominated by the daily struggle to get food for family and friends. Her fluency in the language she learnt from her governesses brought her into contact with the occupying forces. She has spine-tingling stories of how her quick-witted decision to divert German soldiers from searching a monastery where she knew partisans were hiding meant hundreds were saved. Another time she pretended her younger brother Gino was 'feeble minded' (her words), to prevent some officers from taking him away to interpret for them. At one point during the occupation she was required to report daily to Fascist headquarters as she was told she was 'under suspicion'. Eventually she discovered that a girl, jealous of the attention Luisa was receiving from an admirer, had made up some stories and reported her to the authorities.

As for art history, it was not an ideal subject at this time: the great collections were inaccessible, important works of art had been hidden away and the bronze doors of the Baptistry and other monuments were covered with sandbags to protect against bombs and bullets. Luisa switched first to archaeology, then to Greek literature, and achieved a First for her thesis on the origins of tragedy. When she was awarded a postgraduate scholarship to study in Germany – Italy's wartime ally – her father began introducing her to well-connected people in the hope that she would find work closer to home. Some anti-fascist friends took her to meet Bernard Berenson, who was in hiding in the outskirts of Florence, a target for the Nazis as both an American and a Jew, with a covetable art collection. Two years later, restored to his villa I Tatti and hearing that Luisa was ill and malnourished, he asked the same friends to find her. She arrived

Luisa with Bernard Berenson.

at his door with a fever and was slowly nursed to health. She remained at I Tatti, engaged as Berenson's assistant, until her marriage.

My father Ben had studied with BB (as he was known) before the war. In 1944, he travelled through liberated Tuscany as a British Army officer, determined to find his old mentor. He arrived at I Tatti, where the door was opened by a liveried butler, as if little had changed. It was here that my parents met and connected over their love of art history, and their admiration for Berenson. Twelve years on, at my birth, my parents asked Berenson, then already over ninety years old, to become my godfather. When I was introduced to him, as a baby, I apparently peed in his lap.

Luisa had been romantically involved before she met my father. She had embarrassed Nonno by breaking off an engagement to Pippo, a Sicilian medical student whose brother Vito was married to Maria, her cousin. Luisa had met Pippo on the occasion of Vito and Maria's engagement party. Luisa was sent with the chauffeur to collect him from the station.

'He was so handsome,' she would remember wistfully. 'And on the way back to the villa he asked the driver to stop in front of an expensive patisserie. I thought he was buying something for the family, but when he got into the car he said, "this is for you," as he presented me with a beautifully wrapped tray of delicacies.' She was smitten.

The war meant separations and an engagement only made bearable by the long letters they exchanged. Just before they were due to marry, Pippo took her on an ill-fated trip to Sicily. Luisa could not understand why he never introduced her to acquaintances they met in the streets of Palermo. She was expected to wait patiently behind him until he was ready to end his conversation and move on. And when she spoke to him about the books she planned to publish, he made it clear that once married she could write as much as she liked as long as she was not paid, for a woman working for money reflected negatively on a Sicilian husband's ability to provide financial security. Then one night Pippo pounced on her. 'He forced himself on me,' she told me years later. 'He was not in control of his sexual appetite.'

She broke off the engagement, resolving to devote her life to academic pursuits.

We took our meals at the Pensione Annalena, the small hotel above Nonno and Nonna's apartment. Every lunch and dinner the four of us climbed up the grey stone steps to the second floor and sat at our table in the corner of Annalena's dining room. Our napkins, held in place by coloured rings decorated with pictures of Florence, were kept on our reserved table and changed twice a week. We ate whatever we were presented with; usually the standard fare of pasta or soup followed by roast or grilled meat with potatoes and vegetables. Fish was served on Fridays, a day I dreaded, and pudding usually consisted of a plate of seasonal fruit.

The dining room was small but often busy, and this provided some distractions. I clocked every change of guest, especially children my age, and what the waiters, Irma and Giuliano, were up to. I never saw them dressed in anything other than their uniforms: Giuliano in black trousers and a white jacket with gold buttons, Irma in a black dress with a small apron pinned to her chest. She was a plain woman, probably in her late thirties, with a lower jaw that jutted out beyond her upper lip, and unruly black hair that escaped from the clips she used to contain it. Who knows what Irma's story was, where she came from, whether she had a family, and what she did when she was not working. I presume she wasn't married. But these questions didn't occur to me then. For me, as a child, she existed only in the Pensione. The dining room was Irma's stage, and she covered every part of it. I marvelled at the way she weaved around the tables, plates balanced along her arms, aware of everybody and what needed to be done. She was the star of the restaurant, unlike Giuliano, who spent most of his time loitering, especially when a table of guests included a pretty girl. Hands clasped behind his back, he would lean on one leg and then the other, chatting in his broken English, infuriating the diners who were trying to attract his attention.

'He's a good-for-nothing idiot,' Nonno bellowed with predictable regularity while I shuffled on my hard wooden chair, feeling hungry, waiting, hoping no one could hear.

After a very brief and unhappy stint at an exclusive private school for rich Florentine girls, followed by a year or two at 'Miss Burbidge's English School', I was sent to St Michael's, now known as the International School of Florence, whose motto is 'Believe, Achieve, Succeed'. This was much more fun. Every morning we sang three national anthems: English, American and Italian, reflecting the three nationalities that made up the student intake. I was truly trilingual, speaking Italian at home, English at school and American in the playground. I celebrated Halloween in October and *Carnevale* in February. I liked school and made friends. At the end of the day the school bus – American style – delivered us home. It would let me out in the lay-by next to the Boboli Gardens entrance, and I would shout 'goodbye' to my friends before crossing the road to Nonno and Nonna's apartment.

It's 5 October 1964: I am eight years old. As usual, I climb out of the school bus clutching my satchel, ready to walk across the road to that familiar front door. Suddenly there is a noise like a roar and I am hit, hard. A woman screams a strange cry, muffled, as if through water. When I finally manage to open my eyes I am on the ground surrounded by worried faces.

'Where's my satchel?' I panic. I have to find it. My homework is in there and to lose homework is a punishable offence. But I can't feel my legs. A man in a white coat is picking me up.

I think quite calmly that I am going to die. There is a lot of blood and I feel weak and faint. I am vaguely aware of hearing a woman crying. I think it's my mother. Then I am on a trolley in an ambulance with my mother sitting by me, looking agitated. It occurs to me that I must say goodbye to her – and then I close my eyes, and as I drift in and out of sleep I hear a siren wailing through the streets.

I hate the hospital. The nurses are unkind, the ward full of noisy kids, staring at me. I crave silence and solitude. A little boy in the bed next to mine whimpers constantly until one of the nurses tells him that she will cut off his tongue if he doesn't shut up. It works. My head hurts, everything hurts.

I have been run over by a motorbike coming round the corner at high speed. As well as a blow to the head, I have a broken nose and injuries to my back and my right leg. I find it hard to turn over in the hospital bed, and I am desperate to be discharged. Finally I am allowed to go home and convalesce. Luisa moves out of her room and I am allowed to sleep in her big, comfortable bed. Meals arrive on trays, as do decorated letters from all the children in my class. I am read stories and given a new doll.

Best of all, Luisa invents a game which from then on becomes the standard amusement when I need to be distracted. It involves hiding a small present in her bag – a new set of coloured pencils, perhaps, or a colouring book – followed by a question.

'Have you been good?'

When I nod vigorously she begins chanting and waving her hands over the bag. '*Abracadabracadoo*, let's see what you can do ... Now, I wonder if the fairy has left you something?'

She rummages around until a treat emerges in her hand. It is magic.

Every so often there won't be anything for me in the bag, and she says, 'Oh dear, the fairy hasn't left you anything this time!'

I know that the present depends on my being good.

I also believe her when she says that the white marks on my nails represent the lies I have told, the size of them relating to the size of the lie. However much I try to be truthful, these little white marks appear like dreadful stigmata. I become obsessed with them. Slowly it dawns on me that maybe the white marks reflect my bad thoughts. How can I censor the resentments and jealousies that come into my head? They just arrive, and then it is too late, another white mark is forming. In the end I have to accept that there will always be evidence that I am not – and can never be – a perfect child.

From left to right: Luisa, Nonna Giovanna, Nonno Giacomo (behind sofa),
Nori and Vanessa.

Ben was a loving, if absent, father. A whole year or more might pass between our meetings, but affectionate letters and cards would arrive and be stored in my 'Letters from Daddy' folder. Around Christmas and birthdays he might tell me to look out for a parcel, although sometimes the present took ages to get to Florence, or arrived broken. There was the saga of the toy typewriter, something I had repeatedly asked for. I wanted a typewriter like my mum, so I too could write 'books', but she wasn't happy about it when it finally came.

12 September 1963

Dear Ben,

The typewriter arrived but I had to pay 35/- custom duty on it. However, Vanessa was thrilled. Unfortunately, when we tried to use it, it typed all the letters on the same spot so we had to give up the attempt. I enquired among the toyshops in Florence. They have Italian typewriters for children, they cost 16,000 lire and seem to work. I have packed your present up and shall bring it back to London. Vanessa wanted to keep it even though it didn't work but that does not seem sensible. You can give it as a Christmas present to Nigel's children and pay me 16,000 lire for an Italian one.

For Christmas I suggest you send her books. Maybe Homer, or stories from King Arthur's round table.

The following summer Ben wrote to me:

Dear Vanessa

It is lovely to think that you will be coming to London soon and that I shall see you again at last. I want to take you to Sissinghurst and other places. We'll have a little motor car and drive about together. I am so excited! It is so long since I saw you, I have a dreadful feeling that if I saw you in the street I wouldn't recognize you! I haven't seen a photograph of you since the one Mummy sent at Christmas. I am sure you have changed again and now look even more grown up. I shall have to get used to a new Vanessa altogether! You will find me much the same. I have not got bigger, or smaller, or thinner, or fatter, or cleverer, or stupider. I don't feel as if I've got older but I suppose I must have.
    Much love and kisses,
    Daddy

PS You will have an extra present waiting for you – do you remember what it is? The one you should have had last year. I have made sure the letters work on this one.

'I hardly recognize you!' he said every August as the air stewardess handed me over.

Then we'd go back to his flat for the night and the following morning I would be sent off to those friends with children who were willing to help out, or be put on the train to Staplehurst to stay with my cousins at Sissinghurst Castle. Timetables of pick-ups and delivery were devised and the arrangements sent to Luisa in advance for her approval. She still has them. One ends: 'you will be entirely relieved of her until I deliver her back on the 14th of the following month.'

The summers were long. The custody agreement in their divorce specified that Ben would have me during August, but where was I to go while he had to work? This was under constant discussion, as was the amount of time I should spend at Sissinghurst Castle. It became part of Luisa's most protracted, most focused campaign.

In June 1962, six months after my parents agreed to divorce, my grandmother Vita died. Luisa presumed that Ben's inheritance would mean a generous alimony. But Ben decided to sell some of the land and property he inherited around Sissinghurst Castle in order to help his brother Nigel with the significant sum of money required 'to hand over the whole property to the National Trust in good condition and with an adequate endowment'. As compensation for Ben's donation of £10,000, a lot of money in 1962 (the five-storey house in South Kensington was sold for less that same year), Nigel offered Ben the permanent lease of a cottage within the grounds called the Priest's House, sometimes referred to as the 'dining-room cottage' because Vita and Harold had taken their meals there.

Ben worked out that once it was transformed into a self-contained cottage it could be let for about £300 a year, a sum Luisa could receive and have deducted from the final settlement of the alimonies. Luisa was not happy with this, anticipating problems with tenants and upkeep that would cause the income to be unstable. Neither was she pleased with the suggestion that the cottage could be a place for me to spend the holidays, with one or other of my parents. Letters were exchanged between London, Sissinghurst and Florence, trying to reach a solution.

Sissinghurst

My dear Luisa,

Vanessa must always feel that she has a welcome here. I know that you want her to take pride in her English half-parentage, and so do we. It is better that she should associate that part of her life

68

with Sissinghurst than with a flat in Holland Park. It is for that reason that I suggested, soon after my mother's death, that you or Ben should take over the dining-room cottage here as your own, so that Vanessa could come here with either of you whenever you wish. That idea didn't work out, but the best alternative would be if either of you brought her here at least once a year, to live with us and our children just as if she belonged here.

Yours ever,
Nigel

Luisa answered immediately saying that she saw only two alternatives, 'if we want to reach a lasting peace between us'. The first was to return the endowment Ben had made to the National Trust. If that was not possible she made clear that:

Sissinghurst must be provided with a housekeeper, who knows that one single and one double room are always at our disposal and we only need to tell her who is coming and when. You should not feel that you must be there to entertain us, as long as there is a housekeeper to feed us and look after us; and we should not require you and the children to be there.

As you know, Ben meant to tie up some money for Vanessa's education, but could not dispose of any capital having given what he could dispose of to you for Sissinghurst. This was quite enough of a sacrifice. I hate quarrels but only fools accept to be paid with sheer good words. Indeed, it would be a pity if Vanessa were to discover in her own uncle the embodiment of the worst British image abroad: that of people whose talk is all goodness and virtue while they push the poor foreigner out of business. I promised to bring up Vanessa as a good British subject, loving her father and his family. I have miraculously succeeded so far; some day she will discover by herself that her father is an eccentric; it would be worse if she discovered that her uncle was an exploiter.

My very best wishes,
Luisa

An 'exploiter'! In response, Nigel appears surprisingly measured, at least at first. He points out that Sissinghurst Castle and farm were left outright to him and that Ben had agreed to contribute to the endowment in order for the National Trust to accept the property. He also explains that the sale of his London house was earmarked to pay for his children's education.

> From this you will see that I cannot repay Ben what he gave me for putting Sissinghurst in order, even if he asked for it, which he doesn't. It is his contribution towards saving for the nation a house and garden which our parents created. He made this contribution willingly, and he does not now regret it. No conditions were attached, but I voluntarily suggested that Ben might like to have the Priest's House for Vanessa. This offer was declined by you. In later negotiations with the Trust, when they were anxiously trying to find other sources of revenue from the place, I suggested the Priest's House might be let. The National Trust would get the rent, not me. But now I find that my offer has been converted by you into £300 worth of hospitality which I owe Ben!
>
> Do you really wish your quarrel with Ben to embrace his whole family? Do you really want to charge me with cheating, when all I did was to accept for the interests of Sissinghurst and all it means an offer which my brother made voluntarily to me, and from which neither you nor Vanessa suffer in the least? If your answer is that you do wish to quarrel with me over this, then for heaven's sake don't let it harm your child. Let her come here this summer, and be received in the friendly spirit of my last letter to you, to which you have replied in such dreadfully mercenary terms.
>
> Yours ever,
> Nigel

Despite his generous words, he was reluctant to have me come to Sissinghurst at all. I found this out, years later, from the correspondence filed away at Sissinghurst between Nigel and my second godfather, John Sparrow.

7 April 1965

Dear Nigel,

Luisa was at I Tatti, with Vanessa, who is a delightful child.

She is worried about Ben's plans – or lack of plans – for a summer holiday. Sissinghurst is, from Vanessa's point of view, so obviously much the best holiday place – and Luisa thinks that Ben has some claim on it for her (Vanessa I mean) for holiday purposes. I must not interfere in family affairs, and am myself only interested as V's godfather and a friend of both her parents. I promised I'd do what I could!

Best wishes,

John

Nigel replied immediately.

About Vanessa. There is a slight froideur between Philippa [Nigel's wife] and Ben. They are not each other's sort of people, although there has never been anything approaching a quarrel between them. He is sweet to her, and she takes infinite trouble about him, just because their relationship is not naturally sympathetic. But Vanessa is one cause of this feeling. Philippa thinks her a spoiled child, and she thinks that it is very wrong of Ben and Luisa not to tell the child that her parents are divorced, as it will be all the bigger shock later. Philippa also thinks that the presence of Vanessa might spoil our own children's summer holidays, since she does not really get on with other children, as we found last summer when we took them all down the Thames from Oxford to London. ('Oh Vanessa, you must come on deck. Windsor Castle has just come into sight.' 'I don't want to. I've seen it before in a photograph.')

Anyhow since getting your letter I've had another talk with Philippa, and she agrees that Vanessa should come here for a week in August, unless there is measles or no nanny or some other disaster. I'll tell Ben this as soon as he gets back, and if you are writing to Luisa, please mention it too – but not the bit about Philippa and Ben or Windsor Castle.

Yours ever,

Nigel

When I did go to Sissinghurst, I was apprehensive. I dreaded the moment when Nigel would deposit me in my aunt Philippa's sitting room after the uneasy car journey from the station and leave us in awkward silence.

Philippa was beautiful in a groomed and coldly immaculate way. She was like an English version of my Italian aunt Nori. I can picture her clearly, sitting in the small sitting room next to the 'drinks' room, the gold packet of Benson and Hedges at her side, placing her cocktail down on the table as I approach. I am six, seven, nine, eleven, it's always the same scene. I stand there worrying about whether I am supposed to kiss her in the way I would Vannozza and the Italian relatives, or not. When I get close she smiles stiffly and picks up my hand.

'Darling, look at your nails!' she exclaims in her aloof, cut-glass voice. 'Hasn't your mother ever told you how to keep them clean? And you shouldn't bite them. I know what you need.' (I received a manicure set from her every Christmas for several years.)

Then my cousins Adam and Juliet appear, clattering down the wooden stairs, bright and blonde and bantering. What did they make of me, their dark, mongrel cousin? I can imagine Nigel taking them to one side before I arrive. 'You must be kind to Vanessa when she gets here, you know she is so very shy. Make sure you are nice to her ...'

Nigel and Philippa did not have much to do with the daily grind of childcare. This responsibility was left to Shirley, nanny in charge of little Rebecca, my youngest cousin. Shirley kept an eye on us as well. She made sure we were ready in the morning and took us to the dining room for breakfast, where chipolatas and bacon prepared by Mrs Staples, the cook, sat under domed dishes on hot plates. Conversation was not required at this time of day, as Nigel liked to have his toast and cigarette in peace while hidden behind *The Times*

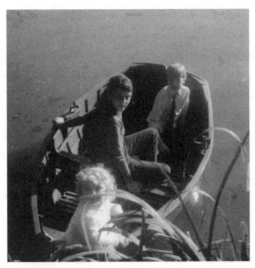

In a boat on the lake at Sissinghurst with Rebecca and Adam, August 1965.

and Philippa was absent, taking her breakfast upstairs in her bedroom.

Lunch was a more intimidating affair. Nigel sat at the head of the long oak dining table and, if there were no guests, I was placed next to him. The chairs were like the atmosphere, stiff and uncomfortable.

'So Vanessa, what books do you like reading?' Nigel might ask. A reasonable question, but all the books I loved that came to mind – *The Princess and Curdie, Little Women, Ballet Shoes* – seemed instantly inadequate and childish.

'Umm, I can't remember, I think ... maybe ...' I would mutter bashfully.

'Surely you must know which books you like! Ha!'

That little snort of amused derision haunted me even as an adult. When he responded in that way I would feel I had said something unforgivably stupid – which I probably had, out of sheer trepidation. Unease about being thought 'dull' or a 'bore' – unforgiveable sins for the Nicolsons – permeated my visits, although now I see that Nigel, too, was shy. He was just as self-conscious as I was.

The sense of falling short, of being second best, of failing to do what was desired or expected, was with me from very early on. I hadn't realized until now that this was actually documented in my family's letters. After one weekend with Vita and Harold, Ben wrote to his mother, 'our visit to Sissinghurst was a success but I wish Vanessa could be more natural with you and Daddy as she is with us. I can't understand this coyness, it is most depressing.'

I was only three years old.

As an older child I became less shy with Hadji, as my grandfather Harold was known in the family. He appeared to have got over his disappointment in my gender and sent me sweet, affectionate cards addressed to 'Vanessablessa'. I answered them in a mix of Italian and English.

'Dear Hadji,' I wrote from Florence in 1963, 'I am about to start school again. Mummy bought me a new satchel, a new pencil case and shoes, all blue. She says you know French better than Italian but you can read: *ti mando un segnalino e tanti bacini* [I send you a bookmark and lots of kisses].'

Hadji and Vanessa at Sissinghurst with Tony King-Deacon (Hadji's nurse) and the architect Francis Pym, September 1964.

By the time I was eight or nine, poor Hadji had become frail, his sense of fun diminished. He was still mourning Vita years after she had died, and his sudden fits of weeping were unsettling. Years later, when Nigel complimented me on my 'control' at my own father's memorial service, it occurred to me how painful Hadji's outbursts must have been for him to witness.

Sissinghurst
17 April '66

Dear Ben,
    No real news from here. Daddy shouts at the visitors to the garden, who respond with startled amiability. But it is getting a problem. On Polling Day, I drove him to the village to vote, and gave him a lecture beforehand about not shouting in the Polling booth. He promised faithfully not to. We got there. He made his cross (in the wrong place, so I got him another voting slip). He then, relieved by the fulfilment of his civic duty, started yelling. 'OH, OH, OH, OH, OH – poor me, poor me, poor me!' It was all most embarrassing.
    Yours ever,
    Nigel

At the end of August I would be back in Florence, and because Luisa's long research trips continued (she went away to America, to Mexico, to England), it was Nonna who looked after me much of the time. Nonna was not demonstrative but she was a calm and gentle presence, a welcome contrast to Nonno's irascible character. If I was not at school I would wait until Nonno had gone out and lead Nonna to the sofa in the library. And perform. I sang and danced and, with the help of dressing-up clothes and my toys as props, I become the heroine of stories I invented or had read in my books. The fact that Nonna was often distracted by her sewing helped – I was able to express my imaginative world without worrying that she was assessing my performance. I could just 'be'.

When we went out, we linked arms as we walked along the street, Nonna and I. In the summer months we might only get as far as the bar on the corner of Via Romana, where the old man piled extra ice cream on a cone, '*cioccolato e limone*', which I licked with concentration, worried in case a scoop might topple off. I had a system which the bar owner was aware of: the *cioccolato* had to be put on first so that I could push it down into the cone with my tongue, once the lemon was finished. (Still now when in Italy, I feel a pang of childish disappointment when the lemon is applied first and I know I won't be able to enjoy the chocolaty biscuit at the end.)

At other times we set off to do errands, perhaps to collect a piece of jewellery Nonna was having altered in one of the shops huddled together on the Ponte Vecchio. If there was time she let me linger at the window of the toyshop on the way home – it displayed enormous dolls and carnival clothes, and although we never bought anything it was enough to look and admire.

One rainy day we waited to cross the road near the bridge when a car screeched to a halt to let a pretty girl pass. The good-looking young driver was smiling but as soon as Nonna and I began crossing behind the girl he accelerated, sending us reeling back into the puddled gutter.

'Get out of the way!' he gestured, his face twisted with disgust as he sped off.

'Why did he do that?' I asked Nonna, perplexed.

'*Eh bé, gli uomini sono strani,*' she sighed. 'Oh well, men are strange.'

It was as if the knowledge that something bad was going to happen was with me from an early age, like a spell or something etched into the palms of my hands. I didn't have a name for it, I simply felt it as an underlying dread of something inevitable and beyond my control, always under the surface of things, worse for my not knowing what it was going to be.

And then it happened. When I was nine years old Nonna was taken to hospital.

After weeks of nagging, Luisa agreed to take me to see her. It was upsetting to see Nonna in that unfamiliar bed. She was trying to smile but I could see that she was in pain. She could not even raise her head to look at the drawing I had spent all afternoon colouring for her, so I put it on the bedside table and waited for her attention. She hardly spoke. I looked down at her hands folded on the bedspread. An old woman's hands: veined and mottled. I was going to tell her about the story I was saving up to perform for her once she was home, the one about the good and bad sisters, but Luisa interrupted with 'say goodbye to Nonna', and we had to leave. I did not want to say goodbye. I wanted to pass her the familiar purple dressing gown hanging on the back of her door and walk her out of this place that smelt of the dentist.

'*Voglio la Nonna*,' I wailed as we left the hospital.

But I wanted the Nonna I knew, not this old lady with watery eyes. One night Luisa heard me crying. I could not stop. She came to my room and Nonno followed. At that moment I was crying not so much because I missed Nonna but more because I didn't want to have to go and stay with Luisa's cousin Vannozza and her children again after school.

'I want to stay at home!' I sobbed.

'How could you be so selfish when we are all so worried about poor Nonna?' they answered, incredulous that I could be so unreasonable.

So I learnt that at times it was better to avoid the truth if it meant being told off. The next time I was upset because I did not want to be sent away again I said it was because I wanted Nonna back. Which was the truth, of course, but not the whole truth.

25 May 1966

Dear Ben,

My mother's agony goes on and on. She now has a night nurse as well as a day nurse specifically for her at the nursing home. Now the gangrene has started in the second leg as well. She does not recognize me. My father copes but occasionally has some

hysterical rages. I am very frightened about the future. Please
could you find out if a boarding school in England could take
Vanessa a year early in September.

    Yours,

    Luisa

Nonna did not recover. I only discovered that she had died weeks
after the event. No one would answer my questions.

'Is she better now?' I kept asking. Luisa and Nonno would look
away.

I never tired of nagging.

'*Quando torna la Nonna*? When is she coming back?'

Then one day Luisa blurted it out.

'*La Nonna é morta.*'

What? How could that be? When did she die?

'A few weeks ago.'

We were sitting on the sofa, the one Nonna always sat on to watch
my performances. I looked at my mother, trying to take in what she
had said.

'Now why don't we play that game?' Luisa continued. 'Let's see if
the fairy has left anything for you. I'm sure she has, you've been a good
girl. Get my handbag, it's on the chest of drawers in my bedroom.'

I got up silently to get the bag and brought it to her.

'*Abracadabracadoo.*'

But I didn't want to play the game any more. Finding the drawing
book gave me no joy.

After Nonna's death, Nonno's cantankerous moods worsened. The
meals at Pensione Annalena were never much fun now that his explo-
sions of rage had escalated into something more frightening. We
avoided him as much as possible but there was no escape at mealtimes,
when Nonna's chair sat empty and Nonno ranted.

'*L'ai uccisa!* You killed her!'

It was late July and the room was full of holidaying hotel guests
pretending not to look. My cheeks burnt with shame.

'Please ... don't ...' Luisa whispered under her breath, as the accusations got louder and more intense.

'Hello everyone!' he announced to the room of disconcerted diners. 'This is my daughter. Take a look!'

A few guests gave us sideways glances.

'This ... this woman you see here ... she killed her own mother!'

I wanted to vanish from the room. I turned away from my raving grandfather and weeping mother and spotted Irma the waitress, standing immobile in the centre of the room. She was holding our plates of food, looking horrified. I darted her a look of such pleading and misery that she put the plates down on a side table and rushed towards us, gently helping my mother out of the chair and beckoning me to follow her into a private room at the back of the Pensione. She settled us down and brought us our meal. It was an act of pure kindness, but neither of us touched the food Irma placed in front of us. I sat in that strange dark room wondering what to do.

I had seen my mother sad, I had seen her distant and preoccupied, but I had never heard her cry like this before. An internal voice was telling me to offer her some comfort, hug her maybe, but I felt coldly detached. The reality was that I felt nothing except a longing for this to be over, for someone to explain how I was supposed to behave.

Luisa and I left our home after that. We went to stay with Nicky, who had been Berenson's companion, and her sister Alda, until I was sent to England and boarding school a few weeks later. I didn't see Nonno again for two years. In the residential home run by Irish nuns just outside Florence he was unrecognizable, cutting a pathetic figure as he sat hunched in an armchair next to his metal-framed single bed. I stood awkwardly in the school uniform I had put on to show him.

'*Che bella signorina inglese,*' he said with a gummy smile.

His sunken cheekbones made him seem like the oldest person in the world, ancient and defeated, buckled in on himself. The life force had escaped from him like the air of an abandoned balloon.

Nonno pointed at the bed and I sat down uneasily while Luisa remained motionless by the open door as if we were just popping in. She couldn't wait to leave. Nuns in white habits bustled along the corridor. There seemed to be nothing left to say so I passed over the oranges we had brought him and he picked one out of the bag. He held it in his hand while I looked at my mother for reassurance and then he passed it back to me.

'By the time this fruit becomes rotten, I shall be dead,' he said.

And so he was.

1991

Ellie and Rosa aged four and two at Horserace.

My children meant – and still mean – everything to me. After my first daughter Ellie was born, nine months after my thirtieth birthday, I looked into the cot at the little creature with the crumpled face and jet-black hair and felt the most overwhelming sense of love and purpose I had ever experienced in my life.

Two years later Rosa arrived in the same delivery room. Unlike Ellie she was plump and bald. I was so tired, and this time I worried that I felt nothing for my baby. Back home, I talked to the health visitor about it.

'Relax, you just need to rest,' she said.

And then, a week later, it happened.

I gave Rosa a bath in a large washing-up bowl and then enveloped her in a towel. As I distractedly kissed the top of her head, it came like a flush of warmth – that intense feeling of love and protection, and with it the same promise made to Ellie, that I would do everything within my power to make her life as happy and safe as possible.

My girls aged four and two: so different, both in looks and character. Dark, restless Ellie, fair, dreamy Rosa. Ellie liked wearing trousers, Rosa pretty dresses. Ellie enjoyed attention and distractions, Rosa was happy to play on her own. I frequently got cross or bored but I tried to be a 'good-enough' mum, engaged and present. No secrets, no atmospheres, no pretence. I worked part-time on an art and antiques magazine, but on my days off we went on picnics or visits to the zoo or the park. Andrew worked long hours on a newspaper but took over early in the morning at weekends so that I could catch up on sleep. And at weekends we would leave London and go to Horserace, to enjoy some country life.

One day we were crossing a busy road in London. I had taken Ellie by my right hand, and Rosa by my left. I was looking right, towards the traffic.

'Come on, we can go now,' I said, still looking right towards the momentarily empty road.

I tried to start walking but Rosa was not budging.

I turned to find her standing motionless, looking far away, as if a pause button had been switched on. I tugged at her hand. She stood still for another few seconds, and then she came back to me.

'Come on, dreamy girl,' I smiled. What a funny child.

I am sitting in the kitchen with her 'All about Me' book on the table. I have found it, like a forgotten treasure, in a drawer of her desk, and I have brought it downstairs to savour it once again. She was four years old, and had just started school when she asked for my help to fill it in.

I read out the questions and wrote down her answers.

Favourite toys and games: my hippo, dressing up.

Favourite stories: Sleeping Beauty and Spot.
Favourite songs and rhymes: 'How much is that Doggy in the Window?'
Favourite TV programme: Sesame Street.
Things I like doing: painting, stickers, going out to tea, gardening with Dad.
Best friend: Steph.
Pets: Tiffy.
What makes me happy: Swimming.
What makes me sad: Not going swimming.

At five and seven, Rosa and Ellie were both at the same school and seemingly settled. We had made a permanent move to Horserace, deciding it was a healthier place to bring up children, with those fields in front and woods behind. Andrew was making a beautiful garden out of the remnants Vita had left. We joked that soon it would resemble a messier version of Sissinghurst, with woodland weeds – and sure enough, a number of times we found a Japanese tourist or two lost within it.

Andrew and I were married, after all those years of saying we wouldn't pander to society's expectations. Somehow it had gradually dawned on us that it was something we wanted to do. We got a dog, and later a cat. We did ordinary things. Trips to the supermarket and the playground, children coming over to play. I organized birthday parties. On family holidays the girls made scrapbooks. We had become like the families I envied at my boarding school, all those years ago, even though I was far from a perfect mum. 'I don't bake cakes,' I once said pompously to the mother who asked me to contribute to the school fete. But I did my best, and produced a disgusting confection which, incredibly, got sold.

No, I was not perfect. But I had achieved ordinary life and security within my own family, and found a kind of peace.

Occasionally Rosa seemed distant and in a world of her own. But she was gregarious and a great character, known for making funny comments and voicing exactly what was on her mind. One Christmas when Uncle Nigel asked whether she had liked the book he had given her, she answered truthfully, 'No! I wanted to throw it in the fire!'

I told her off, but was secretly amused by her candour.

She had a lovely teacher called Mrs Mahon who did everything to encourage creativity. Her classroom was an Aladdin's cave of hanging mobiles and sculptures and crazy things the children had made. One afternoon she took me to one side.

'I am a bit worried about Rosa.'

Rosa? My happy, sunny girl?

'Why?' I asked, bemused. Was she being naughty?

'I think she may be suffering from petit mal absences.'

'*Petit mal*? Absences? What does that mean?'

'It may be an idea to get her checked by your doctor.'

I made an appointment with our GP and reported Mrs Mahon's concerns. 'I don't understand. I thought she was just a bit dreamy. What is "petit mal"?'

He looked serious as he scribbled something in the medical notes.

'It's a form of epilepsy,' he said, looking up, 'like a temporary disturbance of the brain caused by abnormal electrical activity. I shall make a referral to a specialist.'

Epilepsy? Where had that come from? I didn't know anything about the condition. We left the surgery, with Rosa skipping along beside me, oblivious. A friend, Alison, called out 'hi!' across the car park. As she came closer she noticed me looking upset.

'You OK?' she asked.

My lip quivered.

'Yes, it's just that the doctor has suggested that Rosa has a form of epilepsy.'

Alison gave me a sympathetic look. Her little girl had just been diagnosed with diabetes.

That is when we entered an unfamiliar hospital world of tests and appointments. EEG, MRI, initials that meant nothing to us a few months previously soon became part of our vocabulary. Rosa was made to stare at flickering lights, to hyperventilate, to look at fingers coming towards her, away from her, and so on. It was all a game for her, but the medication she was prescribed made her tired and gave her headaches. At her check-up I reported the side effects to the doctor. The good news was that the absences had ceased.

'I think we can wean her off the medication now. I'm sure she will be fine. Children often manifest this mild form of epilepsy and then grow out of it.' He seemed confident.

Six months later Rosa had her first grand mal seizure: complete loss of consciousness and convulsions. She was now six years old. Andrew brought her back from school and carried her into the house. She was still wearing her Viking Day costume. It was a day she had been so looking forward to: dressed-up actors were doing workshops in the morning and various events were planned for the afternoon. And then at break-time she fell off the bench where she had been sitting with her friend. At first Agnes thought she was mucking about, with all that frothing and shaking and grunting. Then she got frightened because Rosa wouldn't stop, so she called the teacher.

We put Rosa to bed. I sat by, tenderly stroking her forehead until she fell asleep.

This is how it is since she died. I wake up in the morning and lie very still. My consciousness moves into the stiffness of my neck and shoulders. On a good day I haven't got a headache. But my throat is always dry, parched with dehydration. It feels as if something has stuck there like a stone, making swallowing difficult. I look to my right, to the bedside table, glance at the clock, remove the earplugs. Take a sip from the half-filled glass of water. Think about getting up. Don't move.

It's not as if I don't remember that she is dead. I know it only too well. But I lie there and I can see her as if she were alive. I imagine her in bed in the student house on the Cowley Road, wondering what to wear that day, having a quiet moment before getting up. On the floor beside her is the discarded detritus of a nineteen-year-old girl: dirty pants, tights, a bangle or two. Except that now she would be almost twenty-one and looking forward to her birthday party, wondering how much booze to get in, what music to play. Whether she should wait till Saturday to buy herself a new outfit, something sexy her boyfriend Adam will like. I imagine her stretching long limbs, pushing the duvet off.

What present would we be choosing for her? A big present for a special birthday, although when she turned eighteen she pleaded, 'Can I have a big party now, and I won't have one on my twenty-first?' I'm sure she would deny saying that now. And we would have wanted to buy her a big present anyway. A second-hand car perhaps, if she had ever managed to pass that test. Or a trip to Top Shop, like on her nineteenth birthday, when she chose a gossamer skirt with a design of black butterflies on it.

I have caught that butterfly skirt and sewn it onto a piece of pink Thai silk and folded it into a framed box. To preserve that moment.

I'd like to get out of bed but I seem to be pinned to the mattress. I can't move. That familiar boulder is pressing down on my chest. There is a taste of mud in my mouth.

Andrew is walking into the bedroom with a mug of hot water and lemon. He is sweet, the way he does this every morning, silently, with no comment. We may not always be able to talk, but he never misses the hot water and lemon. Sometimes if I'm really bad he just leaves it on my bedside table, and

when I finally haul myself out of bed I gulp it down lukewarm and – for a
split second – it makes me feel better.

I have a spiral-bound notebook where we noted down every seizure, with all its characteristics. When the policewoman interviewed me after Rosa's death, I rushed to bring it out as proof to her (and to myself) that we had been caring, vigilant parents.

Every page is full of jottings like these:

5th Jan. 5.30 p.m. Three-minute seizure, head back, gurgling, left foot twitching, then left hand. Very groggy on gaining consciousness. Stays awake. Asks for orange juice.

29.9. 9 a.m. Hear noises from bedroom. Is unconscious. Grunting, chewing motion. Lasts three mins. When awake complains of headache.

22.10. Lunchtime. Collapses at school. Bangs head badly, bites lip. Had been saying 'the windows are melting' just before having seizure.

11.12. Appointment Dr B. Says results of MRI show generalized pattern of 'difficult to treat' epilepsy, tending toward front of brain. Advised introducing second medication.

10.5. Has three seizures in succession. Get ambulance. Spend night in hospital.

This notebook came with us to every consultation. We passed on the information but it never seemed to lead to any new insights. There might be no seizures for a couple of months, then three in one day. The health professionals seemed as much at a loss as we were. Andrew and I were both working – he had negotiated a contract with his newspaper so he could work from home. I completed an MA and was writing a commissioned book, part of a series on British sculptors – but the management of Rosa's epilepsy felt like the real job. Every few weeks there were scans and assessments, notes taken, changes made to the medication. A hospital in Surrey for the EEG, an MRI in London.

I also dragged her to innumerable alternative practitioners: cranial osteopaths, homeopaths, nutritionists, Chinese doctors who pre-scribed strange-looking herbal concoctions she refused to drink. How annoying all this must have been to her. One highly recommended man instructed me to brush her back thirty times every night with a small paintbrush. This was supposed to 're-educate the neuron trans-mitters in the brain', or something. We did this for weeks but the seizures continued. Andrew despaired at the waste of time and money but I had to make sure we had not missed anything that might help.

When we went out in the evening we worried about the babysitter coping if Rosa had a fit. We began making excuses for not socializing with friends. We felt detached from concerns that seemed irrelevant to us. We did a lot of 'taking turns' and built up resentments over who had done more. One of us needed to accompany her to the endless medical appointments, and be present on every school trip and sports match (the school insisted). We had to remember the twice-daily administration of medicine as Rosa often forgot. Someone needed to be around to take the inevitable call from the school – 'I'm afraid Rosa has had a seizure, can you pick her up?' Mostly the school was kind, but occasionally a comment slipped out. 'Fortunately the other chil-dren were not upset by Rosa's seizure,' a teacher said to me once as if Rosa had done it on purpose. Then I would be taken to see my daugh-ter lying in the sick room, groggy and confused, bruised from her fall.

The fits could be sudden and alarming. We were constantly on edge, listening out for strange noises, a change in her breathing, the crash in her bedroom or bathroom. We might be sitting together having lunch, sharing a joke, and suddenly with no warning her face contorted, her body was in spasm, limbs jerked uncontrollably, hands curled, eyes rolled upwards, her colouring changed. Andrew and I became practised at dealing with this calmly when it was happening, but once the danger had passed I would be distraught. I never got used to it. It was as if she was experiencing a little death every time, and my tearfulness when it was over was a release of the tension, because during the few minutes that she was fitting it felt as if I had lost my child.

It was hard for the family to know how to help us. Luisa proved to be an exemplary grandmother at times, playing board games and encouraging the children to draw, to make up stories, to dress up. She could be interested, engaged and affectionate, and they looked forward to seeing her.

But she never really took the epilepsy on board. Rosa was a loving and spirited girl but she could also be rude, absent-minded, impulsive and irritable, especially as she got older. Unlike the accommodating child I had been, she was headstrong, opinionated and uncompromising. I tried to explain to Luisa that Rosa's disinhibition was partly due to the epilepsy affecting the part of the brain that moderates behaviour, and advised a bit of indulgence. Luisa made no concessions. 'I will not play with a cheat!' she cried as she aban-

Luisa with the girls at Horserace.

doned the game of Monopoly that Rosa, aged seven, was playing by her own rules.

One Christmas Eve when Rosa was about twelve, my family gathered in the South Cottage, the small house where Harold and Vita used to sleep, at the centre of Sissinghurst Castle garden. Uncle Nigel was holding forth with a story about something he had done during the war. A small group that included Luisa and Tom, my cousin Adam's eldest son, sat in rapt concentration. The rest of us – cousins, partners and children – were milling around between the sitting room and the kitchen, waiting for supper. A log fire spat in the grate.

Suddenly, a crash.

Rosa had fallen to the floor, having a seizure. Adam's wife Sarah, who had trained as a doctor, joined Andrew and me in circling protectively around her. We waited until the jerking stilled, and then Andrew carried her to a bedroom to lie down and recover. The sofa on which Nigel and his audience sat was only a few feet away. But Nigel continued telling his anecdote over the sound of Rosa's grunting. And his listeners continued to listen.

It is something we do not speak about. It's too big a thing.

Our marriage is straining under this weight of grief. We are sealed into our separate hells, incapable of reaching out to each other for comfort or support. My regular tsunami of tears only irritates him, reminding him of what he is trying to keep dammed up. And when it is his turn, and I see the clouds of anguish pass over his face, I want to say, 'Talk to me, Andrew, tell me how it is for you, tell me what you saw. We gave her life together; she is half me, half you. You loved her as fiercely as I did.' But I can't reach him, and I can't ask the questions. Maybe the truth is I don't really want to know.

He prefers to keep busy, to redirect his thoughts away from this pain, whereas I feel like a betrayed lover discovering an affair, wishing to know every detail, needing to visualize the very thing that has wounded us so much.

How did you find her?

Tell me, don't tell me.

Face down? Face up?

I imagine Rosa floating, like that painting of Ophelia, lips parted, ethereal and beautiful. But we do not speak of this.

I am wary here of romanticizing her death, but I will never let go, I cannot let go. I must not let go.

1966

I have just turned ten. I am clutching my father's hand, feeling like I am about to be taken to prison. It's drizzling and I'm in a large, echoing station where everything is grey, from the pavement, the platforms, the porters and passengers to the tiny chinks of visible sky. Dank, cheerless Waterloo, a long way from warm, vibrant Florence.

I am wearing new clothes. The blazer with a 'Mountain, Sun and Eagle' badge on the breast pocket, the light grey pleated skirt meeting long woollen socks at bony knees. My brown lace-up shoes are pinching my feet, my Clydella shirt is coming untucked. A few weeks ago Luisa stood in D.H. Evans uniform department ticking everything on the clothes list while the salesgirl searched for the twelve cotton handkerchiefs, two pairs of hockey socks, big blue knickers, pyjamas and lots of other stuff, all to be labelled with my name printed in neat blue pretend-handwriting.

Ben is towering above me, long and lanky in his pinstriped suit and brogues. Daddy-Long-Legs, I call him, after my favourite book. He scans the wooden Departures board for the right train, his fingers stained yellow from cigarettes, tapping his nose in concentration. Then he steers me purposefully past a whistling guard. I have to skip to keep up with him.

'Here we go,' he says, more to himself than to me, as we approach a huddle of children of different shapes and sizes, nervously clustered around a teacher wearing a corduroy jacket.

I eye them all, hoping they won't notice I am looking. Boys with stick-thin legs dressed in grey flannel shorts and polished shoes, girls like me, with hair pulled off their faces, blazers too long in the arm. No one speaks, but I am pretty sure we are all sizing each other up, deciding who might be friend or enemy.

There is a thin boy with carefully combed hair, sticking-out ears and runny nose. I watch as the drip slowly makes its way down between his nostril and mouth. Another boy with a mischievous look, mud on his soles and shoelace undone, rhythmically kicks the side of a bench. Further up the platform a few older children have set themselves apart from the fresh-faced 'new' ones, girls giggling, boys joshing, catching up with news about their summer holidays.

Ben is speaking to the teacher about the arrival of trunks and tuck boxes. He turns to lean down and pats me on the shoulder. 'Well, jolly good then, have a good term.'

My chin wobbles.

'Try not to make a fuss, Vanessa. I shall see you at the half-term break, very soon.'

And off he goes, mission accomplished, swallowed into the darkness of the station. Something constricts in my chest, a familiar feeling of dread and anticipation. The teacher turns back to his list of names. A breathless mother runs onto the platform clutching the hand of a bewildered girl. They have made it just in time.

A minute later, our train comes into the station. Teacher leads us along the platform and I climb up the step into our allocated carriage. I wonder if the others are as apprehensive about the next few hours, days, months, years; whether they are also missing their parents and thinking about our consolation, the biscuits and crisps and chocolate bars in those tuck boxes being sent on ahead. And inside the gleaming new trunks with our names spelt out in gold letters, the new clothes folded neatly by our mothers, waiting to be unpacked; the brushed cotton Ladybird pyjamas and little gym skirts alongside familiar old Teddy, and those useless handkerchiefs.

The train makes its way out of the greyness, past the concrete of south London and into the suburbs. None of us younger ones speak:

for a group of ten- and eleven-year-olds we are very subdued. Teacher doesn't make an effort either; he has got everyone on his list onto the train and wants to cut himself off for a while. I'm sitting by the window, squeezed into a corner but happy to be there. Across the aisle in the other corner some boys are picking at something on the window ledge. Nose-running-boy is still dripping. I want to put my hand in my pocket and get one of the crisp cotton hankies and hand it over, but shyness overwhelms me.

The train goes on and on. Brown suburbs give way to green countryside. We pass wet fields in the fading light. It's teatime. I long for a biscuit.

The girl opposite smiles at me impishly. I notice that one of her socks has fallen down and is bunched around her ankle.

'My name is Natalie Andrews,' she says.

I whisper my name in return but then self-consciously look back out of the window. She is watching me.

'How old are you?' she asks.

'Ten,' I say, still staring out of the window.

'I'm nearly eleven.'

I don't answer.

'My big brother is called Ben.'

Slowly I look round, back at her. I want to tell her that my Daddy has the same name. She grins. Outside, some leaves fall to the ground. We have almost reached our destination.

A coach meets us at the station and we are driven to the school. I haven't seen it before because my admission had been organized so quickly, through an 'intelligence' test that took place in London. A kindly lady had asked me to look at an illustration of a figure with a shadow drawn at right angles and the sun above.

Lady: What's wrong here?

Me: The shadow is in the wrong place.

Lady: Well done!

I felt like a fraud. As there was nothing else in the picture it couldn't have been anything else but the shadow.

The coach comes to a stop in the courtyard of the school. The

Frensham Heights.

building looks huge to me, like a castle from a story, where princesses are locked away in attic rooms. The girls are dropped off first because our dormitories are in the main building. We are met by a woman in a tweed skirt. 'I'm Miss Brown. Come this way, girls,' she says, leading us through a porch, into a building that smells of polish and something vaguely edible.

The dormitory I am shown into is characterless. It reminds me of my ward in hospital when I got run over by the motorbike. Three metal-framed beds with thin, horsehair mattresses jut out from the wall; the bunk in the corner has a small window above it. White walls with a hint of lime echo the colour of the corridors. The floor is grey linoleum.

The other girls in the dormitory are Natalie, Thea and Jenny; soon to be renamed Nat, Tuppy and Podge. I become Nessa. Then there is Kim, the only one to keep her name because it is too short to change. In the months to come, I think of plenty of names I'd like to call her. She controls and manipulates and the other girls accept it. I have no idea why. Perhaps they are too frightened to rebel or maybe they don't want to appear vulnerable.

I regularly cry myself to sleep from homesickness.

'Did you hear that annoying noise again last night?' asks Kim as she gets dressed in the morning.

Someone answers, 'Don't think so, what was it?'

'Must have been Nessa snivelling again,' Kim sneers with derision.

14 November 1966

Dear Mummy,

Daddy just told me I shall not be seeing you at Christmas. That makes me very sad. I don't like it here. I miss everyone in Florence, especially Nonno. Does he lose his temper often now? I wish Nonna was alive, I think of her when I am going to sleep.

I hate boarding school. Today some horrible children looked at my letters. Please write in Italian next time.

The people I like best here are the ladys [*sic*] who give out the food. They are Italian! I always tell them I am Italian too.

Lots of Love,

Vanessa

Kim also teases Podge, who survives by going home as often as possible, returning laden with biscuits and crisps that she hides under her mattress and munches as silently as she can. The meals at school are so different from those at the Pensione Annalena and I am hungry all the time. Gristly meat in watery stews, stodgy puddings in lumpy custard. It's all horrible. Sometimes Podge notices my longing looks and hands over a few Twiglets or digestives when the others are out of the room. Although I'd rather have Tuppy as my friend because she is pretty and popular, at least Podge is kind. She even writes to my mother.

Dear Mrs Nicolson,

I am one of Vanessa's friends. She was very homesick recently. Her kola [*sic*] comforts her most of all because you gave it to her. She received a letter from you today you should have seen her face she was really thrilled. It is my birthday on Monday and I have invited Vanessa to my birthday table. At the moment we are on my bed and she is licking some Marmite. Happily. Her hair sometimes gets in the way.

My mother answers, expressing her pleasure that we are friends. As I can't go back to Florence for half-term because there has been an awful flood, Podge invites me back to her house. Her parents are friendly and I love everything about their warm home, their garden, their big dog, the Sunday lunch, the sandwich supper in front of the TV, and the smell of leather in her father's new car as he drives us back to school at the end of the week.

After I get back to school, things get worse. There is no escape: the dormitory has become a battleground. Kim breaks my things, steals and hides stuff. I have to rescue a wet and dripping Teddy from the lavatory where she has tried to flush him away. My Koala gets thrown out of the window. She intercepts letters addressed to me and either hides them or opens them and reads them out in her mocking tone. She mimics and parodies. Worst of all, she persuades everyone to send me 'to Coventry', a slow, cruel game designed to make the recipient feel as if they no longer exist by ignoring everything they say.

One afternoon I walk into the dormitory to find the matron standing in the middle of the room, arms folded, eyebrows arched, listening to Kim spinning a story. Jenny is sitting on the edge of her bed, staring miserably at her feet. Nat and Tuppy look on uncomfortably.

'Someone has stolen all Podge's tuck,' Kim says as I come in, her thin lips exaggerating the shape of every word.

'That's enough, this is a very serious business,' says Miss Brown. 'Vanessa, do you know anything about this?'

'No, not at all, I don't ...' I stammer, going red as confusion and helplessness rise up in my throat. How strange to feel guilt when I have no reason to do so.

Miss Brown's eyes linger on me and then she looks around the room. 'If no one owns up you will all be severely punished.'

She taps her black shoe on the lino.

'I told you, I bet it was *her*.' Kim points straight at me. 'She's always sucking up to Podge to get at her biscuits.'

'No, no, it's not me, I don't know anything, I ...'

'Shall we have a look under her pillow then?' Kim interrupts. Before Miss Brown can say or do anything she has swept the pillow off my bed, and there, exposed to all present, is a half-eaten packet of biscuits and some cheesy snacks.

Kim smiles, triumphant.

My eyes widen. 'But I didn't, honest, I promise, I wouldn't, I never . . .' I look around for reassurance, my sense of injustice rising.

Jenny looks hurt, Nat and Tuppy confused.

'Come with me please, Vanessa.' Miss Brown marches me straight to the headmaster's office where I am given a lecture on the evils of theft and dishonesty.

It's another term, and this time I am in a top bunk. My legs dangle over the side of the bed and I am wrapped in concentration, playing with the Etch A Sketch that I got for Christmas. I am trying to create an image of a house out of the horizontal and vertical lines that appear on the screen as I turn the knobs on the red plastic frame.

I no longer share a dormitory with Kim, but every so often she seeks me out. Here she is, coming in.

'You playing with your toys?' she asks sarcastically as she saunters towards me.

I ignore her.

She comes right up to the bunk. 'Let's see . . .' she peers at the Etch A Sketch, and then as I continue ignoring her she tries to grab it out of my hands. But I lift it up away from her, and before I am aware of what I am doing, I am bringing it down forcefully onto her head. The metal toy hits her hard, and a corner of the frame breaks off as it falls to the floor. Kim is staggering around and grabs the doorknob to steady herself. For a second we fix each other across the room like wounded animals. Then she splutters, 'You . . . you . . .' before turning her back and leaving the room.

She leaves me alone after that.

It was during my immersion in boarding school life that I became aware of being truly different. We were all separated from our parents and thrown in together but we spoke a lot about those we missed and had left behind, and I began observing the way other families were configured. I hated being an only child and envied the chat about brothers and sisters. How great it would be to have one, or even several. And a cat or a dog or a hamster thrown in, all contained in a home in Berkshire or Hampshire with a television. I had never heard of the programmes my friends spoke about because I had never watched television. My upbringing excluded me from a whole realm of experience, and not only a familiarity with *Dr Who* and *Blue Peter*. Netball, hockey, Mars bars, 'the Four Marys' in *Bunty*, Racing Demon and jacks competitions; midnight feasts and pillow fights. I had no idea what my new friends were talking about half the time.

Then Loyce Blackmur, one of my new pals, told me she was adopted. I had never heard about such a thing and thought about it a great deal. What would that be like, not knowing who your real mummy and daddy were? Her adoptive parents had explained to her that she was chosen because she was special. Mr Blackmur was an accountant and lived with his wife and a red setter in a clean suburban house outside Reading. With hindsight, remembering Mrs Blackmur's glazed smile and her obsession with cleaning, it may not have been as perfect as it seemed then. But after a visit to Loyce's house I wanted what she had – the same as Jenny and Nat and all the other little girls who invited me home for weekends. A haven. Welcoming parents and a dog wagging its tail. Smiley grandparents who got out large tins of assorted biscuits to have with cosied tea in homes that were safe and warm and familiar.

I only had a hazy memory of my grandmother Vita, towering above me dressed in breeches and lace-up boots, accompanied by Rollo, her Alsatian. But she had gone now. And then there was Hadji, crazed with grief, still weeping over her death years later. And Nonna gone, and Nonno become mad. Was this what happened when you lost someone you loved very much? I wondered. You went mad.

And Ben, much as I adored him, wasn't like other dads, with their shiny cars and the pear drops in the glove compartment. He didn't own a car, or a television, or comb his hair with Brylcreem. He was gangly and scruffy, with unruly thinning hair and long, nicotine-stained fingers. Embarrassing tufts emerged from his ears and nostrils. ('Daddy, why do you have hair growing in funny places?' I once asked. 'Never make personal remarks,' he answered, looking cross.)

I tried to make him fit, and sent him instructions. 'Dear Daddy,

When you come to the Christmas carol concert can you bring Jaffa Cakes and I need Marvel for my tea. Don't forget.'

He didn't forget. But I saw him fast asleep in the carol concert.

These were Ben's arrangements for the Christmas holidays at the end of my first term:

Dear Luisa

My time-table with Vanessa is as follows:

20th Dec. I meet her train from Frensham Heights in the morning and take her down to Sissinghurst early that afternoon – or I send her down in charge of the guard. She remains there with Philippa, Nigel and her cousins until the afternoon of the 23rd (Friday) when I join her for Christmas, until:

27th Dec. (Tuesday) when Laurian and Pierre drive down to Sissinghurst in the afternoon and pick her up and take her to Rottingdean. I travel to London alone on the morning of the 28th.

4th Jan. (Wed.) I pick her up at Rottingdean, return her to London, and deliver her the same day to the Gardiners at Oxford, where she remains until 12th Jan. (Thurs.). I pick her up at Oxford, return her to London, and deliver her the same day to Mrs Heber, Southampton, where she remains until

17th Jan. (Sunday), where Mrs Heber drives her, plus her own daughters who are also at the school, back to Frensham Heights ...

I sometimes felt like a parcel being passed from place to place. Panic would take hold as I waited to be collected from rural stations. I reassured myself that it was acceptable to be quiet, as long as I smiled a lot and interjected 'please' and 'thank you' at regular intervals.

But I always looked forward to visiting the house near Oxford where the Gardiners lived. It had a beautiful walled garden with out-buildings where the children, Josephine and (another) Vanessa, were allowed to play. The kitchen was warmed by an Aga and upstairs there was a big attic room we children slept in. They were my ideal family,

450 Holland Park, W.11
14th December

Xmas 1906

Dear Louise,

I write at once in answer to your letter of the 10th. My time-table over Xmas is as follows:

25th Dec. I meet her train from Frensham Heights in the morning and take her down to Sissinghurst early that afternoon — or I send her down in charge of the guard. She remains there with Phillippe, Nigel and her cousins until the afternoon of the

after Friday 23rd (Friday) when I join her there for Christmas, until:

27th Dec. (Tuesday) when Lucien and Pierre drive over to Sissinghurst in the afternoon and pick her up and take her to Rottingdean. I travel to London alone on the morning of the 28th.

4th Jan. (Wed.) I pick her up at Rottingdean, return her to London, and deliver her the same day to her friends at Oxford, where she remains until

12th Jan. (Mon.) I pick her up at Oxford, return her to London and deliver her the same day to Mrs Heber, Down Ampney, Bassett Green Road, Southampton, where she remains until

17th Jan. (Sunday), when Mrs Heber drives her, plus her own daughters who are also at the school, back to Frensham Heights.

I also said I would spend the weekend of the 30th Dec. — 2nd January at Rottingdean in order to be with her 2 further days besides Sissinghurst but I cannot stay at Oxford or Southampton.

Now I must suggest is how you come over about 27th – 28th

---

the one I imagined could be mine when I closed my eyes, a template for the family I wanted when I grew up: jovial father, nurturing mother, happy children, pets, a welcoming home.

Patrick Gardiner was a Professor of Philosophy, part of Ben's intellectual group of friends, but he was not frightening and remote like Uncle Nigel or grumpy, like Nonno had been. And I loved his wife Susan, who was generous and kind. Shoulder length brown hair framed her thin, almost angular face, and a nervous tic made her head twitch when she spoke. Maybe it was this apparent vulnerability that made her so appealing to me. She engaged with her children whether she was cooking supper, reading goodnight stories or planning activities. Best of all, she treated me as one of her own.

The children, 'Jo' and 'Nessa', seemed positively keen to be my friends. Jo was about my age, Nessa slightly younger. I was baffled by their occasional squabbling, but secretly pleased when they vied with one another for my attention.

When I arrived that early January in 1967 I was met with great excitement. Their cat had just given birth to a litter of kittens in the old barn in the garden, and the girls rushed to show me the latest additions. There they were, a moving bundle of black fur, jostling to get close to their mother. Susan followed us to the barn and held back as we crowded around the box where the cat lay licking her babies.

'Do you think I could hold one of them?' I asked Susan.

'No, me, I want to,' squeaked Nessa, pushing in, eager to make her claim.

'No, it's my turn!' Josephine was not going to let her little sister go first.

'Vanessa is our guest, Jo.' Susan came forward and lifted one of the black balls of fur, placing it carefully into the palm of my hand.

The little thing was soft and warm and I cradled it as the other two stroked it gently.

'I think she wants her kitten back now,' said Susan, noticing the cat looking restless. Slowly I returned it to its mother.

We become obsessed by those kittens, running back to the barn at every possible opportunity to check how they were getting on, stroking their backs and discussing which one was the sweetest, what they should be called, whether they were getting any bigger. We left them water to drink and laughed as they tried to tip the bowl over; we studied their movements and analysed their personalities. It was better than any other game we could have possibly invented.

I was contented, but as the week wore on a familiar sense of dread took hold. I did not want to leave. I became sulky and withdrawn. Jo and Nessa took to ignoring me and began playing with each other as if I had already gone. On the eve of my departure I was passing the kitchen door to go into the garden when Susan called out, 'Vanessa, is that you? Why don't you come in and help me get supper ready? You can put the fish fingers in the pan.'

I walked into the kitchen and she passed me the packet with an encouraging smile.

'I thought we'd have your favourite as it's your last night – fish fingers, peas and rice. And we've got chocolate ice cream for pudding!'

She busied herself around the kitchen, getting plates and cutlery out, filling up a jug with squash, wiping the table. And as she did so we chatted and my mood began to lift. The fish fingers that had been sizzling under my care were almost ready. I looked at her and before the words I was forming had time to register their meaning, I said,

'Susan?'

'Yes?'

'Do you think *you* could be my mummy?'

Susan paused, napkins in hand, and stared at me, her smile frozen.

'Vanessa, I can't be your mummy.'

She said it gently but in a measured, careful way.

'You have your own mummy, and she loves you.'

I turned back to the fish fingers. How stupid of me. Of course she could not be my mummy. *Well I don't want her to be my mummy. I don't need her. I don't need anyone.* Tears pricked my eyes as I dropped the spatula onto the side of the frying pan and ran out of the kitchen, out of the back door, into the garden and to the barn. The cat was there, with her kittens. My favourite one, the one with the white spot on its ear who always kept itself slightly apart, was curled up a short distance away. I started stroking it and as I did so my tears welled up. I wanted to remain in that barn and never come out.

And then a crescendo of anger.

They'll be sorry. I hate them and their stupid house. I hate their kittens and the fish finger suppers, and the bed with the eiderdown, and the bedtime stories, and their Christmas stockings and the doll's house and everything about this place. I don't care, they can keep it, I don't want it anyway . . .

I stopped stroking the kitten and yanked it up by its tail. It was frantically squealing as I spun it around in the air, round and round until it was nothing but a whirling ball of fur. In that moment I wanted to inflict all the pain I was feeling, the frustration and the misery and the rage, onto this small, defenceless being. I circled it over and over again and then threw it down on the floor.

I ran out of the barn and bumped straight into Susan.

'I've been looking everywhere for you! I thought you'd gone upstairs but the girls said they hadn't seen you.' She looked into my face. 'Don't be upset,' she said as she put her arm around me. 'We all care about you very much.'

I buried my tearful face into the apron that smelt of supper.

'Come now, it's cold outside, and those fish fingers need eating.'

Back in the kitchen, the girls were sitting at the kitchen table, waiting. The initial awkwardness was soon forgotten. I wolfed down the fish fingers and had seconds of ice cream. The next morning, as Susan helped me pack my bag, we heard a great commotion outside. Jo and Nessa were bounding up the stairs.

As they came bursting into the room they blurted out in unison: 'One of the kittens is dead, Mummy, it's *dead*!'

My eyes opened wide and in horror, I knew. And as three pairs of eyes turned to look at me I thought that they knew too.

While I was in England, Luisa was renovating a property on the other side of Florence from Pensione Annalena. She bought the apartment just after I started boarding school in the autumn of 1966. Two weeks later the River Arno burst its banks and came crashing through the city causing devastation. During that November half-term at my friend Podge's house, I watched footage of a battered Florence on the news, and wondered when I would be able to go there again.

Luisa's building work was finally completed in the spring. It included a top-floor studio flat, fashioned out of a chicken coop. This studio became Luisa's office, where she worked as a consultant on Old Master paintings and drawings for Christie's, the auction house. She also lectured in Renaissance art at the British Institute. I still come across well-bred young men and women, now in middle age, who tell me they followed her courses in the 1970s.

As a teacher her strictness was legendary. She once came back furious from a lecture. Two of the students had been smooching in the front row, not paying attention to the slides she was discussing. She told me she paused, put the light on, and, pointing a finger at the couple, said in her strongly Italian-accented English: 'If you two, there in the front row, want to make love, you can leave the room now.' Then she waited a minute before resuming her talk.

She was tough. She refused to be undermined by the men who ran Christie's. She was constantly in dispute with her colleagues over attributions or how best to catalogue an entry, or over her expenses. (She still has files stuffed with correspondence about unmet demands or disagreements over Christie's marketing policy.) I remember her understandable fury when, in her late forties, she recalled one of her pinstriped 'enemies' announcing, 'Christie's needs more presentable young men rather than menopausal women.'

She fought to forge her career, and few who came across her forgot her. In my early twenties, at a party in Edinburgh, I was introduced to the head of Christie's Scotland. 'Vanessa's mother works for Christie's in Italy,' said the mutual acquaintance, attempting to kick-start a conversation.

'Oh dear, she must have to work for the terrifying Luisa Vertova,' the man smiled amiably.

'My mother *is* Luisa Vertova,' I answered proudly, as a flush of crimson spread across his horrified face. Yes, she could be frightening. But she was also remarkable.

Luisa on her roof terrace, 1970s.

1969

Riva degli Etruschi, 8 August 1969, my thirteenth birthday. On my bicycle.
Celia, Stefano (crouching), Donald, Andreana, Marina, Daisy, Sandro.

I was reaching adolescence and thinking about boys. My idea of romance came straight out of *Jackie* magazine: I wanted to be the heroine with the sexy fringe and beguiling eyelashes, walking off hand in hand with the boy all the girls desired.

Boys were the key to social acceptance. To be fancied by a boy (preferably a nice-looking one) was the ultimate goal. We were pretty dismissive of the boys at our school and looked to the friends of older brothers, cousins, the sons of parents' friends, boys from home, boys met on holiday, pop stars in magazines: most of them were unattainable, but that did not prevent us from whispering and giggling and crying over them. We carved their initials into our desks and scribbled '*I luv* . . .' over our exercise books and pencil cases. Our conversation was peppered with titillating innuendo and misinformation about sex.

The summer I turned thirteen Ben booked a holiday at Riva degli Etruschi, an upmarket holiday camp situated on the Tuscan coast. It had its own private beach, backed by concrete bungalows dotted around a holm-oak wood with communal buildings for eating and entertainment. Andreana, daughter of friends of Luisa, came too.

It was July 1969 and the world was gripped by the progress of Apollo 11. The idea of man landing on the moon held great significance for my father but left me largely unimpressed.

'Isn't it the most extraordinary thing?' Ben exclaimed daily as he read the newspaper. 'Humans have actually left the earth and are going to set foot on the moon – it's simply astonishing!'

I tried to look suitably amazed. Noticing my obvious lack of enthusiasm he added, 'Your generation has grown up with these achievements, but for us ...'

It was *relatively* interesting, I supposed, but while my father's mind was occupied with space travel, mine was much more concerned with the boys Andreana and I had befriended. While Ben sat on the terrace reading *War and Peace* (he brought it with him every holiday), Andreana and I explored the beach and the nightclub and hung out with our new friends. Andreana was the daughter of an Italian count and a much younger American wife and, like myself, bilingual. Unlike me, she was self-assured and displayed an ease and confidence with boys that I coveted. She was sixteen, as were most of the gang. I was almost thirteen. So whereas I shyly fixed my gaze on the ground the minute a boy came near, she *had things to say*. Oh the envy, when she leant towards Donald and engaged him with her thoughts on French cinema or his obsession, *The Lord of the Rings*. I knew nothing about either; in fact I didn't seem to have a view about anything. If Donald or Stefano were to have asked, 'What do you think about the moon landings?' I wouldn't have had the slightest idea what to reply. I wanted simply to anticipate what *their* opinion was. I hid behind Andreana and smiled demurely at Donald and Stefano and François and Jens, hoping that no demands would be made of me.

Soon a routine was established. After breakfast we would make our way to the beach where we spent most of the day, with a break for lunch and a short siesta. After a shower and supper we joined our friends at the nightclub or 'entertainment centre'. It was all quite innocent, and I stuck to drinking Coca-Cola, although I did try my first cigarette, the butt of which is still stuck into my bulging diary with a great ring around it and an arrow – *My first FAG!* Despite my shyness, it was fun being part of a gang, and my lacerating self-criticism was gradually fading. That is, until the morning when Sandro had a good idea.

'It's boring always hanging around on the beach,' he proclaimed. 'Why don't we hire some bikes and go off down the coast to explore?'

Everyone cheered. 'Yeah, great idea!'

I looked around in a panic. 'Yeah, great idea,' I repeated flatly.

I had never been taught to ride a bike. It wouldn't have occurred to my parents that this was a skill I might find useful one day. On the few occasions when the subject of cycling came up, I had managed to hide my inadequacy with excuses, that I was feeling ill or not in the mood, or would it not be more fun to do something else? No one so far had guessed my secret, the presumption being that everyone, at least by the age of eight or nine, is able to ride a bicycle.

Over the next couple of days the 'hiring bicycles' plan became the focus of the group's conversation. Where to get the best price, which bikes to go for, where we might ride. I thought of confessing to Andreana but embarrassment prevented me and she didn't notice my subdued mood. Sandro announced that he had found a good deal. If ten of us hired bikes, the owner of the shop would give us a good price. There was no getting out of it.

'I'm not feeling very well,' I mumbled to Andreana as I dragged my feet along to the hire shop. 'Maybe I'll give it a miss.'

'But, you can't! We won't get such a good deal if you don't hire one too!'

I followed them forlornly into the shop, compiling a mental list of possible escape routes. Maybe there would be a storm. Perhaps I could pretend to faint. Maybe someone else would faint and then I wouldn't have to go through with this. Maybe I could just run away.

Once in the shop, I hung back.

'You are tall, Signorina,' the owner was saying, 'this one should be a good size for you.' Everyone was trying their bikes out, cycling in circles outside the shop, ringing their bells.

'Not . . . not sure about that one,' I kept saying.

'What about this one then? It's a boy's one, but I'm sure you'll get used to it.'

He passed me the bike and I realized that everyone was waiting for me to hurry up. There was nothing for it – I climbed on, praying that by some miraculous intervention I would put my feet on the pedals and glide off like a swan. But no. As I tried to get my leg over the bar I wobbled and fell over, landing in a tangled heap on the ground with the bike across my legs. Before even looking up, I was pushing the bike off and crying, 'I can't ride a stupid bike!'

'Why didn't she say?'

'She can't *ride a bike*?'

Oh the shame.

'It's OK, nobody minds,' said Andreana, finding me red-eyed, much later, hiding in the bungalow.

But I imagined them all laughing, especially the boys. It was a disaster.

'They just feel sorry for you.'

'But I don't *want* them to feel sorry for me!' I cried.

'Come on, cheer up. Stefano says he's going to smuggle some wine into the club tonight, it will be fun.'

In the end she persuaded me to come out after supper. Stefano had smuggled in not one, but several bottles of wine, and we huddled in a corner of the nightclub taking swigs. I didn't like the taste, but it was making me forget my earlier humiliation. François put his arm around me and I felt warm and hazy.

'You should not be so shy,' he whispered. His face was two inches away from mine.

'Yes, I just . . .' I started saying, but suddenly I was aware of him leaning towards me and – oh no – he had put his tongue in my mouth!

I had no idea what to do. Then it dawned on me. *He's French.* That explained everything. This was 'French kissing'. But by the time I had this revelation, he had removed his mouth from mine.

'You have not kissed ze boy before, I think?' he was saying in his soft accent.

Hopefully the darkness in the club prevented him from spotting my very deep blush. I looked around. The others were dancing.

'You know, Vanessa, you are a nice girl. I like you very much.' His face was coming towards me again.

'No, I'm sorry, I've got to go home!' I cried, and pushed him away. I ran out of the club and raced back to the bungalow. Ben looked up from *War and Peace* as I came in.

'How was your evening?'

Without answering I walked past him into my room, flinging myself onto my bed. What a relief. I could lie in the stillness and

With Andreana, summer 1969.

retrospectively savour the thrills of the evening, while trying to forget the humiliations of the afternoon. And then I made a decision. The following day after breakfast I told Andreana I had to do something before going to the beach. I went back to that bike shop, hired a bicycle and practised solidly, falling off the thing so often that my legs were covered in bruises for weeks. But by the time Neil Armstrong stepped onto the moon's surface I could ride a bike.

I was quite good at kissing too.

A few months later, during the Christmas holidays, Luisa was becoming irritated by me slouching around her apartment with nothing to do, so she asked her neighbour Professor Masciotta to introduce me to his son and daughter.

I didn't go round to meet Eligio and Francesca with high hopes. I knew that they were older than me, he training to be a lawyer, she a doctor, and that they were both engaged to be married. But when I turned up at their door they were friendly and I got on with them well enough. A few days later they telephoned to ask whether I would like to join them and a group of their friends on an outing to an *osteria* outside Florence where they served good red house wine and *fettunta*, the Tuscan speciality that I still find delicious: garlic-rubbed bread toasted on an open fire and drizzled with new season olive oil.

It was a cold afternoon when we congregated outside the Masciotta house. Their friends looked uninteresting to me, apart from a boy who had arrived on a motorbike and looked like James Taylor on the cover of *Sweet Baby James*.

'Who is *that*?' I whispered to Francesca.

'That's Nico, an old school friend,' she smiled.

As we piled into a couple of cars, Nico set off on the motorbike and was already seated in the *osteria* when the rest of us arrived. He met my eyes as I approached the table and pointed to the chair next to him.

If only my friends could see me now.

I smoked and drank and tried my best to look older than I was. Nico asked me about myself and about my life in England. I implied that I was almost at the end of my time at school. From him I learnt that he was twenty-one and a student. I hung on his every word and was flattered that he also seemed interested in me.

Francesca and Eligio were amused by the attention I was getting.

'Watch out! She's only thirteen!' laughed Eligio.

I darted him a furious look.

Nico looked at me in disbelief. '*No! Non é vero!*' But it did not seem to put him off. At one point I nervously dropped the cigarette I was trying to smoke in a sophisticated way and spontaneously opened my legs to allow it to fall to the floor.

He leant over and whispered flirtatiously, 'Isn't it curious how women always open their legs when they drop something, whereas men always close them?'

Fascinating, I thought.

Back at school I counted the days until the Easter holidays. Dreaming of Italy punctuated the dreariness of the chemistry laboratory and the hockey field. Eventually the holidays came round and I was back at my mother's flat. Nonchalantly I phoned Eligio and Francesca.

'How are you, I've just got to Florence ...'

'That's great, we're just here with Nico and a friend of his, come over ...'

I was thrilled. Wearing my new brown suede mini skirt and matching fringed bag, I sprinted around the corner and yes, he was there – but right next to him stood a beautiful Italian girl of about nineteen, perfect hair and figure, cool and composed, her hand touching his shoulder. We eyed each other up, she with disdain, me with despair. I could never hope to be as alluring and confident as this rival.

Nico seemed unperturbed. He played up to me as soon as his girl-friend left the room.

'*Sei bella*,' he said sotto voce, and complimented me on my skirt.

Summer arrived. Ben and his friends had rented a villa in Portugal. I yawned at the sightseeing, preoccupied with how my tan was progressing. I hid behind Lucy, the sixteen-year-old daughter of Ben's friend Philip Toynbee, also staying at the villa.

We quickly discovered Sobe-e-Desce, a disco in the local town. Here we could dance, drink, smoke and flirt. I made friends with Julian, a nice seventeen-year-old staying in the villa next door, and followed Lucy around, rather as I had done with Andreana the summer before.

Boys were everywhere – the Portuguese Carlos, Manuel and José, the Americans Rick, Bill, Kid, David and Titch, English Simon, Robin, Chris and Julian. I lived on chips and ice cream, cheap wine and cigarettes. I tasted my first joint with Carlos, lying on the beach one evening, looking at the stars. I had just turned fourteen.

I wrote in my diary: 'I feel so sorry for those Italian girls who are kept inside the house until they are married. They don't realize what they are missing!'

But the only way I was able to acquire a veneer of confidence was through alcohol.

12/8/70

God, last night was terrible. Before we go into the nightclub we always go to the 'Bistro', a little bar with a terrace. Lucy and I went there as usual. When we got there Lucy disappeared and as I noticed that Robin and his friend Dave were there, I started talking to them. I bought a gin and orange and was quietly smoking a fag and drinking and talking, in fact I think I was in the middle of a sentence, when I suddenly felt violently sick and faint. I tried to walk to a chair but everything and everybody was whirling around, then my legs started trembling and I went straight out. Then next minute I found myself in Robin's car being driven home. Sally [Toynbee] gave me a sleeping pill and I went straight to sleep.

The next evening I was back at the disco repeating the same pattern. And the day after that. After yet another drinking session a few days later, I collapsed outside the disco and had to be carried back to the villa. The following evening Ben refused to let me go out – it was the first time he had made a stand about my behaviour. I pretended to be resentful, but secretly I was relieved.

When I returned to the disco two days later they refused to let me in.

23/8/70

Last night they wouldn't let me into Sobe-e-Desce! So Carlos and his friend took me into their tent. I don't really know what happened as they gave me a whole bottle of brandy to drink. But then tonight after nagging and flirting for about half an hour the Sobe-e-Desce people finally agreed to let me in on condition that I didn't drink anything alcoholic. But then the Boss gave me a terrible lecture just 'cos I kissed Bill and Titch for rather a long time, why should he care? Anyway, I still managed to get some drink though I fainted again and when I woke up I was puking like mad. Someone took me home and I fell asleep on the couch. Dad found me there and nearly blew his prick off!

I don't recognize this obstreperous younger self. It's as if I was creating a different character in my diary, fabricating an image of a hard, rebellious teenager in order to convince myself that I was one. It sounds all wrong.

Dad blew his prick off? I never called 'Daddy' Dad. And Ben never raised his voice. I can't match this version of myself to the sensitive teenager I recall, the one who read Kahlil Gibran and Herman Hesse, and who cried over Sylvia Plath's *The Bell Jar*. Maybe that persona only came later.

I was in Italy again and Luisa was worrying about my health.

'Your father hasn't been looking after you at all,' she said when she came to meet me off the flight from Portugal. 'You look terrible. And what about your periods? Haven't they started yet?'

She was always asking me about the non-arrival of my periods. Hers, as she had often told me, began when she was ten and she had found it a traumatic experience. No one had warned her, and when she had started bleeding she thought she was dying.

I responded to her questions with a shrug and for the next few days I mooched around her flat in Florence, going out occasionally to wander about the city.

3/9/70

Today I bought the LP *Hair*, this Parker pen, a pair of sandals and a pair of Levis that don't fit properly. Got a postcard from Julian – he'll be in London by now. This time next week I'll be at school – UGH! I bumped into Eligio and Francesca on the way home. They're nice and they said they would phone tomorrow.

But when the phone rang it wasn't them.

'*Ciao, Vanessa?*'

I swallowed hard.

'*Si. Ciao, Nico?*'

My heart was pounding.

He had heard from Eligio that I was around. His parents, with whom he lived, were still away on holiday. He said he was bored. What was I up to? Could he collect me later that afternoon? Go back to his place, play some music?

I took great care in getting ready. I washed my hair, put on the hipster mini skirt he had admired at Easter and tied a knot in my shirt just under my bra, to show off my flat, tanned stomach. I tried some of my mother's lipstick, took it off and reapplied it more carefully. I practised leaning towards the mirror, to get an idea of what I would look like to him should he kiss me. A terrifying and exciting thought.

He rang the doorbell and I shouted to Luisa that I was going out to see Eligio and Francesca. Nico was standing by his motorbike outside the house, wearing faded jeans and a white T-shirt.

We roared through the streets, my arms wrapped around his waist, leaning into his back. When we arrived at his house, he chased me up the stairs as I giggled and squealed, but in fact I was nervous. The flirtations in Portugal had been nothing more than enjoyable dalliances fortified by alcohol. This felt momentous.

We went into the sitting room and I sat on his parents' sofa. He got me a Coca-Cola bottle from the kitchen and sat beside me, putting his arm around me. I leapt up, grabbed the nearest LP and asked if he could play it. Languidly Nico stood up, put the record on the turntable and adjusted the sound.

'Can you translate the lyrics?' he asked.

We stood there, holding on to the record sleeve as I laboriously tried to find the words in Italian to 'Like a Bridge over Troubled Water'. Then he took my arm. The record sleeve fell to the floor as he kissed me roughly. I felt fear and relief in equal measure. I wanted to slow it down, make it more romantic. I touched him clumsily, tentatively, mixed with a curious sense of resignation. I knew what was going to happen next. I had no say in the outcome.

He took my hand and led me to his bedroom. It was gloomy in there, the shutters closed against the heat. As he pulled his T-shirt over his head, I picked up a comic book, *Asterix*, that was lying on the floor. He came towards me and closed the book, throwing it back down on the bedside mat.

We were on his bed. I was apprehensive, fearful, most of all, that he would think me inexperienced. As he tugged at my clothes he asked me if I had been with a man before. All the drunken fumblings with the boys in Portugal flashed through my mind. What had I actually done with Carlos and his friend in that tent? And now, at this moment, what was I supposed to *do*? I longed for the whole thing to be over as quickly as possible. And when it happened, it wasn't remotely romantic or sexy, more like having a tooth pulled out and then having the wound poked and prodded. The pain was dreadful. I couldn't believe that this was *it*.

We hardly spoke to each other afterwards. I felt dirty. I was worried about getting home. Nico was distant and thoughtful. He sat on the corner of the bed watching me getting dressed and muttered something about how I mustn't tell anyone.

'*Sei solo una bambina*,' he said softly. Only a child.

He drove me back to Luisa's flat, this time in his car, as if symbolic of my development – from motorbike to car, from girl to woman in an afternoon.

When I undressed that night I noticed a spot of blood on my underwear. Creeping into Luisa's room, I said naively, 'Mummy, I've started my periods.'

She got up and put her arms around me.

'You're a woman now,' she said.

Nico phoned the next day, but I had agreed to go out with Luisa. As I was getting ready I realized with horror that I had a large love bite on my neck. Fortunately Julian had given me his silk scarf as a goodbye present when we left Portugal, and I covered up the livid bruise before Luisa noticed it. Nice Julian with his sweet letters and presents.

He was the only one who, I see now, actually cared about me. I had dismissed him because he was too kind.

A new term began. I boasted to my friends about my lover in Italy.

'He's twenty-one, good-looking, has a motorbike ... And guess what? I've lost my virginity!'

So much was true. I left out the part about it hurting and being less than a loving moment.

Nico wrote to me on two occasions. His letters arrived, like evidence in support of my claims, even though he signed himself by his full name, Nicola, which looked like a girl's name. I read the short, indifferent letters until I knew them by heart, attributing great significance to every sentence. As they were written in Italian, I could imbue an innocuous phrase with the passion it lacked in order to impress my friends, and trick myself into believing that he missed me.

I saw him again in the Christmas holidays. He said he was having a party on New Year's Eve. His parents were away. I was almost sick with anticipation. When I got there, the place was full of people I did not know and I began drinking, making a fool of myself by stumbling over everything. I even managed to set fire to a cushion when I nervously dropped my cigarette. 'You always seem to be dropping your cigarette!' Nico said, and I was chuffed that he remembered our first meeting, a year earlier. He was affectionate and we laughed as we tried to save the smouldering cushion.

But by the time I left, an hour or so after everybody else, a coldness had crept in between us. What had I said or done wrong? Was it because he wanted to make love but I had a heavy period? Did that disgust him? Was he angry that he had asked me to stay until the end of the party, and then I had disappointed him? He drove me home. As I got out of the car he said he probably would not see me again before I returned to England. He had an important exam to revise for. His goodbye kiss was distracted, as if he had already moved on.

I received no more letters from him. At first I persuaded myself that

At Harold Acton's villa 'La Pietra', Florence.

the reason was a long postal strike, but when that ended there was still nothing. When I returned to Florence at Easter and asked Eligio and Francesca how he was, they told me he had transferred to the University of Bologna and rarely came back to Florence. The days dragged on.

13/4/71

Too scared to ring Nico's house. I was going to ask him if he wanted to come and see *Morte a Venezia* ['Death in Venice'] but then I didn't. The film was really sad. Today I went to lunch at an old man's villa (he is called Harold Acton) and the garden was really beautiful. The sun has come out at last.

How am I going to see Nico??

It wasn't until the summer that I saw him again. He was sitting on the steps by the Duomo. I stopped to talk to him but our conversation was stilted. A few days later on my way back from the shops with Luisa, I suddenly saw him, coming towards me on his motorbike. He noticed me as he sped past, giving me a brief flicker of a smile and a nod of the head. I stood frozen, bags in hand, a bad taste rising from my throat. He was gone and I knew I would never see him again.

My mother turned round to tell me to keep up, it was past lunchtime and time to get home.

2002

Swimming pool opening, June 1997.

During my years of marriage and home-building, there were times when I felt a physical and mental weakness taking hold. It would creep up on me when least expected and I fought it hard, for the sake of my family. Sometimes I lost the battle, and succumbed to migraines lasting for days, crippling back pain, or debilitating despair. Once I spent a couple of weeks in hospital, unable to function at all. 'What's wrong with me?' I asked the doctor. 'Clinical depression,' he said, prescribing more pills.

Andrew was there to take over. He coped as I was absent, temporarily removed from life.

I hated the depression. I hated Rosa having epilepsy. I was so weak but she was so brave. She refused to let health issues interfere with her being in the netball team, acting in school plays, joining every outing and adventure, going on hair-raising rides at the fair.

She was a happy girl. She adored birthday and Halloween parties, dancing and bowling. Best of all she loved swimming in the beautiful pool Andrew had built with money he inherited when his father died. The day we opened the pool I rigged up a ribbon across the entrance and ceremoniously cut it in front of Rosa and Ellie and their best friends. My mock-solemn pronouncement, 'I declare this swimming pool open,' was drowned out by the squeals of delight as they rushed to jump in. We still have the faded photograph marking the event.

We rarely saw Rosa upset by her condition except when the school suggested she should forgo the abseiling trip to Wales or when they removed her from the netball team before an important match because the day before she had had a seizure.

'It's not fair, this stupid, stupid epilepsy. Mum, *why* can't I do the same as everyone else?'

I was driving her home when she said this. I kept my eyes fixed on the road ahead because I did not want her to see my tears welling up.

'I know, Rosa, it's hard.'

California. Summer 2000. Ellie left, Rosa right.

128

My friend Alison was a news reporter for the local TV station. She asked if she could interview Rosa for a feature on epilepsy. Rosa was eight years old and loved every minute of the attention.

They filmed her cycling, playing with the dog and going on the swing, pretending to do homework.

'What do your friends think of you having epilepsy?' Alison asked.

'They're jealous, they think I'm boasting!'

Alison smiled and asked a few more things. For the final question she had an earnest expression on her face.

'Rosa, can I ask you – how do you feel about having epilepsy?'

'I don't give a toss,' she answered with a grin, and the cameramen burst out laughing.

'Are you all right, love?'

I'm doubled up on a pavement in the town of Lewes, trying to catch my breath, feeling faint, tearful. I look up. A vision in beige: jacket, jumper, trousers, hair, shoes, all creamy brown. She is probably in her mid-sixties, or perhaps the oversized glasses and the basket hooked around her arm make her seem older than she is.

'Yes, fine, thank you, I'm fine . . .'

'Are you sure?'

She looks genuinely concerned. I stare back down at the ground, swallowing hard.

'You don't seem it,' she says.

'I'm fine,' I say again.

Go on your way. Let me be invisible.

I had been with my friend Jeremy and saw some pretty boxes and thought they would be perfect to store Rosa's most treasured possessions. The sales assistant had looked bored as she wrapped them. I wanted her to be respectful – I needed her to understand. 'I'm buying these boxes for my dead daughter's things,' I said. She had looked up, taken aback. I choked and stumbled out, leaving Jeremy to pick up the pieces.

The beige lady does not move.

'I'm OK, honestly, thanks.'

'Have you got a friend nearby?'

'Yes, my friend is just in there.' I nod at the shop behind her. 'He is buying something for me.'

Her hand touches me. She keeps looking into my face. Go away. Don't go away. I'm feeling tearful. Please help me. I'm trying so hard to keep the wail down, trying to breathe. She seems kind. I look straight into her eyes.

'It's just . . .'

She doesn't say anything. She waits.

'It's my daughter.' I take a breath. Silence again. 'Well, it's just that she died and . . .'

A pause. That unfinished sentence hangs in the air.

'How old was she?'

My watery eyes look up again.

'Nineteen.'

'I'm so sorry.'

We remain there, she and I, for a quiet minute or two, she standing by me. I am still crouched awkwardly on the pavement absorbing her kindness when I catch sight of Jeremy carrying the large bags that hold my new boxes.

'You look after yourself now,' she says, removing her hand.

Jeremy puts the bags down next to me as I watch the woman walk away. She pauses and looks back at me, just before she disappears around the corner.

A letter arrived informing Rosa that her application for entry to the local grammar school had not been successful. She had pinned all her hopes on getting in – Ellie was a student there, and many of her friends were going. She read the letter, and ran upstairs to barricade herself into her bedroom. We pleaded, cajoled, we said everything we could think of to cheer her up, but she was inconsolable.

When I discovered that her friend Sarah had been unsuccessful as well, I rushed to give her the news through the crack in the bedroom door.

'You see you're not alone,' I said, trying to offer some comfort.

A few minutes later we heard the barricade being dismantled and she reappeared, red-eyed.

'Will you appeal?' she asked. The children knew the process so well.

But in the end we did not appeal. We felt it wasn't really the right school for her; it had poor pastoral care, expecting everyone to manage on their own. The medication she was taking was slowing her down, making remembering anything difficult. We thought she deserved somewhere nurturing and less fixated on exam results. Should we have tried everything in our power to get her into that school? Who knows.

The following September she started at a private co-educational school, not far from us. She appeared content at first and bonded with a girl called Hannah who also hadn't got into the grammar school. They were both thirteen years old.

About a month into the term someone had a party, which involved camping in a field overnight. We worried about whether Rosa would remember to take her medication, and what about boys and alcohol? The next morning I collected an exhausted-looking girl and dropped her off at home to sleep before driving Hannah on to her house, which was about ten minutes away. In that short drive I asked the new friend how it was going at school and I was hit by a stream of bitterness: how stupid the other kids were, how bad and mean the teachers. As Hannah got out of the car she stopped and said, 'But that's nothing – you should see what's happening to Rosa.'

Before I could ask her what she meant, she had walked off, and I sat there for a moment gripping the steering wheel, fingers tense with worry.

As soon as I got back home, I went straight to Rosa's room. She was in bed, almost asleep. She seemed to have lost some of her clothes, including one of her shoes. The little box that held her medication had also disappeared.

I sat down and placed my hand on her arm. 'Are you OK?'

'Go away, Mum, I'm tired,' she said, turning away from me.

Rosa became withdrawn. I repeatedly asked her what Hannah had meant but she shrugged off my questions. All she would say was, 'I hate that school.' In the mornings she pleaded headaches or sickness – anything to be allowed to stay in bed. The seizures were increasing and the medication was raised. A side effect was weight gain, exacerbated by comfort eating. I watched her smuggle fistfuls of biscuits under her jumper as she set off every evening to spend hours in front of the TV. Any attempt to persuade her to occupy herself in some other way was met with verbal abuse.

She remained an accomplished netball shooter – her medication probably worked like beta-blockers do for snooker players, making her less distracted. She was picked for the netball team. She was tall now and on Saturday afternoons we watched her six-foot frame catching the ball above everyone else's head, effortlessly shooting it into the net, again and again. But she kept herself apart from the others. We were the only people cheering. The other girls seemed to take her ability for granted, but if she missed the goal they sighed and glared. As soon as the game was finished she wanted to leave, refusing to join in with the team teas. We always had to go straight to the car. 'Drive!' she would spit out, staring fixedly ahead as I fumbled with my seat belt.

On New Year's Eve I found her in tears.

'What's wrong?' I asked gently.

She pinched the fat on her arms. 'If I didn't have this . . .' She shook the flesh at me. 'If I was *thin*, everything would be OK.'

I tried to hug her and tell her she was beautiful but she pushed me away.

We researched other schools but could not find anywhere suitable. Finally we reached an agreement, that if she could just get through the GCSE year, she could start sixth form somewhere else. Once this had been decided Rosa cheered up noticeably. She studied hard and got involved in school drama productions. Very occasionally we even sang to the radio as we drove to school, like in the old days.

Shortly after her death, I am clearing stuff in her room. I move the desk slightly and notice part of a large brown envelope sticking out from behind it. I pull it towards me and see in big letters:
PRIVATE! CONFIDENTIAL!
I start to open it, my hand shaking slightly.

Here it is: the secrets and the self-loathing teenage confessions. Pages of lined notepaper tell the story of that first school party when she was thirteen, and how she had pretended to her new school friends that she often got drunk and had experimented with boys. There was a queue of boys wanting to feel her up. Another party: she got drunk and had been persuaded to strip. The boys posted pictures of her topless on websites, and laughed at her. The girls had called her a slag. Page after page about how she hated herself and wished she could die.

And then, another page. Under the heading 'Reasons not to kill myself':

1). I don't want to miss my wedding day

2) I don't want to cause grief to my family.

1971

Stuck at school, aged fourteen, my diary groans with negativity. 'I should be revising but I can't be fagged. It's so boring in this dump.'

I was doing the minimum amount of schoolwork. I was rude to matrons and teachers. I got into trouble for sleeping in, skipping lessons, for smoking in the lavatories or on the roof with friends.

Smoking took the edge off the hunger I felt from missing breakfast and picking at the disgusting food at mealtimes. For years I wouldn't touch stew, because I associated it with bits of gristle and fat floating in gravy, and the idea of a 'pudding' – the stodge surrounded by lumpy yellow custard – turned my stomach. I was hungry all the time.

I began to suffer from migraines and dizzy spells. Once or twice I fainted in the refectory queue. I was tall and thin and the circles under my eyes had grown darker. But this was a fashionable look and I liked to think of myself as 'willowy'. Waist-length hair framed my pale face like black curtains, and I wore baggy jumpers to hide my body, pulling the sleeves over my hands as I slouched around the school in my patched jeans and black and white baseball boots.

My parents, in their separate ways, were acting strangely. On the rare occasions Ben came to visit, he was remote. That is, if he remembered to come at all. 'Today it was the parents' meeting and I was really upset because I waited all day for Daddy to come but he didn't turn up. I tried phoning but there was no answer. I phoned again this evening and he said he had forgotten all about it! Typical! Lydia's parents came down, so did Ann's mother and took them out to lunch. I was really pissed off because I missed breakfast and lunch and was almost fainting by low-tea.'

Luisa seemed by turn depressed and angry. During the holidays in Florence I would catch her staring at me for no apparent reason, particularly when we were having our meals in the kitchen.

'Why are you looking at me?' I would ask impatiently before she turned away.

Sometimes in that kitchen, listening to my mother ranting about the tourists, the younger generation, the way Florence had changed for the worse, I would realize that I had been sitting for over an hour without having said a word. It was as if I had disappeared, flown off somewhere, leaving my body behind. In some ways it was a relief when the holidays ended and I could get back to Frensham Heights. But there wasn't enough to do at school. There was no structure to our days.

Ben had wanted me to have a different experience of school than the one he had had. His years at Eton had been miserable, and he thought that a liberal, co-educational school would offer a well-rounded education. But the school had changed. From being a progressive school with some boundaries, it had become lawless.

Headmaster Maurice Bridgeland.

This was mostly due to a change of headmaster. Maurice Bridgeland arrived to replace Stephen Hogg, who had died suddenly on the tennis court in 1970. The motion to abolish all school uniform (apart from the games kit) had been passed at a meeting of students and teachers the year before, but Mr Bridgeland went further. He believed that children should be given the opportunity and freedom 'to express themselves' as they wished, and if that meant doing little or no work, then so be it.

The teachers who did try to maintain some control had a hard time gaining respect from the students. One left on the verge of a nervous breakdown after suffering months of taunting; another lost his temper and hit a girl who was playing up, then ran out of the room in a panic when the boys began throwing desks around in a frenzy of destruction.

My schooldays as a teenager revolved around waking late, missing breakfast, and smoking in the lavatories and the woods. I wanted to rebel, but that was hard to do when there were no rules to break. One day a boy came into our common room waving a newspaper.

'Hey, look at this!'

We crowded around him as he read aloud:

Hippie's Paradise at £966 a year school

Frensham Heights, founded in 1925, is an independent school charging £966 a year for boarders (Eton fees are £990). It is in 170 acres of countryside and was a pioneer of progressive education in Britain.

A spokesman said: 'Being a progressive school we do not have many rules, although, of course, there are some. Pupils are not allowed to smoke or bring drink into the school. They are allowed to go into the village only at certain times and must not leave the school without exeats. Classes must be attended and they are not allowed to hitch-hike.'

We all laughed. What rules? We broke them all but no one was taking any notice, except maybe some of the parents. Within a couple of years the governors had replaced Bridgeland with a new headmaster, but I had left by then.

The summer holidays came around again. I was almost fifteen.

This time I was accompanied by two slightly older girls on the plane back to Italy. Cathy, the daughter of Luisa's friend Priscilla Gore (who had run the nursery school I had attended in London), and her friend Marcia were coming to stay in the studio flat above my mother's apartment while they followed art history courses at the British Institute.

Cathy looked like a Botticelli Venus, with long, reddish-blonde hair and a peaches and cream complexion. Luisa, who tended to divide people into three categories, 'Good, Stupid and Bad', thought she was wonderful, and definitely in the first camp. She was sweet, polite and accommodating. She smiled demurely at everything my mother said, which irritated me intensely and then made me feel unloveable and mean.

A few days after arriving I received a letter from my schoolfriend Emma, asking if she might stay with me in Florence since her mother was in hospital with jaundice and they had had to cancel their holiday in Portugal. We settled her into a nearby pensione, as there was no more room in Luisa's apartment.

In the course of a warm evening, Emma and I met some American hippies on the steps of Duomo. Larry was not particularly good-looking. He had a big nose, thin lips, aviator-style glasses and shoulder-length brown hair. We began chatting about this and that. He was easy to talk to and I was enjoying myself.

'Hey, let's buy some wine and take it back to my house,' I said. 'My mother's away, so we can do what we like.'

We bought a few bottles of wine and I led the way back home. We climbed the stairs up to my mother's roof terrace and then up a ladder, onto the roof. After sitting under the stars drinking and talking, we moved downstairs to listen to music. I liked the fact that Larry wasn't patronizing – perhaps because he was not aware of my real age. He spoke to me as an equal, and I encouraged him by asking questions about his travels and his interest in photography. He told me about racial prejudice in America; the aftermath of the Vietnam War; student politics at the University of Maryland where he was a student. I had little to contribute but I listened. Then he leant over and kissed me.

'Christ, what a night! Larry and I didn't sleep all night long!' I wrote in my diary the next day.

The following morning Larry left with his friends in the camper van they had bought to travel around Europe. Emma returned to her pensione to have a rest and I concentrated on clearing up the debris from the night before since Luisa was due to come back from a work trip to Lugano.

Emma (left) and me in Florence, 23 July 1971.
Photo taken by Larry.

She returned in a good mood.

'I had a very successful trip. Everything all right here?'

'Yes, everything's fine.'

'Good, well why don't we all go and have lunch near Emma's pensione?'

Something went wrong during lunch. Everything Emma said annoyed my mother. She hadn't been keen on her from the outset. At one point Emma tried to ingratiate herself by commenting on the beauty of Michelangelo's *David*, and this irritated Luisa even more. Marcia and Cathy mentioned a classical concert they were going to that evening and Luisa caught the look between Emma and me when she suggested that we should go as well. Suddenly she exploded.

'What's the matter with you? You are *philistines*!' she shouted. 'You are like those fat American tourists who come here and understand nothing! You may as well go home,' she glared at Emma.

We finished the meal quickly and in silence. I whispered to Emma, 'Don't worry, I'll see you after supper and we can go out.'

But Luisa would not let me out of the house. 'It's late and you look tired.'

'Emma is waiting for me, I have to go.'

'Well, Emma will have to wait. And she is going to have to go home. Tomorrow I am going to send a telegram to her father.'

'But why?'

Luisa had an annoying habit of ignoring questions she didn't want to answer. She busied herself tidying something away.

'*But why?*' I repeated loudly after a minute's silence.

'She's a very bad influence on you,' she said without meeting my eyes.

'But she hasn't done anything wrong! You always want to ruin everything!' I shouted and ran out of the room, slamming the door behind me.

When I said goodbye to Emma I felt bad. But my other friend

Loyce had arrived and Luisa's mood had improved. As far as she was concerned, Loyce was definitely in the 'Good' camp. I was relieved that the atmosphere had lightened.

The three of us left Florence for the seaside. We were sharing a room with three beds in a holiday bungalow at Riva degli Etruschi where I had been on holiday with Ben two years before. After supper on the second evening Loyce and I went to the nightclub where I had experienced my first kiss with François.

'Don't be late!' Luisa called after us.

The nightclub was closed so we went for a walk along the beach and sat on the sand, looking at the moon. We had been out for about an hour when we decided to return to the bungalow to have an early night. As we walked into the bedroom I knew instantly that something was wrong. Luisa was lying in bed in her nightdress and didn't look up when we came in.

'Hello!' I said for the second time, but she didn't respond. 'Is anything the matter?'

No answer.

I couldn't understand it. She had been quite chatty over supper. Luisa kept her eyes on her book, and as I stood there looking at her, she leant towards her bedside light and switched it off. Then she turned over as if to go to sleep. Loyce and I shrugged at each other. There was nothing to do but follow suit, but I lay there in the dark wondering why the atmosphere had altered so dramatically. It was my birthday in two days' time and I had a sinking feeling that it would not be a happy one.

The chill was still in evidence at breakfast.

'Can you leave Vanessa and me alone, please?' Luisa asked Loyce icily.

My friend darted me a look and hesitated, but then picked up her book and left.

Luisa turned towards me.

'You've changed so much in a year,' she said. 'A year ago I trusted you, now I won't be able to keep you out of my sight.'

She then slapped me very hard. I felt my cheek and my eyes stinging. *I shan't cry, I will not cry.*

'You *whore*!' She was screaming. 'You are probably pregnant, worse than that, you are likely to have caught a venereal disease. You're ruined! Do you understand that?'

I looked at her in shock, more at the horror of her having discovered what I had done than at the possibility of the consequences she was suggesting.

'I knew, I knew what you were getting up to when I saw that bite on your neck last year,' she went on. 'You thought you could hide it, but you can't hide anything from me!'

My mind raced. She must have read my diary, from when I was writing about Nico, to all the recent stuff about Larry and, oh God . . .

'That filthy, filthy Nicola Papp!' she spat out. 'I could have understood if you had only had sex with *him*, but oh no, this other . . .' She paused, looking around the room, searching for the word, 'Hippie!' she said in disgust. 'You're like a prostitute, picking men up in the street and turning my flat into a brothel! You will be rejected from society, you will walk down Bond Street with WHORE branded on your back . . . and if your father hears about this he could throw you out with nothing. Nothing! You're spoilt and lazy, you're . . .'

Inside I was seething. How dare she read my private things? Had she not seen the statement I had scrawled in my childish hand on the front of the diary: 'PLEASE DO NOT READ and if you do, I think you are the most nosy, horrible, annoying git to have ever set foot on this earth'?

I fumed silently, letting her rant. But she kept pushing it, finally making me cry. When she seemed exhausted, I got up and walked out. Loyce was sitting on a plastic chair on the veranda and looked up anxiously from her book.

'The holiday is ruined,' I said quietly, trying to control the tearfulness and the layers of guilt, misery, fear and fury battling inside me.

Luisa's appointment diary, found by me forty years later, states simply: '3 August 1971. Read V's diary. Horrified, desperate, sleepless night. 4 August 1971. Talk to V – she cries but won't change.'

I was still only fourteen.

*

As anticipated, the first few days were hell. Luisa refused to let Loyce and me do anything without her and insisted we return to our room every evening as soon as supper was finished.

My fifteenth birthday came and went without celebration. I tried to work out what to do. If only I could get back to London and find Larry. But I had no money and my mother had filed my passport away somewhere. Could I get to England by hitch-hiking across France? Or work my way back, getting odd jobs in cafes and restaurants along the way? I even went as far as searching for my passport in Luisa's bag when she was out of the room, and thought about stealing money from her purse. But I couldn't find the passport and I needed more money than I could steal. And Luisa was bound to tell the police, as I was a minor. Perhaps I should phone Ben and explain how miserable I was? But then I would have to tell him what had happened and he would want to know what Luisa had read in my diary that was so terrible.

She had in fact already informed him in a letter that I had 'picked some hippies or something like that off the street and temporarily turned my flat into a brothel'.

Ben wrote back: 'It must have been a terrible shock to you. What really worries me slightly is that since you are not supposed to know, will Vanessa hesitate to reveal to you that she has missed a period?'

He needn't have worried. My period arrived before his letter did. Luisa found me clutching my stomach one morning.

'What's the matter?'

'I've got terrible period pains,' I groaned.

'Well, that's one less thing to worry about,' she muttered.

Loyce had returned to England and we were back in Florence. One day everything was fine – Luisa produced my present two weeks after my birthday and it was exactly what I wanted, 'a new record player with a fantastic sound!' I wrote in my diary – but the next, we were back to arguing about my clothes or my hair, or my 'insolent and irresponsible' attitude.

I had taken to wearing a long hippie 'maxi' dress and no shoes. After afternoons of aimless meandering, I would return, the soles of my feet jet-black from the city's dirt, before slumping sulkily on her sofa. There were rumours of a cholera epidemic in Italy that summer.

'Now you are bringing the cholera off the streets!' she screamed one day when she noticed my lack of footwear.

Poor Luisa. She had a point.

Soon it was September, and despite Luisa's suggestion in a letter to Ben that 'maybe a convent would be best for Vanessa', I returned to my school to start the sixth form. Not surprisingly my exam results were terrible, which only reinforced Luisa's low opinion of me.

Florence
19/9/71

My dear Vanessa,

I have been writing to you in Italian during the past months and I see that you did get some benefit from it, because at least you've passed that exam.

I am so disappointed in you – and yet I cannot say that your failure took me by surprise. It has been a difficult year, a hard year for you: ever since Portugal really! You've suddenly thought you were grown up, you were a woman, you should taste the life of a free, uninhibited woman, you should smoke, you should seduce or be seduced and all the other nonsense that teenagers fall for. In fact, to start having ones periods does not mean anything but the beginning of a harder life. Scarlet fever and chickenpox one can get over with the help of doctor and Mummy. From your age onwards Mummy and Daddy can help much less. I can suffer in silence – and you'll never guess how much I have suffered for you – because when you hurt yourself it hurts me dreadfully.

I liked being in the sixth form. I was studying subjects for A-levels that interested me – Sociology, Italian literature, English. We had a common room with threadbare armchairs where we were allowed to smoke, and a kitchen where we could make cups of instant coffee and slices of toast. There were newcomers – I felt a bond with Alison, who had come from a school in New York and had an American boyfriend called Josh. And there was Remy, half from Sierra Leone and half from Islington, who showed a zest for life that was in refreshing contrast to the apathy manifested by most of the kids at the school. He found it hard to sit still, and when talking would suddenly leap up to give emphasis to a point, whether it was about music, or politics, or poetry – his enthusiasms were wide and various.

Larry.

Amazingly, Larry did write. Long, detailed letters about his background, his present life, his plans and studies. He confessed to an on-off relationship with a girl called Judi, something he had omitted to tell me when we met in Florence. This did not bother me, as he sandwiched the information between compliments and romantic declarations. 'Firenze – greatest place in the world, and you made it such.'

I wrote long letters back, telling him about school and how I wanted to visit America. I also shared with him the problems I had had after Luisa read my diary.

'I'm really sorry that our night together caused problems between you and your mother,' he replied. 'When I see you again don't write it down in a diary – we'll keep it in our heads. If she ever talks to you about me, tell her I'm not a hippie, but an intellectual college student who will become a millionaire one of these days!'

We exchanged photographs and promises to meet.

'I shall return to England and come and get you,' he wrote. 'I have pretty much decided to get a job in England when I graduate.'

I really wanted to believe him.

Being in the sixth form meant spending most of our time in the smoking room. We would settle in there after breakfast – if breakfast was had at all – and hang around waiting to see who drifted in and out. I found myself looking forward to Remy's arrival, because his anger and his passions brought energy into the room. He had an originality of thought, a confidence in his beliefs, that made his presence felt, and whether I agreed with him or not, he was stimulating company. He was proud of his black roots: his uncle was a minister in Jamaica's government; on his mother's side there had been prime ministers in Sierra Leone. This seemed much more intriguing than the usual home-counties backgrounds of the other students, even if I had in the past envied their stable family lives.

Remy's relationship with his mother was a troubled one. 'Mum's never at home and when she is, she doesn't give a damn,' he would say. His way of coping with a difficult family life was through drawing and writing poetry, and when I showed some interest he let me see his work. I admired it. Mostly he talked and I listened.

One day in May, I found an envelope addressed to Vanessa on my study desk. I opened it up and began to read.

TO A FRIEND

You've confused me and confusion turns me paranoid.
Feel like I'm stepping between you and your lover.
I'd rather step into the gutter.
So we'd better say goodbye,
But don't worry about dropping around sometime . . .

I will walk out in the morning—
I will smile,
Thinking of you
And though you may be far away,
We will be,
What we will be.

I did not know what to do, so I did nothing. The whole thing was all too embarrassing. I avoided Remy as best I could; I stopped going into his study and in our English class I dodged his glances in my direction.

Friends kept giving me messages in a flurry of teenage excitement: 'he wants to talk to you', 'he really likes you', 'he's waiting for you ...'

When he came into my study a few days later we both avoided mentioning the poem. This went on for a week: we would spend time together but the big unspoken question hung between us.

16 May

What do I do now? I finally mentioned the poem. We were alone and the silence was unbearable. 'Thank you for the poem,' I said and then he started going on about how he liked me so much and I didn't know what to say and I left and then later he asked Ann to give me a pile of paper and they were all poems he had written to me. I can't believe it!

I felt shattered from lack of sleep and the next day I skived off double English.

As I walked to my study, Remy ran up to me.

'Where were you? Are you ill?'

I stopped and looked him straight in the face.

'No, just worrying too much lately,' I answered.

A second's pause and then we both started laughing. He put his arm around me and we walked together into the study block. Later that evening my friend Ann came into my dormitory.

'You two going out together then?'

'Hmmm, I'm not sure.'

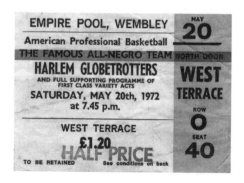

On 20 May I was off to Wembley to see the Harlem Globetrotters. The athleticism of the basketball players and the way they ducked and dived and shot their goals was incredible. Normally I had little interest in sport, but this

was like watching dance, and for the hour or two that it lasted I became completely wrapped up in the game.

As the coach made its way back to school, my thoughts returned to Remy. I realized that I was looking forward to telling him about the outing. As soon as the driver stopped in the school courtyard I ran straight to a sixth form party held in one of the larger studies. Remy bounded over, a drink in hand. I was touched that he looked so pleased to see me, and when we said goodnight at the bottom of the stairs leading to the girls' dormitories, we kissed each other for the first time. I didn't care who saw us, the opposite in fact – I was proud to be with him.

I wrote to Larry telling him that I now had a boyfriend at school. As soon as I sent the letter I realized it had probably been unnecessary, but we had been discussing his plan to look for a job in England, so I thought it only fair. It crossed with a letter from him. 'About me coming to Europe. I won't be able to because I'm graduating soon and I don't have a job and I have no money. I've got to work for some time before I can come. What we had in Florence was unbelievably beautiful but I am not the same easy-going, irresponsible person I was when I met you. I hope you can understand and I still want to be good friends.'

I was relieved, and relaxed into my relationship with Remy. It felt good, being loved. I was like other girls, like those in *Jackie* magazine – I had a proper boyfriend to walk around arm in arm with.

In half-term we arranged to meet in London. He arrived late, stewing with pent-up rage because he had been stopped and searched by police. He railed about it for five minutes.

'There was no reason for them to do that!'

'Why would they do it then?' I asked ingenuously. 'Do you think they were looking for drugs?'

'It's because I'm black, of course! I told you, they're bastards!' He punched his fist into the palm of his other hand.

'You think they stopped you just because you're black? Come on, we're in London, not Alabama!'

He sighed. 'You'll never be able to understand.'

*

A little later, in Florence, I instantly recognized Remy's writing on the bright orange envelope in the mailbox. But it was addressed to Mrs, not Miss Nicolson.

I handed it to Luisa.

'Umm, Mummy, I think this is for you.'

I watched her open it, with growing apprehension. She paused, then began reading out loud: 'Dear Mrs Nicolson, I am very sorry not to have communicated to you, prior to this letter. I hope you will forgive my lack of etiquette however, and accept my due apologies. As this in the main is a letter of introduction, I will introduce both myself and my background. Firstly, in all humility I will present myself . . .'

He proceeded to give his full name and family tree going back several generations, including details of his maternal grandfather's cousins who were prime ministers of Sierra Leone, and their status as Kamand chiefs of the Mendi people, and his father's education and religion, and so on. The explanations took up five pages.

Luisa finished reading. I waited, unsure what she was going to say next.

'Well, that's nice,' she said drily as she carefully folded up the letter and placed it back in its envelope.

Years later I found the carbon copy of the short note she wrote back: 'It was very nice of you to write to me and to give me such a detailed account of yourself and your family: I wonder how much Vanessa has told you about hers?'

On my sixteenth birthday in August I received a card with an illustration of a girl with long black hair – like mine – sitting in a field of flowers. Inside Remy had written a poem comparing me to a rainbow. I clutched it to my chest and rushed to my room to savour the words, again and again. At the end of the summer I actually looked forward to going back to school. Remy and I were going to share a dark, gloomy study in the upper sixth student block. I had plans to make it feel warm and homely.

My diary entry for 12 September was brief: 'Went back to Frensham. I'm too happy to write. Everything is just beautiful.'

Two days later, it was Remy's eighteenth birthday. We holed up in the study with the bottle of whisky I had given him. I had created a love nest in the corner of the room out of Indian bedspreads and velvet cushions.

The next day I went to our study but there was no sign of him all morning. I did not see him at lunch either. Late in the afternoon he came in, slamming the door behind him.

'Where have you been?'

'Nowhere.'

He pulled up his chair and started looking through the papers on his desk. I kept my head down and pretended to study until I couldn't take the tense atmosphere any longer.

'What's wrong?' I said, looking up.

'Nothing.'

He was impenetrable. Should I get up, put my arms around him? Ignore him? I was paralysed by indecision. Oh to be anywhere but here.

'Well, I'll see you then,' I said abruptly as I walked out of the door.

25 September.

He is being a bastard. I really yelled at him today. He has got so bossy. And then he was going on and on about becoming Chairman of the sixth form committee. Big fucking deal.

The following day I went into our study, dreading his bad mood. He sat with his head in his hands but looked up when I came in.

'Vanessa, I'm sorry, I don't think I can share with you any more. I can't think. I've got too much to do. There is the sixth form committee and ...'

'But the other day ...' I mumbled, remembering the declarations of love as he caressed my body.

'Yup, well that was the other day. John has agreed to swap studies with you.'

That afternoon I moved my things out. I hid in my dormitory and sulked for the rest of the weekend. A few days later I noticed him hovering outside the door of my new study. I deliberately ignored him. In the end he walked in and stood by my new desk.

'You want to come for a walk?'

'No.' I refused to look at him.

'Come on ...' He grinned sheepishly.

Oh, those deep brown intelligent eyes. How could I resist?

The following week I went to my appointment with the school doctor to get the pill. I pretended it was because of period pains. The doctor was a reedy middle-aged man with a cadaverous face whom I had known since starting at the school. None of the girls liked him. When we were younger he would get us to line up in our knickers to be weighed and measured, giving us a little tickle or playful slap on our bums as we walked past.

'Take off all your clothes and get on the examining table.'

He stood watching as I did so. He proceeded to give me an internal examination and then put his hands on my breasts.

'Does that feel nice?' he asked as he rubbed them vigorously.

He looked sweaty and old. I felt flustered. It seemed such a strange question to ask, and what was he doing, rubbing like that? Maybe he was checking for something? What could he be checking for? I turned my head away and stared at the white surgery wall, trying to detach my mind from the unpleasantness of the situation.

'You can get dressed now,' he said brusquely.

He then disappeared for twenty minutes. I stood around, fully clothed, wondering where he had gone. I moved to the chair in front of his desk, looking around, expecting to hear him come in. Should I leave the room to find him? Eventually he opened the door again. He didn't look at me as he wrote out the prescription for the chemist.

I rushed back to Remy's study waving a packet of contraceptive pills.

'Look what I've got!' I shouted as I skipped through the door. 'They take a week or so to take effect and oh God, the doctor, it was awful ...'

He spoke slowly to the wall in front of him. 'I'm sorry, Nessa, this isn't going to work.'

Don't do this to me again. Please, not again.

My grin froze into a grimace as I swivelled away from him and opened the door I had just come through. I walked in a trance to my dormitory, chucking the pills I was still clutching in my hand into the waste-paper bin before throwing myself on the bed, distraught.

18 October 1972, Wed.

Ran away to London. Went to Julian's place. Dad not too angry. Smoked a lot of dope with Adrian, Julian and Dad. Quite funny. Got awful lifts when hitching – three sex maniacs in a row. Never hitching by myself again.

Remy and I weren't speaking to each other. I was incapable of concentrating on my schoolwork, I was missing more meals and lessons; I could not eat or sleep or function in any way. Our English teacher Mr Ramsay had cornered me after assembly – or 'morning talk' as it was called – to remind me that my presentation on *King Lear* was coming up. The prospect was terrifying. I hadn't prepared a thing, I

© *Alison Turnbull*

Remy, September 1972.

hadn't even got to the end of the play. I could not possibly speak in front of Remy and his friends. I imagined them smirking and me making a fool of myself and Mr Ramsay getting cross. I wanted to vanish into thin air.

I took the decision at the very last minute, the night before, without telling anyone. When I was alone in the dormitory I stuffed some clothes (plus my diary and my little address book) into my rucksack and pushed it under the bed. Feigning illness, I went to bed early. Under the sheets I was fully clothed and in the morning stayed covered as the others got up for breakfast. They were used to me missing breakfast and in the last few weeks I had often missed morning talk as well. Once it was quiet and I could trust that everyone was in the refectory, I rose, pulled the rucksack out from underneath, slipped into my desert boots and out of the fire door on the landing and down the back stairs.

It seemed so peaceful outside.

It was early and the weather was fresh but sunny. I strode away from the school, past the autumnal trees, across the playing fields and down the long road to Rowledge, the local village. As I approached the Hare and Hounds pub I saw that the bus to the nearest town was arriving so I jumped on. I had no fully formed idea about my destination, I just needed a break from the torpor that had beset me for the last few weeks and felt that if I moved away, I might possibly leave some of the gloom behind.

After twenty minutes or so the bus stopped outside Farnham station. I grabbed my rucksack and walked into the station buffet. I approached the middle-aged woman behind the counter. She smiled as I paid for the watery coffee and the square of fruitcake wrapped in plastic. Her friendliness encouraged me.

'Could you tell me how to find the road that goes to London?'

'Yes, of course,' and she proceeded to offer complicated instructions.

I gulped the coffee and cake down quickly as if I was late for an appointment. I wanted to get going while the woman's directions were fresh in my mind.

I had no idea exactly where I was going apart from a broad sense that London was the place to aim for. Nor did I know what I was going to do. Maybe I would meet some new people – perhaps a van full of travelling hippies. Or perhaps a nice-looking guy would stop and whisk me off into another life. After all, my friend Lydia had met her current boyfriend, the lovely Simon, by hitching a lift in his Morris Minor. Hitch-hiking in the early 1970s represented freedom and adventure. But for me, simply getting away was the main thing. It wasn't so much wanting to be somewhere else as wanting not to be at school. Anywhere else would do.

I stuck out my thumb and tried to smile as each car approached. An hour later I was still standing there and it was getting harder to smile. I thought of my friends, some probably sitting in the common room by now, some making their way to lessons. Would they be wondering where I was? Most importantly, would Remy be worried about me?

By the time a battered pick-up truck pulled up, I felt hugely grateful.

'You going to London?' I asked through the passenger window. The driver nodded and I threw my rucksack into the open part of the truck and climbed in.

'Thank you so much!'

He was a thin, weedy man with very pale skin and sandy hair. The front of his truck smelt of stale cigarettes and beer. From my limited experience of hitch-hiking, I had learnt that you quickly needed to assess whether a driver was a talker, a listener or preferred silence. This one seemed to be the silent type, as he kept his eyes fixed on the road, and that was fine by me. We drove for about half an hour and I looked out of the passenger window. We were travelling along the Hog's Back, a stretch of road that used to make us giggle at school, as did our previous headmaster's name, Mr Hogg. Mr Hogg, who had a heart attack as he was playing tennis with a girl in my year called Ruth. She was very good at tennis. My mind wandered. How long would it take to get to the outskirts of London? What should I do then? I had very little money on me. The reality of what I was undertaking was slowly dawning on me. *Where shall I sleep? What will I be able to get to eat?*

As if reading my thoughts, weedy-man suddenly broke the silence. 'Would you like five pounds?'

He was still looking ahead with his eyes on the road, as if too nervous to gauge my reaction. It was the first time he had spoken, and it was almost to himself. I'd got so used to the silence that it took me aback. I turned my head slowly. He sensed my gesture and glanced at me.

'You can have five pounds if you look at it.'

'Look at what?'

'You know . . .'

'I'm sorry, I really don't.'

He took his left hand off the steering wheel and started tugging at his flies.

'Oh no . . . I don't think so!' I laughed nervously.

'Please! Please just look at it.' He continued to whimper as he pulled at the zip.

I felt a bit sick. 'No, I don't want to look at anything! Can you stop doing that, please?'

'But you only have to look at it and then you'll have five pounds . . .'

For a heartbeat I thought, *I could do with five pounds*, and hesitated. What harm could it do?

'Pleeease . . .' he whined.

I pulled myself together. 'Stop the truck!'

He didn't slow down.

'*Stop* right now!'

Thankfully, the second time I shouted he did as I asked, and I opened the door and leapt out. But just as he began preparing to edge forward to get back onto the road I realized I had forgotten my rucksack.

'Hey!' I banged on the roof of the truck.

He slammed on the brakes and I managed to snatch the bag, just as he accelerated away again.

I took a deep breath and raised my thumb. This time a car stopped almost immediately, a spotless, smart car that smelt of leather. The driver looked like somebody's father: middle-aged, suited, glasses. He began telling me that he was a manager of something, a bank or a business. I didn't care, but listened politely to him talking about his home in Surrey, his wife, his two boys.

'And what's a young lady like you doing hitch-hiking to London? Shouldn't you be at school?'

I made up some story about it being almost half-term and how I was allowed out early as my father had been taken ill and the money he had sent for my train fare had not arrived. The driver kept asking questions, and as I embellished I almost believed the lies I was coming out with. Then slowly it dawned on me that he had driven off the main road onto smaller and smaller lanes. I interrupted my story, feeling slightly anxious.

'Where are you going?'

No answer.

'What are you doing?'

He braked suddenly and leant over to grab me.

'What the hell?'

'Come here and shut up.' All his politeness had gone in an instant.

I started kicking him and thrashing about with my arms. This seemed to excite him even more.

'Proper little wildcat ...'

I grabbed his glasses and threw them across the car.

'You bitch ...' he began fumbling around trying to find them, and as he did so, I seized the rucksack at my feet and shakily managed to open the door.

I had no idea where I was. I ran without stopping, terrified that the man was going to pursue me in his car. I ran until I tired, and then slumped down on a bank by the road to catch my breath. I realized that I was not too far from the main thoroughfare as I could hear traffic in the distance.

I was hungry. I didn't want to hitch-hike any longer but I had hardly any money and there wasn't a station or bus stop in sight. It didn't occur to me to give up my escape, to try and get back to school. It was too late. I was trapped, unable to go backwards or forwards.

To cap it all, the sunny day had now been replaced by greyness and drizzle. I thought of my friends, of Remy, of being lost and far from anything familiar. *I could have been raped, murdered, and no one would know or care. I'm sixteen and I wish I were dead . . .*

I noticed that a car had stopped near the bank and a young man, probably in his mid-twenties, was leaning across to the passenger window and calling out.

'You all right, darling? Want a lift somewhere?'

'I just want to get back to the London road,' I answered miserably.

'I'm going that way, I'll drop you off.'

Thinking, *Please God, don't be another weirdo*, I hoisted the rucksack onto my back and slowly walked to the car. He appeared smooth and good-looking and smiled as I opened the door. It was only when he was driving again that he asked me where I'd come from.

'You seem upset. Boyfriend trouble?'

And then it all came out. I confessed everything – Remy and the running away and not having any money and not knowing what to do and the guy who wanted me to look at his penis (he laughed at this) and the older guy . . .

'So what kind of man do you go for?' he asked.

Man?

Remy was still in his teens, I hadn't thought of him as a man.

'I don't know – sensitive, creative, passionate . . .'

The driver didn't respond and I felt I had given the wrong answer. So I changed the subject.

'What do you do?'

'I'm a photographer.'

'Oh right. What kind of photography?'

He smiled again but left the question unanswered.

After a pause, he said, 'You know, if you need some work, you could do some photos for me. It's all very tasteful. Course you'd have to clean yourself up a bit, you're a bit scruffy, but that shouldn't be a problem, you could earn some good money.'

My heart sank. 'I'm sorry, that's not really my scene.'

For a second I had visions of him getting nasty and aggressive and of never being able to get out of his car. But he was quite calm, indifferent even, and just shrugged.

'That's all right. I'll give you my number and you can call me if you change your mind. I'll drop you up there, this road carries straight on into London.'

I was back on the main road, with the scrap of paper holding his number in my pocket. The road was busy now and I felt heartened by the realization that I was not far from the outskirts of London. The thumb went out again and five minutes later a lorry came to a stop. It looked huge, and from my position on the road I could hardly see the driver.

'You getting in or what?'

'London?'

'Jump in.'

I levered myself up into the passenger seat. I was holding my rucksack on my lap and looking around without moving my head, nervously chewing my lower lip from the inside as I used to do as a child. My eyes darted up, down and to the right, taking in the family photographs and the packet of cigarettes on the dashboard, the well-thumbed road atlas on the floor, a crumpled copy of the *Sun*. I looked sideways at the driver, a burly man of about forty-five, side-burned, wearing a donkey jacket. His black hair was curly and his hands were smeared with black grease. There was a toolbox between us. It was closed and I started wondering what kind of tools were inside it. I felt my breath getting shorter as I imagined the instruments of torture that would soon come out of it. A hammer to knock me on the head, maybe, masking tape to cover my mouth, fat screwdrivers to dig into my neck, something nasty to threaten me with as he drags me into the back of his lorry and rapes me. When would anyone realize I was missing?

'You all right, love?'

As the thoughts had come into my head, my eyes had grown wider, my grip on the rucksack tighter, and I had edged so close to the passenger door that I was virtually out of my seat. My palms felt sweaty.

'Sorry, yeah, I'm OK,' I squeaked.

'I'm not gonna hurt ya, darlin', you look like a frightened rabbit!' He had a deep, coarse laugh.

I tried to relax my shoulders a bit but wasn't convinced. I bit my bottom lip again.

'What ya gonna do in London?' he asked.

I realized that I had absolutely no idea. That I would probably never get there anyway.

'I'm going to see my father.'

He glanced at me, then back to the road.

'How old are you, love?'

'Sixteen.'

'Does your dad know you're hitch-hiking?'

'Er, no, but I don't think he'd mind.'

'You sure about that?'

I didn't answer. I just wanted to know when he was going to turn nasty and drive off the road and rape me. *Let's get it over and done with.*

He sighed.

'Look, love, I don't usually pick up hitch-hikers. I'm not so keen on hippies and the like. But I've got two daughters and one is about your age. I wouldn't want them to be hitching, specially on their own. Not with the maniacs that are around.' He shook his head.

This is where he pretends to be all kind and caring before he leaps on me.

'You don't have to say anything. I just want you to know, don't worry. You're safe. I'm not going to hurt you. Don't be scared. But you gotta promise me you won't do any more hitching, at least not on your own. We'll be near London soon and I'll drop you off by a tube or bus station, and you can get to your dad that way.'

His warm cockney accent felt reassuring and the knots of tension in my shoulders began softening. He seemed genuine. I smiled.

'Are those your daughters?' I was looking at the faded photograph of two plump girls aged about twelve and fourteen grinning at the camera.

'Yeah, they're a bit older now. Nothing but trouble! Drives me wife mad!'

I laughed and relaxed. For the next half an hour or so we chatted about his girls and his job on the road. Eventually he pulled up near a bus stop. We were at the outskirts of London.

'Thank you,' I said, grinning broadly, feeling a wave of gratitude for this big, kind, rough-looking man who hadn't hurt me.

'Take care, love. No more hitching, mind!' His lorry rumbled off.

I was on the pavement in the middle of a thoroughfare. Two old ladies were standing by the bus stop. I asked them in which direction the bus was going. They mentioned names I'd never heard of.

I was cold and hungry and no bus was coming.

I decided to call Julian Rankin.

Julian was the boy I had met two years earlier, during the summer holiday in the Algarve. Our villa had been full to bursting with my father's friends – the Toynbees, the Kees – but Julian was on his own in the villa next door with his mother and stepfather.

His stepfather, Adrian Reid, was a writer and roué who had made money with a book called *Confessions of a Hitch-hiker*. It featured a pho-

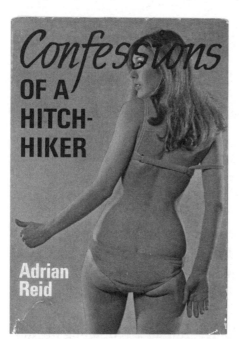

tograph on the cover of a curvy blonde girl wearing a yellow bikini and was based on the story of a young girl Adrian met in the late 1960s, a 'free spirit' who hitch-hiked around Europe with another 'cool chick', having adventures along the way. Adrian was probably the same age as my father – early fifties – but thought of himself as quite the hipster. He had straggly white hair and a florid complexion, and peppered his classless drawl with references to 'birds' and 'chicks'. Men were 'cats'. He talked about wife swapping and dope smoking. I don't think my father had ever met anyone like him, but they struck up a friendship on the Portuguese holiday which continued for a while back in England, as it turned out they lived close to one another in west London.

The inside of the phone box smelt of cat's piss and ash. A couple of panes of glass had been smashed. I fished my old address book out of my rucksack and dialled the number.

Beep, beep, beep. I pressed some coins into the slot.

'Hello? Julian?' I said breathlessly.

'Sorry, Julian isn't here at the moment, it's his stepfather Adrian.'

'Oh hello, it's Vanessa,' the disappointment clear in my voice.

'Hi, baby, you at school? What's up?'

'No, I . . . I don't know where I am, I ran away and . . .'

'You ran away? Where are you phoning from?'

'I don't know! Somewhere near London.' I peered out of the telephone box window.

A man waiting outside shot me an impatient look. The pips were going again and I shoved the last of my small change into the slot.

I felt tearful again. 'I . . . I don't know where I am . . . what to do . . .' my voice trembled.

'Now baby, don't cry. Do you think you can find a taxi?'

'I think so . . . maybe.'

'You get into a taxi and come to Abbotsbury Road. You got any bread?'

Pause.

'How much will a taxi cost?'

'I'll pay, don't worry. Then we'll work something out.'

He sounded almost excited.

I pushed the phone box door open and stood at the intersection of two main roads thinking, maybe I should just hitch again, but I didn't know which direction to take. Finally, dithering, I spotted a black cab in the distance. Its orange 'For Hire' light was on.

'What did you think you were doing?' Adrian asked, filling my mug with coffee.

He had just paid the taxi driver what seemed to me a very large sum. I told him my story – including the weird men who had picked me up on the road.

'Jesus, man! What you going to do now?'

I shook my head. 'Don't know really.' At that moment I just wanted to find a bed and go to sleep.

'Right, we're going to do this. First, I'll call the school to tell them you're here ...'

'No, you mustn't do that!' I shouted, panic rising.

'But they'll be worried, they've probably even called the police by now.'

'I don't want them to know where I am ...'

'They need to know you're safe.'

'They won't even have noticed I'm missing,' I said.

We sat in silence.

'You want more toast?'

'Please, I'm starving!'

I shoved more toast and pâté into my mouth as if I hadn't eaten for days.

'You're a hungry girl! All right, I won't call the school. But you must let me phone Ben. He can be the one to tell the school, and then he can come over here from work. Julian will also be back by then and we can all have supper.'

I cringed at the thought of involving my father, but agreed.

Two hours and a lot of toast later Ben arrived, having left his office early. He looked concerned but did not seem cross. Adrian opened a bottle of wine and when the bottle was finished he opened a second. Julian arrived looking surprised and pleased to find me there.

After supper Adrian rolled the first joint.

'God, this is so embarrassing, what's Daddy going to do?' I thought as Julian passed it his way. Ben took it in two fingers, looked at it curiously and pulled on it, taking a long drag.

'So what's all the fuss about this stuff? Tastes like a bonfire to me,' he spluttered as he examined it in his fingers, slowly letting the smoke escape from his nose and the corners of his mouth.

'You're supposed to pass it on now,' said Adrian, nudging him.

Julian and I caught each other's eyes. Several joints later we were falling about laughing over Ben's story of how he had telephoned my school, and the person answering had no idea that I was even missing.

I turned to Adrian triumphantly. 'I told you so!'

The school suggested Ben keep me at home for a week. 'It sounds like Vanessa needs to sort her head out,' was the view of Nick Reynish, my bearded sociology teacher and so-called personal tutor. For the rest of the week I had long lie-ins while my father went to work, and then spent the afternoons hanging out at Kensington Market.

I was feeling adrift. My attempted escape had got me nowhere and I couldn't concentrate on my schoolwork. I confided in my diary. 'Everything is pointless.'

For days I recorded my gloom. 'Can't stand it any more. Can never stop crying. I'm lost, feel suffocated. Want to feel better but don't know how ... Am so sick of pretending to be cheerful.'

Then, for a while there are no entries, until: '23 November 1972. Went to Farnham – bought pills. 24 November 1972. Took overdose of sleeping pills. What I imagined hell to be like as a little child seemed to come to life.'

I planned my escape from life much as I had planned my escape from school, without telling anyone, and with little emotion. On Thursday afternoon I calmly walked to the village and took the bus to Farnham. From two different chemists, so as not to arouse suspicion, I bought as many over the counter sleeping pills and painkillers as I could. When I got back to the dormitory I hid them under my mattress.

That night I lay in bed clutching the little bottles to my chest. This was strangely comforting. When the others in the dormitory had stopped chatting and been quiet for a while I poured the pills out and swallowed them one by one, with the large glass of water I had carefully placed on my bedside table. It didn't occur to me to grind them into a powder to make them easier to wash down. I only got as far as thinking, *I'll take the pills and go to sleep and not wake up and all this pain will be over.*

The glass was soon empty. I wondered if I had taken enough. Should I get some water and swallow more? Not wanting to draw attention to myself, I waited until I felt quite sure that everyone was asleep.

I was beginning to feel dozy but I forced myself to get up. I poured some more pills into my hand and with the empty glass in the other went to the bathroom. I was standing by the tap filling up the glass when in walked a girl from the year above.

'Can't you sleep either?' she said.

Panic welled up. I couldn't answer.

'Are you OK? Your hand is shaking.'

I looked at the hand holding the glass as though it belonged to some-one else. It was shaking so badly that water was spilling everywhere.

Look normal. Normal.

I stared at her and opened my mouth but nothing came out. Her face was blurring. There was buzzing in my ears. I felt faint.

'You look terrible, what's wrong?'

The room was out of focus. Suddenly my legs gave way, my fist opened and the pills fell to the ground.

'What have you done? Have you taken pills?'

A sob escaped my mouth as I collapsed. The girl ran to call matron and the two of them dragged me to the sick bay. The school nurse began forcing glass after glass of salt water down my throat.

I retched and vomited for what seemed like hours until I felt so weak, I was begging her to let me go and lie down. But she kept forc-ing more salty water down. She was furious. 'What on earth did you think you were doing? You silly, silly girl.'

I knew I had to pretend the whole thing had been an accident, so I repeated the story that I couldn't sleep and hadn't been able to get rid of a headache so I had kept taking the pills. The nurse knew I suffered from migraines so perhaps it didn't seem such an unlikely tale.

Finally I was allowed to go back to bed.

'Sleep it off tomorrow, and no more of this nonsense, please.' And then she laughed, shaking her head. 'It really is unbelievable that you could be so stupid as to do such a thing!'

There are no more diary entries for the rest of the year.

Rumours went around about what I had done, but I kept my head down and nobody asked me about it apart from my sociology teacher Nick. He cornered me in the refectory a few days later to tell me that he had heard I had taken an overdose by mistake.

'Are you sure it was an accident?' he said.

'Oh yes, sure,' eyes fixed on my tray.

'Hmm,' he said, staring at me intently. 'Well, you know if you need someone to talk to . . .'

I looked at him and thought, *Why would I talk to you?*

17 Feb 1973

Went to Portobello Road with Ann and bought a pair of jeans and some very nice grey loons. Had drinks at Adrian's house – he has invited us to a play tomorrow. His wife is ill.

18 Feb 1973

This morning Dad took me to a pub in Islington where a friend of his sings the blues. It was really good. Had lunch with the singer, he is called George Meley [*sic*]. After lunch we smoked thousands of joints – I've never been so stoned in my life. I really thought I was going to faint and on the tube I was getting really paranoid. Went to see the play with Adrian and we had a Chinese meal with some of the actors. Was so stoned all the way through!

When my father told me that his art critic friend sang in a pub, I thought it would be amateurish and awkward, but I loved it. We all went back to the Melly household for lunch and I sat next to George. He was sweet, asking me about my interests, and when I told him I liked the Liverpool poets – Brian Patten, Roger McGough, Adrian Henri – he got up and returned with a handwritten poem by Adrian Henri, *Footnote to 'Autobiography: Winter poem 1971'*.

The poem appeared under a picture of a heavily bearded Adrian Henri sitting in some sort of domestic interior. Under the dedication 'For George and Diana Melly, Adrian Henri', George scribbled 'and for Vanessa (who likes A.H.) from George and Diana'.

I was touched. After lunch Diana, George's beautiful wife, brought out a box and began rolling joints of very strong grass. Then everything

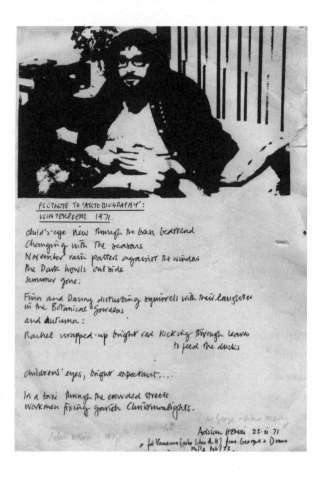

FOOTNOTE TO 'AUTOBIOGRAPHY':
WINTERPOEM 1971.

child's-eye view through the brass bedstead
changing with the seasons
November rain patters against the window
the Park howls outside
summer gone:

Finn and Danny disturbing squirrels with their laughter
in the Botanical Gardens
and autumn:

Rachel wrapped-up bright red kicking through leaves
to feed the ducks

childrens' eyes, bright expectant....

In a taxi through the crowded streets
workmen fixing garish Christmas lights.

Adrian Henri 25·xi 71

is blurred. I remember making some excuse to go back to Ben's flat in
Holland Park so that I could lie down. I got into the right underground
train but kept missing my stop, passing Notting Hill Gate and going
around the Circle line, getting off and taking the right direction back
but then missing the stop again. By the time I got to the flat, Ben was
already home, seemingly fresh and sober. My father never seemed
altered by either drink or cannabis.

The play we went to see with Adrian that evening is not memor-
able. It may have been something he had written himself. He certainly
seemed to know the actors well.

'Darling, she's perfect!' screeched a very tall actress as she joined
our table after the show, putting her hand on Adrian's shoulder and

167

looking at me at the same time. She had so much stage make-up on that it was difficult to judge her age. Late twenties, probably. I looked at Adrian for guidance.

'Yes, I told Ika about you. She is saying Franco Zeffirelli is looking for a young girl to play Mimi ...'

'But I can't act or sing or anything ...' I stuttered, terrified that I would be called upon to audition in some way.

'Oh, that doesn't matter!' Ika had sat down next to me now. 'You're young and you look vulnerable. That's good, exactly what he is looking for.'

As the evening ended she squeezed my hand. 'Promise me to think about getting in touch with Franco. Adrian has my number.'

The next day Adrian rang up. I noted in my diary: 'I'm going to Adrian's studio tomorrow afternoon. He says he wants to talk to me. I'm a bit scared actually.'

Adrian had rented a room somewhere in Kensington. 'I need a place to write,' he explained. Perhaps he used it to entertain the actresses who appeared in the films he wrote for producer Stanley Long, like *Sex and the Other Woman* – a vehicle for soft porn with bad dialogue and wooden acting.

'Come in, darling, come on in,' Adrian said as he opened the door.

His studio was tiny, with only enough room for the single bed that doubled up as a sofa. The typewriter on the small desk was surrounded by paper. He had prepared a joint, which lay next to a notebook. He lit it and passed it to me.

'Sit down,' he said, indicating the bed.

20 Feb. 1973

Oh God, it was so horrible. I went to Adrian's little studio – he gave me a joint and oh Christ he kept kind of putting his hands everywhere, saying I was a beautiful chick and that I can come and see him anytime but that I mustn't let him seduce me. He won't have to worry! I was really glad to get out! Jesus!

Yet when I got back to school we started writing to each other. No mention was made again about his 'wandering hands'. I thought it best to ignore it. I filled my letters with complaints about life at boarding school, my problems with Remy, my worries about what I was going to do next. I found it therapeutic to write to him, knowing he would not be judgmental.

Nessa darling,

You write rather good English – did you know? I mean, even a letter about nothing much, like your last one, was written in clean prose – a lot of people can't do that, my dear. So write a fucking novel. I'm always trying to sell you things, aren't I? Write, act … Well, why not? Write the story about your lover. '*La vie d'une jeune fille.*' Much better you write it than me, because you are the *jeune fille* and I'm not. And novels by chicks under twenty are always well received.

Did you ever write to Franco Zeffirelli about playing Mimi in *La Dame Aux Camélias* – Ika's brilliant idea – you didn't, did you? Thought not. Hum.

Great stresses at the moment re the play – producer wanting one thing, me another. Makes me schizoid. Last night I freaked out and got pissed at the Chelsea Potter, a rumbustious place full of chicks with developed sex drives and cats with developed career drives.

I've just finished a second draft of the play I was commissioned. It's as unfunny as ever. I'm having lunch with the producer in half an hour, and no doubt he will tell me this in his own words, and that will be the end of that little assignment.

Stanley Long rang me this morning to say that the sexploitation movie I wrote for him last summer is an all-time floperoo. Which doesn't surprise me. A series of rather unappetizing ladies in the nude writhing in simulated copulation seems to me the biggest turn-off ever. Can the British public be tired of unappetizing ladies writhing in the nude? And if so, whatever do we give them next?

It was Adrian who gave me the idea of what I should do on leaving school.

> Vanessa dear, no one knows what to do when they leave school except those blessed with a sense of vocation. Don't exile yourself to Florence. Dream up some gentle after school course. There are worse things than art history ... Though it's no good me trying to give people pep talks, darling. xx

Maybe Adrian was right. There were worse things than art history. I had spent my teenage years dismissing my parents' art historian profession, yawning in art galleries, looking the other way during sightseeing trips. But despite myself, I began picking out some of Ben's books from his library. Once, when he came into my room unexpectedly, I quickly shoved Gombrich's *Story of Art* under the covers so that he wouldn't see what I was reading. I didn't want to admit that I was becoming interested in anything he might approve of.

With Ben on Founders Day, Frensham Heights, June 1973.

2005

I can't sleep, and when I do I have bad dreams.

The worst are the baby ones. You are the baby and I'm looking after you, I'm carrying you or feeding you, but in the next scene I'm anxious. I've left you somewhere and I can't find you, and when I do, I see that you have turned into something else. Last night I dreamt that I found you in the sink, and when I went to pick you up you had turned into the doll I had as a child. You were still in the same baby clothes that you had been wearing earlier in the dream as a live baby. But your head had turned into plastic and your eyes were glassy, staring at me lifelessly.

Something changed in Rosa that summer of 2005. Now sixteen, it was as if she had decided to reinvent herself for the new school. Determined to lose weight, she began to watch everything she ate. She stopped snacking and started cooking carefully planned menus, with no carbohydrates.

The days on the sofa were over. Now she never kept still, going for long walks and runs. When the weather was warm she swam fifty lengths of the pool; when it was raining we would hear her dancing upstairs in her bedroom. At first we encouraged her desire to get fit. By September she had lost all the extra weight and started the new school looking wonderful – six feet tall, long limbed, brown-eyed, healthily toned and tanned, with glossy hair. It was how she wanted to look, how she felt she was meant to be.

The dieting, however, had become an obsession. She pored over cookery books, reading recipes until late at night. She measured and weighed everything like a scientist. I pointed out that healthy diets include some carbohydrates and that now she had lost the excess weight, she needed to maintain a balanced intake of food. She ignored my pleas and I saw with increasing alarm that it was taking her hours – literally three or four hours – to get through a small plate of food. I found weight charts and laxatives in her bedroom; she set about keeping a notebook documenting everything she was eating and how many calories each item represented. At the bottom of each page was her recorded weight, now falling at an alarming rate.

She began leaving lists of strange beans and grains to buy from the health food shop and had tantrums if I was unable to get exactly what she asked for. One morning as we arrived at school, we had an argument about mung beans.

'I need mung beans.'

'I'm sorry, I can't get them for you today, I'm going to London.'

'Don't they have mung beans in London?'

'Rosa, I do have other things to do than search for mung beans. I'll get them tomorrow.'

'But I need them today!'

'Well, you'll have to wait until tomorrow.'

'I can't!' she shouted. 'I *have* to have them tonight!'

She slammed the car door, and I, angry and upset, reversed the car in order to drive away. I hit something behind me, and to my horror realized I had backed into her while she was opening the boot to get her school bag.

She screamed and I leapt out of the car, panicking. She was shouting at me, telling me I was an idiot and that I had hurt her foot. One of the teachers was walking by, and we helped Rosa hobble up to the matron. The foot appeared bruised but not broken.

The matron took her blood pressure. It was very low.

'Rosa, have you had any breakfast?' she asked.

'She never eats breakfast,' I sighed.

'Get on the scales,' the matron ordered.

Rosa climbed on and I was faced with the reality of how much weight she had lost over the past few months. She was no longer slim – she was emaciated.

The following week I took her to our GP. Visits to doctors had been a regular part of her life for ten years, and she came along without a fuss.

'You've lost a lot of weight, haven't you, Rosa?' he said as soon as we walked into his room.

'Yes, it's great, isn't it?' she answered.

He gave me a knowing look and suggested I bring her in regularly for weigh-ins. But the weight kept falling, and a few weeks later he referred her to the Child & Family Mental Health Service. A doctor confirmed anorexia nervosa. I began taking her out of school for weekly appointments with a psychiatrist, and would sit in the waiting room while she was being seen, wondering how to help her. What was she saying to the psychiatrist? Both Andrew and I felt completely impotent; this was beyond our experience. It was as if she had been possessed by something independent of herself, much like the epilepsy seemed at times.

When I asked her whether the psychiatrist offered any insights, she laughed.

'But are you able to talk to the doctor? You know, about how you feel?'

'Oh, I tell them any old story!' she laughed again.

The next time we went, I asked the nurse if I could speak to the psychiatrist.

'No, that isn't possible.'

'But why not?'

'Patient confidentiality.'

I read disapproval and suspicion in her eyes: *Here is another hopeless, controlling parent responsible for causing all her daughter's problems.* I wanted to tell them about the epilepsy, about my theory that Rosa was trying to gain control over something, because over that condition she had no control. Strangely she had not suffered any seizures since she had lost all the weight. Was there a connection? I lay awake at night wondering. And then, all the nagging thoughts about my inadequacies as a mother would come. Had she been affected by my mood swings? By my withdrawal when struck down by migraines or depression? By my own issues with body image? I had always associated giving food with offering comfort and her refusal to eat felt like a rejection of my maternal love. Maybe the very thing I wanted to give her – nurturing love – was what she felt suffocated by.

We began family therapy but only managed two sessions. She came along but refused to say a word. Andrew looked distracted. Ellie was away, travelling on her gap year, somewhere in Africa. I sat between my silent husband and younger daughter and talked. Rosa remained mute and Andrew hardly spoke, and when he did he was guarded.

One of the therapists in the room responded with: 'Vanessa, you seem to be carrying all this on your shoulders. You need to look after yourself and develop your own interests. The best thing you can do is back off ...'

Back off ...

We heard this over and over again. Back off. What were we supposed to do? Pretend all this wasn't happening?

My own interests seemed irrelevant. I had published a book on a sculptor called Maurice Lambert and I was researching a second, on another sculptor. I had been to Scotland to study his work, and his widow was keen for me to start writing. I made an appointment at the Henry Moore Institute in Leeds to do some research in their archive. A nice apartment 'for scholars' attached to the Institute was put at my disposal.

I didn't feel like a scholar. I felt like a fraud. My thoughts were not of art but of my daughter. What was happening back home? Was she eating? How was Andrew coping? Should I phone to check, again?

Back off, back off.

I left after two days, promising the director of the Institute that I would be in touch. I never contacted her again.

Rosa had an appointment with her psychiatrist. We were sitting in the waiting room and I smiled at another woman accompanying a pale boy in a hoody. She looked exhausted. Rosa and the boy ignored each other as we mothers commiserated over parking difficulties. Once Rosa and the boy had both been called away, the woman glanced at me sympathetically.

'Anorexia?'

I nodded. It was pretty evident.

'And your son?' I asked.

'Drugs, keeps getting into trouble.'

We talked and she said something about him 'getting in with the wrong crowd'. She sniffed. 'He was such a sweet little boy,' she said, hands trembling while she searched for a tissue in her bag.

'I'm so sorry,' I mumbled. 'My daughter was sweet once too.'

As the weight nosedived, the tension at home escalated. At least Ellie, still travelling on the other side of the world, was spared the rows and slamming doors, the cold, tense silences. I tried to keep out of the way when Rosa was in the kitchen preparing her strange meals, but one evening I lost my temper. I was hungry and tired, and impatient to start cooking supper.

'You always take over the kitchen and make such a mess!' I said, exasperated.

She ignored me.

I tried to walk past her to get to the fridge and we bumped into each other as she turned, causing her to spill a handful of the quinoa goo that she was transferring from pan to plate. It sat in an unappetizing lump on the floor.

'Look what you've done now!' she screamed.

I took a deep breath. 'Clear it up – right now.'

'You clear it up – you made me do that,' she shouted back.

'Just clear it up.'

She tried to push past me. '*Just fuck off.*'

I grabbed her arm. 'Don't you *ever* speak to me like that!'

She gave me a look of such disgust, of pure hate, that I was silenced.

I decided to write her a letter. It made me feel better. I wrote that the reason I nagged and lost my temper was because I loved her, but I hated this illness and what it was doing to her. I pleaded with her to talk to us. I left the letter on her desk but I don't know if she ever read it. It disappeared.

She was spending more time in bed, less time at school, and physically she was very weak. She no longer had any friends. At home we were either shouting or ignoring each other. When he wasn't working, Andrew anaesthetized himself with gardening, tennis, TV and football. He didn't want to talk about it, but he suggested taking Rosa out to interesting restaurants, indulging her obsession with food by offering her a different venue every Saturday lunchtime – just to find a neutral territory, to encourage her not to see us as the enemy. Usually we took turns, as she did not like to be with both of us at the same time. 'You gang up on me,' she said.

We pandered to her every whim if it meant she would eat something, driving for miles to find new restaurants, and then sat watching her bony hands playing with minuscule portions of fish. Whatever we tried, the weight continued to fall. She stumbled like a young giraffe, as if those long legs could no longer hold her up. Her face grew elfin and furry. Her hair began to drop out. Her periods stopped.

The consultant psychologist in charge of her case said we had reached crisis point. Rosa's blood pressure was dangerously low, her pulse very weak, her BMI way below the healthy minimum. The psychiatrist wrote to our GP, with copy to us: 'I am concerned about the risk of cardiac arrhythmia related to her low pulse.' We were informed that at any moment she might have a heart attack. She would have to be hospitalized.

It was a gloomy March day as Andrew, Rosa and I approached the specialist adolescent unit. There was nowhere to sit in the waiting room because of building work. As we looked around at the posters advertising support groups and the Samaritans, a gaunt young girl with piercings walked past us, followed by a nurse who led us into a bleak, fluorescent-lit room.

The Director of the unit was waiting for us. She tried to talk to Rosa about her anorexia, but Rosa wouldn't speak, and when she finally did, it was to say that she liked being thin. She no longer felt hungry nor did she feel ill. She couldn't see what all the fuss was about. The Director explained that the stress she was putting her body through was dangerous. She was told that she would need to be put on the 'Re-feeding Menu', which included being made to drink a great deal of milk.

'I don't drink milk,' Rosa said flatly. 'It makes me feel sick.'

The nurse, who had been watching the proceedings, looked weary. She must have heard it all before.

'Drinking milk is basic to the treatment plan. It's non-negotiable.'

Rosa shrugged. 'Well, I'm not drinking any milk,' she said, 'because I'm not coming here.'

The nurse gave her a 'we shall see about that' look as the Director began imparting information about timetables and rules and visiting hours and menus.

'I'm not coming here,' said Rosa, again.

Her bony, drawn face made her look hard and determined. The Director then asked us if we were willing to give permission to section her. I nodded, yes. I didn't want her to die.

In the ensuing silence we all turned to Andrew.

He shook his head, 'I can't do it.'

Rosa looked triumphant. A pause. Finally the Director addressed her.

'Listen, Rosa, we'll make a deal. We'll keep your allocated bed free for three weeks. I won't let anyone take it, but I want you to know that there is a high demand for these beds, and you will be in it if you don't do as I say. If you manage to put on half a kilo every week for that period of time, and continue weekly check-ups with your doctor, you can remain at home.'

I felt desperate. 'Keep her here,' I wanted to say. 'I need some peace in our home. Take her away and return a healthy, anorexia-and epilepsy-free girl. Give back to us the daughter we love: happy, funny, engaged with the world.' I had no energy left to cope with the rows, the fighting, the anxiety, the strain on my marriage.

The journey home was tense. I felt sure we were just putting off the moment when we would be driving back to incarcerate her, to have milk forced down her throat and be psychologically damaged for life.

Andrew insisted that we must give her one last chance to pull herself out of the spiral. 'Maybe someone believing in her is what she needs,' he said.

He was right. Rosa agreed to spend an afternoon with Nicky, her nutritionist cousin, and they devised a plan. With the same will and determination she had applied to losing the weight, Rosa set about putting it back on. It was not easy, because as soon as her weight increased, she panicked that it would get out of control and that she would 'be fat again'. But the image of that hospital and the milk seemed to work. Gradually she reached the required minimum to keep her out of hospital. She remained very thin, but out of danger. We celebrated her seventeenth birthday with a trip to Brighton.

At home she still refused to eat with us and cut everything up into tiny morsels but her hair stopped falling out, her periods resumed and she began to get involved with school. At last she was making

Rosa, in the kitchen at Horserace, summer 2007.

friends. She went shopping with the girls and flirted with the boys and it all felt wonderfully normal.

Our latest worry was over her ambition to be a model. She had got some shots of herself taken by a professional photographer who suggested a modelling agency. They signed her up and she went off for a few shoots but none of it led anywhere as she couldn't take on jobs while at school.

We didn't forget the psychiatrists, 'Back off, back off,' and so we kept quiet. Is there any 'right' way to be a parent?

Finally Rosa made the decision to give up on the modelling to give priority to studying for her A-levels.

What a relief.

1974

What would Rosa have made of what I am about to write? Would she have shrugged with indifference and said, 'That's the way it was,' or would she have judged me as harshly as I now judge myself?

I was twenty when women marched for equality and independence, for control over their bodies, for 'women's right to choose'. I shouted as loudly as anyone. Was I shouting to reassure myself?

I never thought of those babies as just cells without a soul, even though I paid people to destroy them. Their legacy remains with me. The significance of every one of them has affected me, and a residue of guilt and longing has haunted me all these years. Every so often I work out how old they would be now, what they would look and sound like, how they might be doing. Curiosity about who they might have been has punctuated my thoughts for decades, but it's much worse now that Rosa has gone.

I need to remember them.

The first of the fathers was a stocky twenty-year-old with curly brown hair called Leon. He started talking to me outside a second-hand bookshop in South Kensington. It was the summer I would turn eighteen. I was standing in my green chenille poncho and patched jeans, glancing through the books in the cardboard boxes on the pavement. I noticed him noticing me, and buried myself in the book I found closest to hand – a battered edition of Sylvia Plath's *The Bell Jar*, a copy of which I already had at home.

'That a good book then?' was his opening line.

He had never heard of Sylvia Plath and he wasn't quite as tall as me, disappointing on both counts, but I still agreed to meet him in a pub later on.

I had just finished my year at a crammer in Oxford, taking art history A-level and retaking sociology. My father had been amazed when I announced I wanted to study art history.

'Art History?' he repeated, twice. 'But you hate sightseeing and art galleries and museums. You always have done! What about in Portugal, when you looked the other way when I was trying to point that church out?'

'Well, I can't think of anything else to do,' I mumbled, not wanting to give him the satisfaction of knowing about my developing interest in his subject.

The college in Oxford was called St Aldate's. I moved to a house with some friends, Henry and Cherry, from school. There were a couple of other girls staying there too. I had a tiny room on the ground floor with a desk, a single bed and a huge poster of Jimi Hendrix in

With Pat (in cape) at Frensham Heights, May 1973.

pink satin trousers and a brocade jacket. One of the younger girls in the house was obsessed with David Bowie, and I was struck by her telling me that when her boyfriend asked if she would swap never seeing him again for one hour with Bowie, she said she'd take the hour with Bowie.

I had another friend from Frensham Heights called Pat whose parents lived up the road in Headington. After the exam retakes she would come and stay with me at Ben's flat in London. Within a few weeks of meeting Leon he had become her boyfriend, not mine, but the three of us continued to spend most of our time together.

If Pat's parents went away, we would hitch-hike from London and spend the weekend there. One such evening we had polished off a bottle of wine when the cramps I had been experiencing that afternoon started getting worse. This did not surprise me. A few days earlier I had gone to seek the help of a doctor who looked like my father.

'My period is late,' I had told him.

It had been a couple of months since my last one. Initially I hadn't given it much thought, as my periods were often irregular, but after missing the second one, I thought I had better talk to a doctor about it. At first I wasn't sure how to find one. I had tended to avoid doctors after my experience with the school one, but I checked my father's address book under 'D' and made an appointment with Dr Someone-or-Other, whose surgery was situated opposite the house in South Kensington where my parents had lived before their divorce. Ben never consulted doctors, and had probably never set foot in the surgery, but the receptionist seemed happy for me to make an appointment.

'Do you think you could be pregnant?' the doctor had said drily from behind his desk.

Pregnant?

This possibility hadn't occurred to me. In our brief relationship, Leon and I had always been careful. Although there was that one time on my birthday when we were drunk and stoned ...

'Umm, I suppose so ...'

'And if you were pregnant, would you want to keep the baby?'

'Oh no,' I answered quickly. 'I'm going to university next year, I hope.'

I wanted him to know I wasn't an irresponsible and ignorant girl but an intelligent one with plans. Something about his demeanour made me feel he disapproved of me.

'These should do the trick,' he had said in his patrician tone after examining me.

What were these pills he was giving me? I didn't dare ask, but took them from him, muttering, 'Thank you, thank you very much.'

I had left the surgery before I realized that I hadn't asked him if in his opinion I *was* pregnant.

The following day on the way to Oxford, I felt the familiar aching I had been longing for, and when we got to the house I was relieved to discover that something was happening. At last!

But the cramps were really bad. I left Pat and Leon making tea in the kitchen and went back up to the bathroom upstairs. I crouched on the floor, my back against the wall, knees pulled up to my stomach, face looking up at the ceiling, jaw clenched in pain, and stayed there for what felt like forever, vaguely conscious of the music coming from downstairs. Oh God, the pain! I fell sideways into a foetal position and then became aware that my jeans were soaked. When I tore them off, I saw with horror that despite the sanitary protection I had in place, my thighs were covered in streaks of blood. I pulled myself up to sit on the lavatory seat and as I clutched the sides of the seat, the blood seemed to pour out of me in thick clots. My breath was short and I began feeling very frightened. After a while I grabbed a towel from the rail, wrapped it around myself and staggered down the stairs. Pat and Leon were on the sofa. The room smelt of dope.

'I'm not well,' I stammered, clutching the doorknob.

Pat looked up and screamed. 'You've got blood over Mum's best towel!'

'Shit, I'm getting an ambulance.' Leon was leaping up from the sofa and striding towards the telephone.

'But they'll know we've been smoking dope!' Pat wailed. 'The neighbours will tell my mum . . .' Leon hesitated on his way out of the sitting room door, then kept going.

'Just phone the ambulance,' I whispered to the floor.

It was a relief to get to the hospital, where I felt safe and looked after. I was cleaned up, examined, samples of blood and urine were taken and I was given a bed with lovely starched white sheets. The woman in the next bed smiled at me.

'You need to get a good night's sleep, love,' the nurse said. 'The doctor will see you tomorrow.'

Leon and Pat appeared just before the doctor's round. There was only one chair by the bed and Leon sat on it, with Pat on his lap.

Then the nurse appeared, with the doctor behind her. 'They can stay,' I said, indicating Pat and Leon.

She drew the curtains around the bed.

The doctor was talking to his clipboard. 'I'm afraid you've lost your baby. It's an incomplete miscarriage, so we shall have to perform an evacuation D and C; we can organize that for tomorrow morning.'

I nodded, wondering what D and C stood for. The doctor glanced up at Pat and Leon and then back at me.

'Does your husband know you are here?' he asked.

I hesitated. Pat giggled.

'Um, I don't have a husband ...'

'I see,' he said and I caught the look he exchanged with the nurse.

After the operation the doctor came back to see me. This time he was a bit more solicitous. 'How are you feeling?'

I felt groggy and sick.

'So-so.'

'It's very curious, although your pregnancy test result was still positive, we found nothing on operating. So you must have miscarried everything.' He smiled. 'Well, rest now, and I shall see you tomorrow,' he said before leaving my bedside.

I noticed the woman in the bed next to mine, watching me.

'I couldn't help overhearing. I'm sorry you've lost your baby,' she said softly.

Quickly and without thinking I answered, 'No, it doesn't matter, I didn't want to keep it anyway.'

I had to strain to hear what she said next.

'Oh I see.' She paused. 'I'm here with my third miscarriage, we're desperate to have a baby.'

I looked at her, silenced by the realization of what I had said. How could I be so callous and insensitive? It was as if I had absorbed the indifference of my friends and the detachment of the doctors and was acting like one of them. 'I'm so sorry ... I didn't mean ... um, that is,

I hope . . .' But it was too late to apologize or wish her a healthy pregnancy in the future. She had already turned away.

Two days later I was discharged and I took a taxi to Pat's house. Fortunately it was close by. I had period-like cramps and felt weak, so I didn't have the energy to get as far as Ben's flat in London. Pat's parents were still on holiday and she and Leon had settled in like an old married couple. They wrapped me in blankets and settled me on the sofa as they went to prepare supper.

Later that evening I was curled up watching the television with a plate of food on my lap, when the doorbell rang. I froze, hearing Pat's surprised tone and the familiar voice coming closer to the sitting room. It was Remy.

'Yeah, hi,' he bounced around nervously. 'Henry said you'd been in hospital and that you were here now, so I thought I'd come and see how you were doing.'

Pat and Leon exchanged a knowing look and left the room as Remy took his place next to me on the sofa.

'How did you get here?' I asked.

He ignored the question. 'So you been getting yourself into trouble then?' he grinned as he put his arm around me.

We had a nice evening. He was tender and funny, as he could be. He didn't ask for details and when I tried to explain what had happened, he interrupted with, 'I just want to know you are OK.'

It got late and we made up a bed on the floor with the sofa cushions and blankets. I fell asleep fully clothed on his chest, feeling peaceful and protected, sleeping deeply for the first time in a long while.

I woke in the morning alone. I looked around to see if Remy had left a note. Nothing. Was he in the bathroom or the kitchen? I staggered to my feet, searching in the rooms, but the house was filled with silence. I got back under my blanket and let my head fall on the cushion.

This has got to be the last time I ever let him do this.

It wasn't. Intermittently over the next ten years Remy would turn up, always unexpectedly. It might be the telephone ringing, 'Hi, was just wondering how you are?' or the doorbell: 'Was passing so I thought I'd say hello.' He had an uncanny knack of appearing at difficult times in my life. A conversation, sometimes a meeting, was followed by promises of keeping in touch. And then a letter would arrive, making it quite clear that no emotional dependency was to be established. Or no letter at all. I learnt to expect nothing, and not to mind.

Decades later, married with my two daughters, I read something about Remy becoming the headmaster of a school for excluded kids. I sent a card congratulating him for doing something so worthwhile. 'I always knew you would,' I wrote. 'No need to answer.' He responded by phoning me at home, and we had a long and intense chat, 'catching up'. He was married too, with three children.

'Can I write to you?' he asked as we said goodbye.

'Yeah, sure,' I answered, knowing he wouldn't.

He never did.

I let Ben know about the miscarriage to explain why I had been away longer than intended. He was understanding, in his neutral way. I made him promise not to tell Luisa for fear of sending her into another rant, and he agreed that it was best not to worry her.

My friends commented on how liberal my father was, and I did appreciate the way he left me to my own devices without moralizing, but I remember at the time partly feeling this was because he was unconcerned with my welfare. I think now it was more a desire not to meddle and seem authoritarian, but my eighteen-year-old interpretation meant I was loath to share my feelings with him and ask for advice and support.

The truth was I didn't know what to do next. Back in west London I wandered from his flat to friends' houses, increasingly terrified of my uncertain future and the negative thoughts in my head. I confided in my diary.

2 September 1974

Went to the doctor today who prescribed some weird medicine 'to lift you out of your depression'. I'm sure I'm going insane, I spent two hours today staring at the ceiling, my mind a complete blank.

10 September

I don't know if it's these pills but I feel in such an anxious state all the time. It's terrible, like I'm perpetually stoned and can't come back down to reality when I want to. And my head is either blank or full of bad thoughts. Last night, I had a nightmare of a man trying to kill me with a gigantic needle. I think I'm going to stop taking these pills.

I knew I couldn't keep finding excuses not to go to Florence. I was aware of Luisa's wish for me to live there for a while, perhaps follow some courses or help her with her administrative work for Christie's. My fear was that once I got there I would have no excuse to leave.

I finally confided my worries to Ben, and he came up with a solution. 'I have to go on a research trip to Sicily and southern Italy. Go to Florence, then come and join me. You can keep me company.'

I ditched the pills and flew to Florence, then met him in Naples, where we took the boat to Palermo. I followed him around remote churches and museums, waiting for him to finish taking notes for the book he was writing on the followers of Caravaggio. Often I would go outside to soak up the late summer sun, to recover. He allowed me the freedom to choose what I wanted to do. On 1st of October I noted in my diary, 'Saw many beautiful things this morning with Daddy. We left Palermo after lunch – stopped in Cefalù, saw the Cathedral and walked along the sea. Then I went by myself to a ruined castle in the mountains. It was wild, with no tourists, so peaceful.'

How did I get to this place in the mountains on my own? I can't recall. But I do remember that on this trip that later took in Malta, Reggio Calabria and Rome, Ben introduced me to some beautiful works of art and sights. 'The most important thing for an art historian to develop is an "eye",' he would say. 'Look at what is actually there in front of you, see how the artist has managed to convey light and texture, and how he is telling the story.' Ben's approach was rooted in the kind of art history now deemed old fashioned, based on training visual memory; basically learning to look. And I did begin to look, and I think

Ben in the early 1970s.

Ben was gratified. At other times he would be wrapped up in his own thoughts and we might stand together silently for some time before the 'old' Vanessa whined, 'Daddy, can we go now?'

We also had fun. We shared good food and jokes, laughing over the hotel managers who referred to us as husband and wife and insisted on giving us rooms with interconnecting doors, while winking at Ben when he referred to me as his daughter. We made up stories about the other guests. 'That lady,' Ben might say, 'has an incurable disease and wants to spend her last days in Italy.' I would dart a glance and whisper back, 'No, she has left her husband and is waiting for her Italian lover, but he isn't going to show up ...'

With the eye of an anthropologist, Ben described the life I was leading back in London in a letter to his brother Nigel:

Vanessa is developing in the most interesting way imaginable – in a way very strange and unfamiliar to me or to you, but remembering how odd we were at eighteen in a different way, I am fascinated, keeping my correct distance as a parent should. She is almost entirely indifferent to what is going on in the world – inflation, political corruption, whatever you like to think of – and is totally engrossed in a small group of devoted friends, boys and girls with whom she constantly stays (in Oxford and Sussex) and who are constantly staying with her (at Holland Park).

Her bedroom at night looks like the remains of a package tour to Nicosia – bodies sprawling all over the floor wrapped in blankets, male and female, you can never tell which because both sexes have equally long hair which flows over the carpet by their pillows of knapsacks. Some of them are *bedint* [a Sackville term denoting 'working class' background or taste], some ordinary middle class – I believe they make no differentiation between classes. I provide breakfast for all of them but only some arrive because the others are too lazy to get up. I think after I go off to my office they make cups of tea periodically because at night I find stacks of cups piled up in the sink. They treat me with polite deference. Whenever I go into the room where they are all chattering, suddenly total silence descends as I reach for a book and carry it to my own room (which mercifully they do not invade). They telephone and are telephoned incessantly. They are all (so Vanessa tells me) falling in and out of love the whole time, and she gets almost as depressed or exhilarated by their emotional entanglements as by her own. I suppose I witness a mere cross-section of the general, worldwide, attitude of youth: 'The world is going to pot, and all I care about are my friends, their loves and my loves.'

He was right. I had many friends and would have done anything for them. I just didn't quite know what to do with myself.

I ended up going to Reading. Loyce, my childhood friend, was living there with a musician called Jonny. She invited me to visit them at the house they were sharing with Jonny's younger brother Paul.

I was attracted to Paul. I liked his long fair hair, his androgynous features and boyish body, his soft, gentle voice. He was eighteen like me, and sensitive. Initially he watched me warily and was hesitant in conversation. But when Jonny and Loyce went to get more cigarettes and we were alone, he opened up, telling me about his love of song-writing and poetry and his dream of going to drama school. He picked up his guitar and played me some of his songs and when he finished, I told him they were beautiful – lyrical and tender.

A week later the telephone rang for me at Ben's flat. It was Loyce.

'Nessa, can you get to Reading? Paul has locked himself in his bed-room and says he won't speak to anyone else but you.'

'Why me?' I was flattered.

'He says you're the only girl he has ever met who listens and understands.'

'What do you think is wrong with him?'

'He seems very depressed. And you've made quite an impression on him. Perhaps you can help?'

'I'm not sure . . .'

Loyce pleaded, 'At least try and talk to him? We don't know what to do.'

I was on the next train. Being wanted and needed felt good, and I was susceptible to poetic boys. We stayed up late into the night sitting on the mattress on the floor of his bedroom and when the wine and cigarettes ran out I waited for him to make a move. *That's what boys do*, I thought. *If they don't, it means they don't fancy you.*

We had stopped talking and he was playing with some cigarette papers. Then he smiled and muttered a word. 'Frigid.'

'Oh no, not really,' I said hastily. 'You see, it's because of my mother . . . she's really uptight about sex . . .' Paul looked bewildered as I tried to explain.

'You see, she read my diary a few years ago, and . . . and was really angry, and whenever . . . you know . . . whenever I'm with a boy . . . I kind of sense her watching me . . .'

Paul was still looking at me blankly. I took a deep breath.

'Well, what I'm trying to say is, it's not really that I'm frigid, it's just . . .'

He threw back his head and laughed. 'What? I said *fidget*, 'cos I was fiddling with the cigarette papers . . .'

'Oh no!' I blushed crimson and buried my face deep into my hands, refusing to re-emerge, despite Paul putting his arms around me and telling me not to worry.

'Come on, let's go to bed. No pressure. Relax.'

Within a week Paul and I were an inseparable couple.

Early on, he introduced me to his parents, Mr and Mrs Carr. They had moved from Newcastle to a modern estate in the south and Paul visited them regularly. His mother, thin and sharp-featured like her

Walking with Paul to Ben's flat in Holland Park, 1975.

sons, had dyed blonde hair piled up in a bouffant. She worked at the Lancôme counter of the local department store. Her husband had been a policeman 'up north' and now worked as a security guard. Whenever I went with Paul to visit, his mother was in the same position, sitting with her feet up in front of the TV, her long manicured fingers holding a cigarette, the small brown table next to her covered in empty mugs. Ashtrays overflowed with dog-ends wrapped in red lipstick.

I had never met people like them. I liked their friendliness, the way they called me 'pet', the homeliness of their warm house, the endless cups of tea, even their telly. It was unthreatening and secure. I didn't feel I had to be clever or entertaining. I never felt I had to guess what they were really thinking.

Meeting the Carrs brought home the fact that I had never been north of Oxford. I began to feel the need to see something more of life, to give something back. I was embarrassed by my privileged background and aware that I had no idea how the majority of the population lived. So I decided I would do something to widen my experience by researching organizations that offered opportunities to volunteers. I started adventurously, with kibbutzes in Israel and the Voluntary Service Overseas. But these would take me far from Paul. Then I heard about Community Service Volunteers, based in Britain, and I sent off for an application form.

Would I prefer to work with: the elderly, young people, children, or the disabled? I chewed my pencil as I read the form. I felt uneasy around the unpredictability of children and the disabled, so I went for the old. What are your hobbies? Pottery, drawing, writing stories. Yes, I was available immediately. The following week a woman with an encouraging voice rang me and asked me the same questions all over again.

'Would you be willing to travel?' was the final question. Yes, definitely.

A letter arrived three days later.

Dear Vanessa,

I am pleased to be able to write to you with full details of the project we have arranged for you. You will be going to a new project for Community Service Volunteers and therefore I don't have a great deal of information concerning it – I shall be relying on you to keep me well informed. You will be working in Napier House, a residential home for the elderly. It is in quite a deprived area of Newcastle but most of the residents will have lived in the area all their lives, so you should have a great time listening to their stories of what it was like. Your role there will be to generally help out and maybe spend time with the residents doing creative activities. For this you will get board and lodging, travelling expenses and £4.00 a week pocket money.

Good. The idea of Newcastle appealed to me. I liked the coincidence that Paul's family was originally from Newcastle. I imagined a house full of elderly versions of the Carrs, grateful and responsive to my attempts at getting them to make things and tell their stories.

I didn't inform Luisa about my plans. I imagined her attitude would be, 'What on earth are you going to *do* up there?' For Luisa, social work was for well-meaning but downtrodden spinsters with limited intellect. No one in my family had ever done anything similar apart from my mother's cousin Elena, whose tendency to rush and help whenever there was an earthquake or flood somewhere was always slightly ridiculed by Luisa.

But Ben understood what I had decided to do and was concerned.

'It will be hard,' he kept saying. 'You have no experience in this sort of thing. You don't know anyone there. Why don't you think it over? Sleep on it? Maybe you could try a bit of charity work here in London first?'

No, I had made my decision, and a week or so later I was saying a tearful goodbye to Paul at King's Cross station.

'You don't have to go,' he said.

I shook my head. 'It's only for a few weeks, and I'll come down again soon.'

Napier House was in a bleak part of Newcastle, a world away from the bay-fronted, white stucco houses of Holland Park. It was 1975, years before the large-scale regeneration that transformed the city. Some of the slums had been cleared, but soulless, brown brick constructions had emerged like mushrooms in their wake. Napier House was one of these: functional and clean but lacking in character.

The Director of the home, a professional woman in her mid-forties, opened the door and shook my hand. 'Hello, I'm Mrs Hooper, nice to meet you.'

As I walked in I was hit by the noise of the TV blaring in the day room. Twenty or so elderly women and a couple of men sat motionless in Draylon-covered chairs semi-circled around; none of them was actually looking at the screen.

Mrs Hooper waved her hand towards the room. 'This is where our residents like to spend most of the day,' she said, adding in a stage whisper as she began climbing the stairs to the next floor, 'I hope you will encourage them to take part in various activities other than TV watching.'

I nodded behind her back, lugging my suitcase up the staircase and through the fire door. She paused in front of one of the institutional-looking doors that appeared at regular intervals along the corridor.

'Here we are.'

As I followed her in, I noticed a sign hanging on the outside of the open door: 'Community Relations Officer'.

Mrs Hooper was drawing back the curtains.

'So what do you think?'

'Thank you, it's lovely.'

It had everything I needed. A single bed along the wall, a bedside table with a lamp on it, matching white laminated chest of drawers, a desk, a pine wardrobe. A basin under the mirror. Off-white walls. Outside the window was a small car park.

'Well, the bathroom is down the corridor, and you can use the staff kitchen downstairs for making tea and coffee. I'll show you where everything is later. I'll leave you in peace now to get yourself unpacked.'

'Yes, thank you. Um, could you just tell me what exactly you would like me to do with the residents?'

No one had actually given me a job description.

'We can go through that fully tomorrow but our staff will let you know how you can help. Essentially, you are not required to assist with nursing tasks but it would be good if you could encourage some creative activities. You know, basket weaving or things like that. I'm sorry you have just missed occupational therapy day, always on a Wednesday. The CSV people tell me you are quite artistic?'

I felt a pang of regret for the 'pottery' and 'drawing' I had listed under 'Hobbies' on the application form. My recent evening classes in Golders Green had resulted in a lopsided sugar bowl and a wonky dish that I had given to my father. And the doodles on my exercise books could hardly be classed as 'drawings'. My friend Lydia had suggested I put all that down. 'It will make you look creative,' she had said.

I nodded at Mrs Hooper again, trying to appear enthusiastic.

'Yes, well I've applied to university to read History of Art,' I said, though to be honest I wasn't sure how this would help the residents of Napier House. 'Er, another thing, could you tell me what exactly is a Community Relations Officer?'

'Oh, you mean the sign? Don't worry about that, we put that on your door because we don't want any of the residents bursting in on you. They respect a title.'

'Right.'

'You just make yourself at home. I'll see you later.' The tight smile lingered as Mrs Hooper left the room.

Basket weaving. I sat down heavily on the candlewick bedspread. I already missed Paul and the friends I had left behind. I craved a cigarette. I looked around the room for an ashtray but couldn't see one. Maybe I could have a sneaky one out of the window? But what if someone spotted me? I sat immobile for about five minutes staring at the wall, then slowly got up and lifted my suitcase onto the bed. As I carefully transferred the layers of clothes into the chest of drawers, a note in Paul's writing fell to the floor.

'Safe journey. Miss you already. Xxxx'

A bell was ringing. I opened my door to a familiar boarding school smell of cabbage and stew.

Mrs Hooper was bustling down the corridor. 'Hello there! Come with me.'

She led me down the staircase and through the swing doors into the dining room. The residents were being helped along from the day room; some were already seated and bibs were being tied around their necks. A large woman with a hard face and lank hair scraped back into a ponytail was wheeling a metal trolley around the room. Some of the diners were shakily managing to manoeuvre a fork or spoon into their mouths, while others needed more help getting food into the right place.

Mrs Hooper walked confidently up to a table.

'This is Vanessa,' she said to a group of orderlies. 'She is the volunteer I was telling you about.'

With that she was gone. I sat down and smiled awkwardly around the table, then looked around for the metal trolley. I was hungry.

'I'm getting married on Monday,' said an elderly lady in pink, with rouge on her cheeks and badly applied lipstick.

'That's nice,' I answered. 'Is your fiancé a resident of Napier House as well?'

Two of the staff glanced at each other and laughed loudly, while another one spluttered, 'Maisie thinks she's getting married every week!'

'Oh.'

I moved my shoulder to let the dinner lady slam down a plate of food in front of me. The swill of brown stew and cabbage looked unappetizing. I began stabbing the overcooked carrots. The nurses were still smirking but Maisie took no notice. She was happily humming, 'I'm getting married in the morning'. I watched two of the other diners dribbling onto their bibs.

A sinking feeling hit my stomach. Maybe I would feel better the following day.

I didn't, and by the third day, I knew I had to leave.

'Vanessa, you're late for lunch!' Mrs Hooper was walking down the corridor towards me. And then the lie took shape and there I was, blurting it out.

'It's my boyfriend Paul, he's been depressed for a while and he didn't want me to come and now my friend has phoned and she told me he's taken an overdose and I have to get back immediately to see him and I don't know how to get back and ...'

'My dear girl, come, let's go and sit down,' and she led me back to her office, pointing to the chair by her desk.

'What do you think you will do?' she was saying gently. 'Would you like to go home and return to us when you have checked out the situation?'

But the lie had taken hold, and I elaborated all the reasons why this might not be possible. 'I don't think I'll be able to come back, you see he needs me there and then I have to go away to university, and ...'

'Yes, I do see, I'm so sorry, we'll work something out,' and the genuine concern in her voice was like a knife piercing me with guilt.

Several hours later I was sitting next to my suitcase at the coach station, waiting for the late coach to London. The journey was uncomfortable as I sat in the row of seats at the back, surrounded by football fans singing and shouting and teasing me. I was the only young woman on the coach. But I didn't mind because the further I travelled down the motorway, the closer I was to London and home.

As I unlocked the door to Ben's flat I heard him going into the kitchen to fix breakfast. We came face to face in the hall. He looked surprised and confused.

'I'm back,' I said sheepishly.

'So I see,' he replied coldly. 'I have to say, Vaness, this is the first time in my life that I haven't been pleased to see you.'

In my uncle Nigel's file marked 'Letters from Ben', I have found the following:

4 May 1975

My dear Niggs

Vanessa has taken a job in Social Services in Newcastle, looking after old ladies. I'm keeping my fingers crossed, although on the telephone she said the atmosphere was strange and unfamiliar. All her friends told her she would be back in a week, which has strengthened her resolve to make a go of it. The girl has mettle.

Love from Ben

I had proved him wrong. He was as disappointed in me as I was with myself. But I was determined not to sink back into depression. I had to get out there, to try something else. The following day I made an appointment at Brook Street employment bureau.

'I think we may have something for you,' the woman there said.

An hour later I was at Reed International in Piccadilly, wheeling a huge urn of tea around their offices. Paul was not impressed. 'Why are you doing this in London?' he asked on the phone from Reading. 'They have employment agencies here as well, you know.'

So at the end of the first week I let the agency know that I would be signing on with their branch in Reading.

'I'm going to stay with Paul for a while,' I told Ben.

The following Tuesday saw me checking numbers on spreadsheets at a company based in an industrial estate near Reading. The number columns danced around my eyes and the fluorescent lights gave me headaches. It was soul destroying, and on Thursday I called in sick with a migraine and stayed in bed, feeling a complete failure. At six o'clock Paul was waking me up.

'I've got some good news!'

He had spotted a notice in the window of the boutique next to the furniture shop where he worked. 'Here, I copied it down.'

VACANCY Part-time Assistant 10–3 Tues–Friday. All day Saturday. £13 a week. Immediate start.

The manager was an American girl called Chris, only a few years older than myself. She didn't seem to mind when I confessed that my record for employment wasn't impressive. We chatted, and got on well.

'You can start on Monday? The job is yours.'

'I've got the job!' I called out when I heard Paul coming home. He changed out of his work clothes and we went off to the pub to celebrate.

I liked my job at 'Naturally'. It was a small shop packed with clothes: two rails of cheesecloth shirts, denim waistcoats and hippie dresses from Afghanistan, peacock feathers, Indian jewellery, sandalwood, jasmine and patchouli oils. The smell of incense mingled with the sounds of 10cc ('I'm not in Love'), the Bee Gees and Marc Bolan. Best of all, the boutique was near Paul's furniture shop, and he came in regularly during his breaks to say hello.

For the next few months I felt settled and contented, working and going home to Paul. The house we lived in was the last in a row of identical red brick homes on the outskirts of Reading. It had stained carpets and linoleum floors, bedrooms on each floor and a communal kitchen and bathroom somewhere in the middle. The meters were constantly hungry for fifty-pence coins to keep the electricity going. Loyce and Paul's older brother Jonny occupied the top floor, and a friend of theirs called Nick had the bedroom by the kitchen. Jonny was tall and skinny, with blonde corkscrew hair, tight jeans and beads around his neck. Two more things contributed to his coolness – he never smiled and when he played his guitar and sang, he sounded exactly like Jimi Hendrix. Not just like him – *exactly* like him. If you happened to come into the house when he was playing 'Hey Joe' you would have sworn that Jimi himself was there, playing upstairs, even though he had died years earlier.

August 1975. In the kitchen at George Street.

I could never be sure whether Jonny liked me or not. His name for me was Mona. 'How's it going, Mona?' he'd say as I waited in the kitchen for the kettle to boil. I secretly hoped he was referencing my Italian looks and enigmatic smile, but I wasn't sure.

'Does Jonny think I complain a lot?' I asked Loyce.

'What do you mean?'

'Oh, nothing really.'

As the summer wore on, a sensitive subject hung between Paul and me: my plan to go to university. Much to my parents' amusement, I had decided to read Art History, with Italian. 'Not a particularly adventurous choice for someone half Italian with two art historian parents,' I joked with my friends.

At Sussex University Erika Langmuir, the History of Art tutor, had put me at ease immediately. 'Come in, come in,' she had said in her soft American accent as she pulled up a chair for me. It felt as if I had just popped in for a conversation rather than an interview. No tests or putting me on the spot. Towards the end of our meeting she asked for my opinion on the role of the artist in society. Halfway through my speech, I completely lost the thread of what I was saying and stopped mid-sentence. 'I'm talking rubbish, aren't I?' I said grimacing, convinced I had blown my last chance.

'You certainly are!' she laughed. 'And I'd very much like to offer you a place here.'

I could not believe it. We both stood up and she shook my hand.

Just before the term began, Ben took me on holiday to Crete, together with a friend of his called Ginette, and my school friend, Lydia. Ginette, who was celebrating her sixtieth birthday, was very glamorous; stylishly clothed, French accented, menthol cigarettes in a long cigarette holder. She teased and flirted with Ben and told us stories about all the lovers she had had. We were staying in a hotel called Grammatikakis, on a beach in the north. Ben

With Lydia in Crete, September 1975.

was in one room, Ginette in another, and Lydia and I shared the third, but within a few days Lydia had gone off with Nikos the waiter, so most of the time I had the room to myself.

Soon, my first term at Sussex was starting. When the day came, Ben hired a car and I filled it with posters, bedspreads, books, clothes – all my worldly possessions apart from the few I had deliberately left in Reading to show that I was not cutting all ties with Paul. Before I left he gave me a stuffed toy lion.

'His name is Moonglum and he's the only one allowed to share your bed,' he said.

Ben drove very slowly and parked in Brighton so that we could have lunch before going to the university.

'I have booked a table at Wheelers,' he said.

The restaurant was full of other parents with kids doing the same thing. It felt like the days I had out as a child, when Ben would take me to Farnham for a big meal at the Mitre, and I would eat as much as possible before he took me back to boarding school.

After lunch we visited the aquarium, then we had tea. I was feeling apprehensive, but once we arrived on campus I wanted to shoo my father away before anyone saw him.

'Will you be all right now, Vaness?'

'Yes, you can go.'

And then as he prepared to leave, I experienced a pang, a sense of wanting to push away but pull back at the same time, of needing to articulate something to mark the moment. He hesitated, as if struggling with the same feelings. But neither of us said anything. I kissed his cheek and breathed in that familiar smell of whisky and tobacco before saying goodbye.

Dear Luisa

I took Vanessa down with all her luggage (which you can imagine, what with transistor radios, 15 pullovers, 25 pairs of jeans, 50 shirts etc.) took up more space in the car than she and me combined. She seemed very lost, poor dear, at first, but I managed to cheer her up with a good lunch in Brighton and spending the whole afternoon with her. Mercifully she has a friend, Jenny, who is starting this term, and she turned up about half an hour before I had to leave. I telephoned on Sunday and she seemed more settled and less bemused. I am sure things will get all right for her – she has a sweet little room with everything one could wish – bed, hanging cupboard, shelves, wash basin, writing table etc. and at the end of the passage is a kitchen she shares with the others on her landing. I forgot to tell you that she also has a Slumberdown, so there is no problem about cold in the winter.

Love,

Ben

He omitted to mention the orange and brown curtains and match-ing orange plastic armchair. The room was like a tightly packed box but it was functional. Ben was right – I *had* felt nervous, and once alone in my room, I delayed leaving its safety. I began trying to make it my own. I threw my Indian bedspread across the bed and draped another one over the chair. I stuck up some postcards: a Giacometti drawing, a Piero della Francesca painting, a Munch lithograph, the poem by Adrian Henri given to me by George Melly. I began putting some books on the shelves and noticed a piece of lined file paper which had been pushed through the crack in the door.

Dear Vanessa,

This is a note from your friendly second-year sponsor. In other words I am supposed to give you the benefit of all my experience of being a student here, to help you find your way through the first week. If you want to contact me leave me a note in the European pigeonholes. I hope I shall see you at the party tonight in the European Common Room at 6.30 p.m. Yours …

'Euro' common room was assigned to students who were studying a language, as well as their 'major' subject. I hesitated about going, and by the time I walked towards the building I was late, worried about having to face a room full of strangers. As I approached the door, out came a dark-haired girl wearing a hippie dress like the ones I used to sell in 'Naturally'. We literally bumped into each other before I stepped back to let her pass.

'Are you Vanessa?'

How did she deduce that?

'We've got the same "guide",' she grinned. 'You can't miss him! He's in the right-hand corner of the room, waiting for you! See you in a minute.'

She laughed and I watched her run off towards the bathroom.

Inside, a table was set up with glasses and wine. I poured one for myself. It tasted sweet and warm. A girl came up to me with name labels.

'Your sponsor is over there,' she said, pointing to a boy with thickly framed glasses who was holding forth to a group of students huddled around him. I introduced myself.

'Yes, I can see that,' he said, glancing at the label on my shirt. 'I was just saying ...' and he carried on speaking about the clubs and societies we could join. I thought the other students looked very young, and far less interesting than my contemporaries at school.

'I'm back!' The girl was at my side again. I smiled.

'My name's Minky, hi!'

'Oh right.' I had noticed that her label read Briony.

She followed my eyes. 'That's my real name, but my friends call me Minky. My dad named me that when I was a kid – you know, "little Minx!"'

I laughed, warming to her. 'I'm Nessa.'

Our sponsor darted us a look.

Minky.

'I was just explaining,' he said pointedly, 'about the refectories ...'

Minky leant her pixie face towards me and whispered, 'Shall we go and find a bar?'

'Good idea.'

My friendship with Minky was my passport to a social life. People responded to her sociable nature, and because I was always at her side, they showed an interest in me too. I was flattered that she wanted to spend her time with me and relieved that we were to share the same tutorials. She was bright and engaged, and able to combine being a 'swot' with having a good time. She claimed she wasn't doing much studying but always had clever things to say in tutorials. Yet she never missed a party.

I was also – as had happened before, so many times – attracted to her family. When she invited me to her home outside London, I absorbed the warmth of her parents' welcome like a sponge, soaking up the attention, grateful for inclusion. Only once did it backfire. I had stayed overnight in Minky's childhood room and woke to the sound of the other guests talking in the next bedroom, just a thin wall between us. The couple managed a vineyard in Italy and had spent most of the previous evening telling us about Italian wine, food and character as if we had never heard of the place – despite the fact that I had pointed out that I was half Italian.

'She's very strange, isn't she?' I heard the wife say.

'Strange? Who is?' her husband answered.

'You know, that friend of Minky's who's staying.'

Every muscle in my neck tensed up as I strained to hear more, but the woman walked away from the wall and all I could hear was mumbling.

I could hardly look at them over breakfast.

'*Very strange*,' echoed in my head for a long time.

Things had become difficult with Paul. Initially his letters were sweet and supportive. But I was finding it hard to keep my lives separate: my pre-university life of work and pubs, and my new university life of tutorials and film societies and student bars. My new friends at Sussex had different tastes in music; they liked discussing films and books and feminism and politics. They had less restricted outlooks and opportunities than the young people I had known in Reading. One of them, Ed, was gay. I had never had a gay friend – the only gay people I knew were friends of my father.

Paul had been right – I was mixing in a different world. But I had no intention of losing him. I wanted him to remain like a parent in the background, loving me but allowing me to blossom in another environment. This worked while I kept him at arm's-length with letters and phone calls, or when we met on our own. But when he came to visit, I was torn between the self I was with him, and the self I was with my new friends. Paul was suspicious of them and reserved in their company, and I could see my university friends struggling to find much in common with him. He became jealous, possessive and insecure, but I couldn't let him go, and we continued to see each other, in the pattern of my previous relationship with Remy – on, off, on, off.

In June, towards the end of that first academic year, Paul wrote:

> I'm too tired and depressed and disillusioned to go into all the details of how you and I have grown apart. Our tastes are different. When you lived with me, you revolved around me and I around you, but once at Sussex with all your other 'liberated' intellectuals, you have become a typical ordinary, very intelligent, straight personality. You used me a lot recently. Each weekend I was a little sexual holiday camp where you got away from it all. I couldn't believe that you had to go to an exhibition before coming to see me – our relationship was on the rocks but you had to go to an exhibition beforehand. Well you certainly got your priorities right!

I was about to go to Italy with Minky and decided that this was making him feel left out. So I suggested that he meet me in Paris in a few weeks' time – the train stopped there on the way from Florence to London, and I could break my journey. At least we would have some time together to see whether the relationship was worth continuing.

What I hadn't known was that I was carrying his child.

*

It was sweltering in Florence and Luisa was concerned – I was pale and looked tired. Was I having heavy periods?

'No, I haven't had one for a couple of months,' I replied. 'They're always irregular.'

'I also had this problem at your age, it's probably because you are too thin,' Luisa said as we ate lunch in her kitchen. 'I'm going to make an appointment with a specialist. It will be expensive, but these things need to be sorted out.'

A few days later I was sitting in a dark room opposite a middle-aged man at his desk. Why were all the doctors I met middle-aged men? Luisa sat next to me.

'So your mother tells me your periods are irregular?' he asked, looking at me intently.

'Yes,' answered Luisa before I could respond, 'and when they do come, she suffers from cramps and heavy bleeding and terrible headaches. She can be in bed for days.'

The doctor wrote something down. 'When did you have your last period?' He was looking at me again.

I glanced at my mother as if she knew the answer.

'Umm, I'm not sure . . . a couple of months ago perhaps . . .'

Luisa returned my glance, then turned back to the doctor. 'Don't you think it is because she is so thin? I had this problem when I was her age, during the war . . .'

'I'd like to examine you now, Signorina,' the doctor interrupted, getting up and indicating an open door to my right.

'No, Signora,' he said, noticing that my mother had also got up and was following us in. 'Could you wait here, please, there isn't space in my examining room for all three of us.'

He closed the door and I smiled at him wanly.

'Could you remove your lower garments and sit on the bed, please.'

I did as I was told, a brief memory of the school doctor flashing through my mind.

'Now,' he said as he began examining me. 'Can you tell me in your own words why you are here?' He had one hand inside me and one pressing on my abdomen.

'Well, my mother is always asking about my periods, and um ... sometimes I don't have one for ages and then when it comes it's really heavy and painful.'

'Hmm.' He removed his hands. He paused, looking thoughtful.

'Right, you can get dressed now,' he said, moving away from the bed. 'May I just ask, do you have a boyfriend?'

'Yes, yes I have.' I smiled, thinking he was making conversation.

'I see,' he said.

By this time I had put my trousers on, and I was following him back to where my mother sat waiting. She was looking up in anticipation.

'I have examined your daughter,' he said. 'I need some urine samples from Vanessa which will be analysed at the clinic in Santa Maria Nuova.'

From the shelf by his desk he took down three empty sample pots and wrote something on the labels. 'This one, with the red top, needs to be filled tomorrow morning as soon as you wake up. We also need samples from the following morning and evening. You need to bring them back as soon as possible, just drop them off with my secretary. We shall get them checked by the laboratory and I shall write a report based on the results. Then we can take it from there.'

'What could be wrong?' Luisa looked worried.

'Most likely a hormone imbalance of some kind.' He smiled. 'We shall be in touch.'

I duly provided the samples and two days later we dropped them off. I waited as my mother paid the bill presented by the secretary. 'Goodness, that was expensive,' she muttered as we walked out onto the street. 'I hope it's worth it and that we can get to the bottom of what is wrong with you.'

A few days later I met Minky at Pisa, and we took the train to a resort on the coast. My mother's cousin Anna and her husband Vittorio owned a beach concession called 'Moby Dick': rows of deck chairs and a beach bar which Minky and I were given the job of running. The busiest time was in the morning, when we made endless coffees, and late afternoon, when we helped clean the beach. Every evening we fell, exhausted, into the bunk beds that took up the whole space in the hut behind the bar; every morning we were up early, to serve our first customers. We became tenacious *barristas*, and it was fun. But an underlying anxiety was nagging at me. I told Minky about the irregular periods and the expensive tests I'd had done in Florence.

'You don't think you could be pregnant, do you?' she asked. The fear I hadn't yet acknowledged to myself suddenly seemed a real possibility.

We hatched a plan. We would intercept the results. As soon as we were back in Florence we would go to the laboratory mentioned by the doctor, and find out.

The hospital of Santa Maria Nuova was close to Luisa's flat. We told Luisa that we were popping out for an ice cream and rushed to the hospital. I was carrying the receipt from the doctor's clinic that I had found on Luisa's hall table. I could return it later.

'I've come to collect some results,' I told the young receptionist at the clinic.

'Name?'

'Vanessa Nicolson. Here is the receipt from the doctor.'

The girl looked through her files.

'I have a note of your name but the receipt is in the name of Dr Luisa Vertova.'

'Yes, you see that's my mother's name, she paid for it, but the tests are for me.'

'I'm sorry, but we can only give the information to the person named on the receipt.'

I was beginning to feel out of my depth.

'*Per favore* ...' I pleaded. 'I really need to know the results.'

'Then I suggest you come here with your mother.'

'*Non posso!* I can't!' I wanted to cry.

The receptionist looked at me, and I detected a flicker of sympathy.

'*Va bene,*' she sighed, '*aspetta qui.*'

I watched as she went over to a filing cabinet and took out some more papers. She stood reading something and then went to speak to an older woman, indicating the paper and then pointing me out. The older woman marched towards me.

'Signorina Nicolson?'

I nodded.

'I'm very sorry, but as I think my colleague explained, we are not able to give out this information.'

'But it's about *me!*'

'I do appreciate that. Why don't you just come here with your mother?'

'I can't do that!' I was beginning to feel desperate. 'Anyway, it's *my* body we are talking about, not hers!'

'I'm sorry, Signorina, those are the rules.'

'Rules? This is crazy, it's *my* body!' I was shouting now, and could sense I was red in the face.

'Just come back with your . . .'

'Oh, forget it! Come on, let's go,' I said to Minky, defeat sinking into my voice.

I tried to put it out of my mind. In a few days I would be off again, meeting Paul for our first proper holiday, and I didn't want anything to spoil that. Minky was going to join her French friend Christine Azèma in Holland for a camping holiday and Christine's parents had kindly offered Paul and me some rooms at the top of their house outside Paris.

One evening, quite late, Luisa phoned.

'Vanessa?'

'Yes, hello, Mummy! How are you?'

'I am quite well.'

I had a sense of foreboding.

'But I am so angry,' she continued, her voice getting louder. 'These idiots have told me that you are pregnant. I insisted it was a mistake, of course . . .'

Oh help.

'And I have not been able to get hold of you on this number until this evening.'

'Yes, the Azèmas are out a lot . . .' I whispered.

'What did you say?'

I didn't answer, taking in the news.

'So what do you say to that? Why are they telling me you are pregnant?'

I couldn't speak. I just looked at Paul. He had heard her shouting over the phone and was looking horrified.

'Well? Hello? Are you there?'

'Yes ...'

'And so?' There was a pause. 'You couldn't *be* pregnant, could you?'

My voice had abandoned me.

'Well, could you?'

'I, I, I don't know.'

'Either you could be or you couldn't. Yes or no?'

Silence from me.

'Are you telling me it's the Immaculate Conception?'

'Umm ...'

'Answer me, have they made a mistake?'

'No, it's not a mistake.'

The following day I bought a ticket for a flight back to London. Paul followed by train and boat. It was odd, thinking about having a baby inside me. I knew I was not going to keep it but I felt strangely protective. I looked down at my stomach and imagined I could see a swell to it.

That's my baby, I thought, putting my hand over it.

11 August 1976

Dear Luisa

As soon as Vanessa got back to London she had a pregnancy test at a clinic and was told she was thirteen weeks pregnant. She goes to hospital today to have her abortion. Fortunately the young man involved is staying here and will take her to the hospital and bring her back. All three of us discussed what we thought about the abortion, and all of us had no doubt at once that this was the right thing to do, even Vanessa. She does not seem too depressed about the impending ordeal, I think because we have deliberately made light of it, determined not to alarm her. So far Vanessa is not really in need of much psychological reassurance – she is taking it wonderfully calmly. Thank God the young man is here to help.

Yours ever,

Ben

12 August 1976

Dear Mummy

I came out of hospital yesterday and have since been in bed but I wanted to write to you. I am feeling sad and I have bad cramps but I suppose that will pass.

It was an experience I wouldn't wish on anybody. I was one of the last people they did so I had to spend all day in bed not being allowed to eat or drink. Finally they wheeled me in, gave me an injection and the next thing I was in bed again feeling dopey with a pain in my stomach. They let me out very early this morning which I think is stupid because the movement of the underground train made me feel terrible and in the end I collapsed at Holland Park station and the guard had to phone up Paul to collect me. He was going to come and collect me from the clinic but they let us out at 7 a.m. and I felt fine then so I rang up and insisted that I could get home by myself.

I'm all right now. I just feel empty. I should have told you about Paul but I was sure you wouldn't like him because he is so shy and also we have had many ups and downs over the last year and a half. But it is a serious relationship.

I keep wondering whether it was a little boy or a girl.

Daddy has been very kind. He paid the £85 for the abortion. But Paul says he will pay him back, at least half.

I'll write again when I feel better. I hope you are well.

Love,

Vanessa

Luisa responded with three pages of densely typed fury. She attacked my stupidity and immaturity. She was incandescent that I had not checked whether I was pregnant before letting her pay the gynaecologist in Florence. She thought I was idiotic and irresponsible for choosing to go home by underground after such an operation. She was dismissive of my relationship with Paul. She told me I was lucky that my father hadn't 'thrown me out on the streets'. She said I had let him down and not to be surprised if he stopped speaking to me altogether. She added that I had cost both my parents a great deal of money that summer. And I had got what I deserved. Finally she accused me of selfishness and for not being grateful for everything she had done for me. 'Not for one minute have you thought of the miserable reward your mother has received for all the sacrifices she has made from the moment you were born.'

Ben was supportive in a detached way. But there was something else. In his letters to Luisa he had failed to disclose that during the evening before the abortion, when he had sat with Paul and me over supper, I had said to him very quietly, 'Perhaps ... what if I kept it?'

I hadn't thought this through, but I had the urge to hold on, not to let go of this little bit of life that was developing inside me, that was all mine. Paul looked at me, surprised, and made no comment. Ben seemed taken aback as he replied, 'Oh, don't be silly now, you know that's out of the question,' in a tone that precluded any further discussion.

From my diary: '11 August 1976. Am lying here in hospital and they're just about to kill my baby and I'm paying them £85 to do it.'

I stored that loss away but could not grieve it. It wasn't a human being, was it? Well yes, for me it was.

Another layer of self-inflicted guilt had been laid down.

'Move on,' they say, 'move on.'

Two weeks later I took a holiday job at the London Tourist Board, and for the next month I worked at their centre in Victoria station. I got the job on the basis of my fluent Italian and basic French. On a questionnaire I had to tick all the tourist sights I had never got around to seeing – Greenwich, Hampton Court, Kew Gardens – and spent the day before I started rushing from one to the other in order to be knowledgeable when giving out advice and information. I couldn't believe I was being paid to go sightseeing.

My colleagues were mostly students, and we got on well. Receiving tips was a sackable offence, but it was hard refusing the cash offered to us, particularly by rich Arab men. One girl did accept £100 and got away with it. I envied her – I could have paid my father back for the abortion and had some money left over. Paul was unemployed now. He was never going to get enough money together to keep his promise to Ben.

My working hours were long. Paul was still staying with me intermittently at Ben's flat. One evening I came home carrying two heavy bags of shopping picked up on the way home. The moment I walked through the door, Paul was shouting at me in a cold, accusatory way.

'I found the letter!'

'What letter?'

'The one from your boyfriend.'

'What are you talking about?' I put the shopping down wearily on the nearest table.

'Bob, of course!'

'Bob? American Bob from university? He's just my friend, he heard about the abortion. Why would I leave the letter for you to see if I had something to hide?'

And then I felt a rage, like a ball of fire. Rage that it was I who had had to go through with the termination; rage that I was the one earning money, bringing home food, and now was having accusations fired at me. I was wronged. I felt like the ten-year-old at school being accused of stealing Podge's biscuits.

Unfair, unfair. My face burnt with indignation at the injustice of it all, and before I knew what I was doing, I picked out a carton of yoghurt from the top of the shopping bag and threw it at him. He ducked and it smashed against Ben's Flemish Old Master painting hanging on the wall behind him. We looked in horror as the yoghurt dripped its way slowly down the sixteenth-century nativity scene.

'I'm sorry,' said Paul, realizing he had gone too far.

'So you bloody well should be,' I replied and went into the kitchen to get a cloth.

By late September I had returned to Brighton. I had moved into a house share with Minky, our friend Jeremy and Julia, whose parents had bought the house as an investment. Number 9 was halfway down Lower Market Street, a scruffy road in Hove. We considered it well placed, being between the Conqueror pub at the top of the street and the sea around the corner. It was furnished with things reclaimed from skips and bought in junk shops, and had a bohemian, shabby feel to it.

Julia, effectively our landlady, was stylishly 'arty'. Whereas I had continued to wear my school 'uniform' – baggy, sloppy Joe jumpers, jeans and basketball boots – Julia favoured feminine 1950s dresses and had luscious red hair pinned up in the manner of a Toulouse-Lautrec dancer. I was slightly nervous of her and convinced she preferred Minky to me. Her boyfriend Chris was not at the university but lived in the house as well, teaching English to foreign students only a couple of years younger than himself. The other tenants were Wormy the cat and Rabbit the rabbit. We had to remember to put our records away as Rabbit liked sitting on the LPs left on the turntable and inevitably scratched them in the process. He also liked chewing the corners of our essays if he found them lying around.

Chris was a terrible cook. His speciality was liver and bacon, an overcooked piece of meat as tough as the sole of a shoe, usually presented next to some fatty rashers dripping in grease. Even Wormy would leave the leftovers in a rotting pile in his bowl. Minky and I began to invent evening lectures and commitments to avoid Chris's dinner nights, while Jeremy announced he had become a vegetarian. I craved Florentine steaks but my shopping lists from that time (yes, even those have been kept) reveal a diet heavy in pulses and grains bought from Infinity Foods, the wholefood shop in the Brighton Lanes: 'Chickpeas, Kidney Beans, Lentils, Brown rice. Henna.'

My bedroom was painted black. I found it like that when I moved in – a black box. The bed was a mattress covered with an eiderdown and a velvet bedspread, and lots of cushions so that I could sit up and read, although reading was quite difficult in the feeble light. A small window overlooked the yard and a car repair shop at the back of the house. Posters depicting Tibetan gods decorated the black walls and a framed photograph of Ben, laughing, sat on a low desk by the window (I was devastated when years later this photograph disappeared inside a stolen handbag). My clothes hung on one of those free-standing metal rails, and I cobbled together a makeshift bookcase out of a couple of planks of wood and some bricks.

The room was never referred to as 'Vanessa's room' in the way the other bedrooms were 'owned' by their occupiers. It remained 'The Black Room', as if the room's strong identity defied individual ownership. Its blackness seeped deep into my psyche. That cold, dark winter I was often ill or depressed – it's a wonder I ever made it to any lectures or tutorials. The strangest thing is that it took a long time to dawn on me that I could redecorate and change the colour.

Perhaps I felt it suited me in some way.

2007

With her recovery, Rosa was released. She had been buried under so much anxiety about who she was and what she wanted to be, that she had lost her way. And when she reclaimed her life she seemed determined to catch up on the time she had missed. She had set herself free.

The day the A-level results were to be announced, I drove Rosa to school. As we approached we could see teenagers everywhere, chatting and squealing and waving their results around in the air. She was nervous, and refused to get out of the car. She had a conditional place at Oxford Brookes to study 'International Hospitality Management' – her dream was to run a restaurant – but she was panicking.

'I know I won't get the right results, I just know it,' she said, biting her lip.

I tried to reassure her that whatever the results, she had done well, considering how ill she'd been a year ago.

She opened the door of the car, walked into school, collected an envelope and got back in the car. She still couldn't bring herself to open it. And so I continued with my speech about exams not being the be-all and end-all.

Slowly she began to open the envelope. She screamed with delight as she scanned the piece of paper. She had done more than well, far exceeding Oxford Brookes' admission requirements. As she flung her arms around me I felt overwhelmed – so happy and proud, but most of all so grateful that we were over the hell of the last few years. She was in my arms and I was thinking, *We have our Rosa back*. I started the car and she chatted happily all the way home. 'I just need to pass my driving test now! Will you take me out later?'

We got home. Our dog Dotty bounded towards us wagging her tail, as if she knew something good had happened. We rushed straight to Andrew's study to tell him the news.

'Guess how your brilliant daughter has done?' I said as we burst in, interrupting his work. He got up and enveloped her in a big hug before even hearing the answer.

The bookcase by your bed is that old brown one of my father's. J.K. Rowling and Jackie Wilson books have replaced Dylan Thomas and Aldous Huxley. Later, you added the teenage books: Mates, Dates and Tempting Trouble, Girls in Tears; *the series of* Fearless *and* Cafe Club *that you read over and over.*

On top of the bookcase sits your collection of 'Beanie Babies'. Beak: date of birth 8 February 1998, Gobbles the Turkey, Stinger the Crab, Butch the Dog (two of those), Stretch the Ostrich, Freckles the Leopard and Sheets the Ghost. Zip the Cat looks like our cat Dipstick. I could never remember all the names; I only do so now because they still have their tiny labels attached. Your favourite game when you were little was to test me: when I came in to put your lights out you would get me to say goodnight, in turn, to the gang. I'd look at the ostrich and deliberately say, 'Goodnight, Ostrich,' and you would giggle and screech, 'It's Stretch!'

'Goodnight, Stretch. Goodnight, Ghost.'

'No, it's Sheets!' *And so on until I kissed you and told you it was time to sleep.*

Tacked to the walls: posters of bare-chested Justin Timberlake, Orlando Bloom in Lord of the Rings, *Johnny Depp in* Pirates of the Caribbean; *the boys you fancied from* The O.C. *And from your younger years, the presents from your godmothers: the painting of pigs by Kate, a silk Chinese wall hanging from Mary. On the mantelpiece stands a huge drinking glass. On it is written in red ink: 'Hands Off – Rosa's Drink – Happy Eighteenth Birthday'.*

Scarves and belts hang from the wardrobe door; slouchy slippers sit on the carpet, the white towelling dressing gown is on a hook. A 'Coca-Cola' waste-paper basket, CDs, music and story tapes, notebooks, pens, coloured pencils, jewellery, hairbands, make-up, perfume. Tufts of your hair lie in your pink hairbrush, your toothbrush is by the basin. The Top Shop and H&M clothes, the ones that Ellie can't bear to be given away, still hang in the wardrobe. The dog-tooth jacket, the pretty dresses, the skinny jeans, the skimpy tops, the hats and winter scarves.

How am I supposed to dismantle this life, this world? I can picture you in here, kissing me goodnight, brushing your teeth, playing, laughing, gossiping with Ellie or your friends, dancing, shouting at me to 'Get Out Of My Room!' Having seizures, crying, complaining, refusing to go to school, being ill in bed. Bringing you tea and toast or creeping in here with your stocking on Christmas Eve. I see you, getting ready for a party, applying make-up, wrapping presents. Sitting at your desk doing your homework, making cards, composing your funny poems and your sad ones. Trying on new clothes. Practising your dance moves to music.

Being alive.

In September 2007 Andrew and I filled the boot of the car with Rosa's huge spotty suitcase, overflowing with clothes and shoes and some new red shorts stolen from her sister she hoped Ellie wouldn't miss (she did). And then there was the new bedding and kitchen equipment and all the paraphernalia necessary for student life. Rosa snuggled into her duvet in the back of the car and we drove to Oxford.

We were the first to arrive at a small flat in the concrete block. I found excuses to linger – I made her bed, cleaned the communal kitchen and lavatory which had been left grubby by the previous students. I felt like such an anxious mum, not wanting or able to let go.

A blonde girl turned up and Rosa leapt out of her bedroom.

'*Hiya!* I'm Rosa!'

I felt more than tearful, but Rosa was buoyant. 'Can you leave now?' she asked, laughing. As I drove away I saw her framed in the rear-view mirror, striding into the student bar on her own. *You are so brave*, I thought, remembering myself at her age, hesitantly going into the Euro Common Room at Sussex University.

I tried not to cry on the journey home, telling myself to pull myself together, but as soon as we got back I rushed to the two old oak trees in the field opposite Horserace and stood leaning against one of them for support, overwhelmed by a sense of loss and anxiety. Would she remember to take her medication? Eat properly? Change her sheets? Would she make any friends?

We returned to Oxford a few weeks later and she introduced us to tall, lanky Adam, with an asymmetrical haircut and low-slung jeans. I had never seen her so happy, brimming over with fun and energy, exuding confidence and deeply in love. She liked her course, had some great new friends, a social life, and a boyfriend who clearly adored her. She looked terrific – thin but not too thin. She had become sweet and affectionate. Her sense of humour had returned and replaced all that rage and cynicism.

After Christmas Rosa went to stay with Adam and the day she was

Rosa and Andrew, July 2007.

due to return she had three consecutive seizures, the first for over a year. Adam phoned to tell me, his voice shaking. She was taken to hospital, with an anxious Adam spending the night on a chair in a waiting room as he was not allowed to stay in the ward by her side. I drove to pick them up and noticed that her face was covered with thick make-up to conceal the bruises and black eyes caused by her falls from the seizures. But the traces of the battering her body had received could still be seen. 'Oh Rosa,' I said, gently touching her face, but she brushed my hand away.

For the next hospital appointment she dressed as if going to a party, a colourful dress with a sticking out skirt, big earrings and her favourite ballet pumps. When I commented on the outfit, she said she wanted to cheer things up, because 'those waiting rooms are so depressing'. How right she was! She sat in the drabness like a beacon of light.

I pleaded with her to rest, to take care of herself, to moderate her alcohol intake, like the doctors advised. She promised she did not smoke and was not interested in drugs but I knew she liked drinking, and I could understand it was hard to refuse when students consumed alcohol so liberally. She always shrugged off my anxieties. 'Stop worrying so much! I'm *fine*, Mum.'

Towards the end of the summer term, she came home for a few weeks to earn some money waitressing. She asked if she could borrow £150 ('Don't tell Dad!') to make up the difference so that she could go with Adam on a cheap package holiday to Portugal.

I have a little film of her shot by Adam in the kitchen of their holiday apartment. Just after she died I would sit, catatonic, watching it on a loop, two inches from my screen, as if trying to climb in to touch her. She is looking tanned, wearing a minuscule stripy bikini and demonstrating how to make a cocktail. She begins, 'Hi, I'm Rosa Davidson and I'm going to show you how to make ...' She laughs as Adam's camera pans down her body, lingering on her breasts.

I waited by the barrier at Gatwick airport with everyone else meeting passengers off the planes. Rosa was towering above the Spanish family in front of her, wearing a short summer dress, her long, tanned limbs stretching beneath the light cotton material. In her right hand she wheeled her enormous spotty suitcase which must have held her whole wardrobe. Her other hand was gesticulating wildly as she chattered to Adam who was walking by her side. How well and happy they both looked – for a second I felt a pang of regret for not having a camera on me to capture the moment.

Once she saw me she let go of her suitcase in the rush to give me a hug. 'We had the *best* time!'

I returned her squeeze as Adam hung back, grinning.

As I drove out of the airport, they competed to tell me about the holiday, how much younger than everyone else they were, how they had an apartment all to themselves, how hot it had been. 'And it had a balcony! And there was a swimming pool and there was this little town nearby and do you remember ...'

I had been listening and asking questions, so relieved to find Rosa looking radiant that I hadn't been concentrating on the roads, and now we were completely lost. We were clearly going in the wrong direction, so I turned off and we found ourselves in a strange, deserted hamlet in the middle of nowhere that seemed to have nothing in it but a Starbucks.

'You two hungry?'

Adam nodded enthusiastically. I parked the car and we ordered sandwiches and cakes and teas and coffees and even Rosa – always so careful with her food – tucked in, and right then everything seemed well with the world.

A few days later it was Sunday and we drove Adam to the station as he had to go home to begin a holiday job. I waited in the car park as they said goodbye to each other on the platform. When Rosa climbed forlornly back into the car, something made me say, 'Why don't you go and wait with him, the train isn't due for a few minutes.'

Rosa didn't pause for a second. She leapt out of the car to skip back to his side and give him one last kiss.

1977

October 1977. I was studying Italian as well as Art History, so I was expected to spend my third academic year in Italy. My friend Lucy went to Bologna, Clare to Florence, and I had chosen Venice.

I was packing when Ben came into my room to hand over a packet of letters from his friend Nathalie Brooke. She worked for the Venice in Peril Fund, a British committee set up to conserve Venetian works of art and architecture, and the letters were to introduce me to influential people in Venice. Enclosed with the packet came an accompanying note listing the people she had written to, with brief biographical details.

Dear Vanessa,

Ben tells me you are going to be living in Venice. Here are some introductions: I've not 'done' the strictly art world there as I expect your father has! [He hadn't.]

What I should do is when you're settled to write to all these people enclosing my letter and await results! Here's a run-down on who and what they all are:

Sir Ashley and Lady Clarke: Ambassador in Rome for nine years; vice-chairman of Venice in Peril Fund.

Countess A.M. Cicogna: spends most of the week in Rome now, is in deep mourning for her sister, Countess Luling, who lived at Maser.

Prince and Princess Clary: Prince C. is ninety, the Princess is eighty-three but they are by far the most interesting, forward looking and amusing *and* nicest people I know.

Philip and Jane Rylands: was at King's Cambridge, is working on Palma Vecchio.

Joan and Ned Guinness: he is a retired banker, they live in the most beautiful palace.

Rose and Peter Lauritzen: she was called Rose Keppel. Peter is a Henry Jamesian character who comes from Chicago but has written books on Venice.

Cristina and Nanuk Franchetti: live in a wonderful palazzo I'd like you to see.

Sarah Quill: she is thirtyish and has taken a flat in Venice for the winter, for two reasons (1) she is a professional photographer (2) she is sorting out matrimonial problems.

The only person to sound remotely interesting to my twenty-one-year-old self was Sarah Quill.

'Letters of introduction? It's like something out of a nineteenth-century novel!'

'There is no need to be ungracious.' Ben frowned.

I made a face and stuffed the letters into a corner of my suitcase, vowing I would rather starve than contact this ancient clique of the great and the good.

Venice in late October was still sunny. I stood on the *vaporetto* and watched the Grand Canal stretching ahead of me under the bridges, the palaces of pink and ochre on either side creating a harmony of colour and light. Venetians bustled about their daily business and I wanted to shout, 'How can you be indifferent to such astonishing beauty?' I was enchanted.

I got off the boat and lugged my suitcase to the Pensione Dinesan. It was well located, overlooking a quiet canal and around the corner from the Accademia. It also had an artistic reputation. Ezra Pound and Allen Ginsberg had stayed there, as had Peggy Guggenheim, before she bought her own house nearby and filled it with her collection of modern art.

The elderly owner, Signor Cici, was friendly enough. He knew I was not a tourist but intending to stay for a while, and after a week he offered me the spare room in his house nearby.

'We will have to share a bathroom and you can't cook there or have friends to stay, but it is a pleasant room. It would be cheaper for you than the Pensione.' I moved in.

I loved unlocking the front door and going up the stairs to the peace of my room. It was small and the single bed lumpy, but there was a basin and a desk to write on. I bought a heating element from a hardware shop so that I could make myself tea and I smuggled in cheese, bread and cold meats for supper when I didn't feel like eating at the cheap *trattoria* close by.

For a week or so I felt engaged and independent. Wandering over bridges and along canals, I explored every corner, getting to know the galleries and churches. I sat in cafes, read novels and watched the world go by. I registered at Venice University and sat in on a few lectures as I was supposed to do, but it felt chaotic after the Sussex system of small tutorials and seminars. And it was difficult to meet Italian students, as they tended to know each other from school, attending their home-town university. They stuck together in tight-knit groups that I couldn't break into.

Just as grey mists and drizzle replaced the sunny afternoons on the 'Zattere', I began to feel lonely. Now the evenings dragged on and on. I thought of my friends and of Paul, whom I had continued to see intermittently. They felt very far away.

One evening I looked at Nathalie Brooke's letters and thought, *Well, maybe I'll send one off, at least I might get a decent meal out of it.* I picked out the one addressed to Mr and Mrs Guinness, as the big door of their palazzo was opposite my local *trattoria*. The next time I walked past I popped the envelope through the door. Within a few days I had received an invitation to dinner.

I had brought one dress that was just about passable in smart society. It was navy blue, in the style of a 1940s tea dress. I wore it with a black cardigan, tights, flat black shoes, and set off. The palazzo was grand, or so it seemed, compared to the tiny space I lived in. A liveried *cameriere* met me at the door and I was led to the *piano nobile* where Mr and Mrs Guinness were waiting for me. Mr Guinness was tall and silent; his wife seemed on edge. I noticed that throughout the evening she kept checking her watch, a jewel-encrusted affair that looked like a bracelet but had a little lid that she opened periodically to peer into.

We sat at a long table and were served dinner by the *cameriere*. Fortunately they had also invited the photographer Sarah Quill, who was living in the apartment above them. I liked her. She was young and attractive, with peachy skin and a gash of crimson across her lips. She told me about the large archive of images of Venice she was amassing, and of her previous photographic work providing stills for theatre productions and film. It was a relief to finally engage with others, even if I had broken the promise I had made to myself to avoid the English community and only mix with Italians.

Without company, Venice was a melancholy place. And sharing a house with Cici was becoming problematic. One morning I woke to find him standing by my bed stroking my cheek.

I sat up in shock. '*Che cosa ...?* What the ...?'

He rubbed his hands together. 'I was only waking you to say that you have a telephone call, Signorina,' he grinned.

I had tried to dissuade anyone from calling, as Cici kept the phone by his bed. When, once in a while, Luisa rang (as she had this time), he would call me to his room, get back into bed and watch me while I was speaking. His old, smirking face sticking out of the blankets made me feel ill. When Lucy came up from Bologna to see me, I told her about it. 'Eeeghh, how disgusting! What do you think he's doing under the covers? It's horrible! Can't you lock your door?'

'No, there's no lock. I wish! I just try to keep my phone calls as short as possible and not to look at him ...'

'You've got to get out of there,' she said, and I knew she was right.

A week or so later I was queuing in a bank, behind a group of young people my age who were speaking English. They looked like students. I watched them with a pang of longing and envy. Suddenly I heard a voice behind me.

'Is that Nessa?'

I spun around to find myself face to face with Penny, a girl from school. I was filled with overwhelming relief and hugged her like a long-lost friend.

'Oh wow, Penny! How are you? What are you doing here?'

She was in Venice with a group of art history students from Warwick University.

'That's amazing, it's so good to see you! I'm here from Sussex, but on my own ...'

'On your own? Come and join us later, you can meet the others. We're over there at the Pensione Accademia by the bridge, we're staying till the end of term.'

'Great, I'll do that. Thanks!'

Better to have English friends than none at all.

It turned out to be a lucky encounter. The other students were welcoming and included me in their gatherings. I particularly liked a gangly blond boy called Mike, and when in late November he said he would like to visit Rome, I suggested we go together. We set off on a freezing day – potential passengers had been put off by the heavy snowfall – and found our train virtually empty. Just outside Ferrara it came to a complete halt. There was no guard or announcements and we sat there wondering what to do.

'You know, I think we should get out and walk,' I announced, peering out of the window and down the track. 'I'm sure we're not that far from the station.'

I was wrong. We plodded on through the snow for hours, but I didn't mind. The day was still, we were dressed warmly, and the snow-drenched fields either side of the railway track made the landscape beautiful. I enjoyed the adventure and the sense of being in charge and Mike was happy to lope along next to me. Finally we got to the station and managed to catch a slow train to Bologna, where we spent the night with Lucy. The next day we arrived in Florence and Mike went to stay with some friends, arranging to meet me the following day to carry on our journey. When I got to Luisa I explained I was en route to Rome with a male friend.

'And where were you going to stay in Rome?'

I hadn't thought of that.

She sighed. 'I shall book two rooms at my hotel.'

Luisa was spending a great deal of time in Rome for Christie's and had an arrangement with an hotel near their office. It was smart and central – near the Pantheon – and the staff knew her. This worried me slightly, but we went there anyway, and they turned a blind eye when I moved my things to Mike's room.

We stayed for a few days, visiting churches, ancient sites and art galleries, warming ourselves in cheap tavernas. On our final evening, with a few hours to spare before catching the late train back to Venice, we walked into a *trattoria* and ordered a bottle of red wine. Although the place was empty the waiter was unfriendly, clearly disliking our scruffy appearance. When he brought the bottle over, he slammed it on the table. The instant we tasted the contents we had to spit it back into our glasses.

'That's disgusting!' spluttered Mike as he wiped the spittle with the back of his hand.

'*Scusi!*' I called the waiter over. '*Questo vino non è buono.*'

'What do you mean, the wine is no good? We sell perfectly good wine here.'

'Taste it,' I said as politely as I could. 'I think you'll find it has turned, it's gone off. Can you replace it with another one?'

'Another one? You want free wine?'

'No, not at all, we are happy to pay, but this tastes of vinegar – please, try it.' I pushed the bottle towards him.

'Vinegar! Now she says my wine is like vinegar!'

His raised voice had attracted the attention of a fat man sitting near the till. He waddled over.

'What's going on?'

'*A questa "nobildonna",*' – this 'noblewoman' – he declared sarcastically, '*non piace nostro vino.*'

'*Non piace nostro vino?*' The fat man was incredulous that I might not like their wine.

I tried to remain calm, explaining once again that unfortunately the wine had turned to vinegar and that we would appreciate a substitute. Mike sat there, his face expressionless, clearly not understanding much of what was being said.

'We can get you another bottle, but you will have to pay for both,' the fat man said.

'But this is crazy! Listen, why don't you taste the wine, and then you will see for yourself?' I pleaded. The men shook their heads.

I had had enough.

'Come on, Mike, let's get out of here.' Pushing back the chair I stood up, grabbed the offending bottle – I don't know why – and started walking out of the restaurant. Mike followed.

'Hey, what are you doing, you bitch?' the waiter was shouting after me.

'Dirty hippies, they're all the same, disgusting, scum of the earth ...' the fat man echoed.

That was it. The red mist was descending.

'Have your fucking bottle!' And with that I spun around and threw it against the window of the restaurant. A large crack appeared as it smashed against the glass. I stormed off, eyes fixed ahead in rage, ranting to Mike, '... those bastards ... and anyway, it *was* vinegar ... what's wrong with these people? Mike? Mike?'

When I looked round I could see that Fat-man and the waiter now had him pinned against a parked car, roughing him up.

'Stop! What the hell's going on?' I raced back. 'He didn't do anything!'

The waiters let go with a shrug. 'The police are coming, they'll deal with you both,' said Fat-man. Shards of glass sat in a pool of vinegary wine. Mike looked worried. 'I'm sorry,' I stammered, my rage evaporating.

The two *carabinieri* were quick to arrive. Fat-man and the waiter pointed at me and then at the window.

'Look what this wild woman has done! She is probably high on drugs or something.'

One of the police officers took statements and then asked us to get into their patrol car. I tried to reason with them.

'But they were selling bad wine, it was undrinkable. We have to catch a train to Venice this evening!'

'Just get in the car,' the policeman said as he pushed us into the back seat.

Ten minutes later we were following him into the police station. The officer at the desk began flicking through our passports, which luckily we had with us. His repetitive flicking was unnerving. It was as if he was trying to think up how best to deal with us. I was still trying to explain about the wine, but he kept interrupting me to question Mike, despite my speaking Italian and telling him Mike did not understand.

'*Giovanotto, quanto tempo è che stà in Italia?* How long are you staying in Italy, young man?'

'*Mio amico non parla italiano.* He is in Venice temporarily as a student.' I was trying to be calm and reasonable.

'So why are you in Rome then?' He went back to looking at the passports.

'We both study art history.'

This did not impress him.

'Put them in the cell,' he nodded at the man who had brought us in.

'But we have to get back to Venice this evening ...'

We sat, bewildered, on a wooden bench in a cell. I knew Mike wanted to be back for something organized by the university the following day, and then he was returning to London with the rest of the students. He looked stunned, unable to speak.

Half an hour later the policeman unlocked the cell door. 'Come this way,' he said and led us back to the officer at the desk.

'I have spoken to the owner of the restaurant and he has agreed not to press charges if you go back to his establishment immediately and pay for the damage you caused.'

I nodded.

'But don't think you can get away with this,' he continued. 'I have made a note of your names and passport numbers – these will be registered nationwide and you will not be allowed to leave the country if the debt has not been paid. Do you understand?'

I nodded again and nudged Mike, who nodded too, having not

understood a word. The officer handed the passports back and we were out in the cold night air again.

'Thank God!' I laughed, feeling liberated, as we rushed straight to the station and jumped on the last train to Venice. We had caught it just in time.

I should have been worried about the police bureaucracy catching up with us, but something else was bothering me. I hadn't been feeling well for several weeks. I was constantly queasy and suffering from dizzy spells. One minute I was ravenously hungry, the next the thought of food made me feel sick.

My pocket diary on 4 December: 'Mike leaves for London. V. sad. Eat alone, feeling lonely.'

Once Mike and my new friends had gone, I could no longer ignore what was happening. I worked it out. I had been on the pill – one of those three-weeks-on, one-week-off pills. There had been a few days after the one-week-off before I left for Venice but I hadn't seen the point in starting a new course for such a short time. Then I had gone to say goodbye to Paul and stayed the night. Surely the pill would still have been in my system? And also, when I had arrived in Florence after that long walk with Mike in the snow outside Bologna, I had noticed spots of blood in my underwear, so I had presumed my period was starting, although nothing further had developed. I tried not to feel too anxious but this time I knew I needed to get it checked out as quickly as possible.

I had no idea how to get a pregnancy test done in Venice but presumed there were special clinics like the one in Florence. I looked up the British Consulate and walked to a telephone booth on the corner of the canal, because I didn't want Cici listening in. I dialled the number.

'British Consulate,' a voice answered.

''ello,' I spoke in the sub-cockney accent I put on when I wanted to avoid appearing 'posh'. Even if no one knew me at the British Consulate, I had a horror of one of those listed, expat worthies somehow finding out that Vanessa Nicolson could be pregnant.

'I was wondering, er, if you could tell me ... um, I'm English and am living in Venice and I need a pregnancy test ...'

'Are you registered with a doctor?' asked a cold, well-spoken voice.

'Um, no, I'm a temporary resident.'

'Well, there are clinics that can do the test for you.'

'Can you give me an address?'

'There is the Laboratorio di Ricerche Cliniche in Castello. You will have to bring a urine test. If you give me your name and address, I can send you some more inform ...'

'No no, that's great, thank you,' I interrupted quickly, and put the receiver down. I was at the Laboratorio di Ricerche Cliniche first thing the following morning.

'*Per l'esame di gravidanza,*' I said in a whisper to the girl at the desk.

'Fill in this form and come back this afternoon,' she said as she took in the sample.

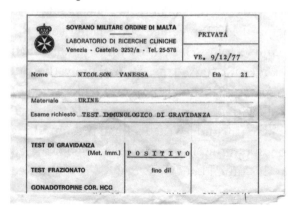

At four p.m. I was back. I passed my 'receipt' to a different girl who disappeared for a minute and then returned with an envelope. I turned away and ripped it open. The word *positivo* stared back at me. I looked away and down again. Maybe I had not read the word correctly. *Positivo*. The girl behind the desk gave me an inquisitive look.

Oh no, please, not again.

I folded the note up and began walking. I knew I was heading in the vague direction of Cici's house but I felt lost, physically and emotionally. I walked and walked, feeling cold and desolate. Finally I sat down on the steps leading to a church and covered my face with my hands.

The last time I had got pregnant, eighteen months earlier, my mother had said that I was stupid and immature and imagined myself the heroine of a romantic novel, but that it was a 'sorry tale'. *She was right*, I thought. There certainly wasn't anything romantic about this. I felt I was being punished – for having sex, for being a woman, for being so damn idiotic.

But underneath all those feelings another thought was simmering. The same thoughts I had had last time. At some level I *wanted* a baby to love and look after. As I sat on those cold church steps a fantasy took hold of carrying a bundle of life wrapped and warm in my arms, of creating a little family unit of my own. Even though the risk I had taken had been so small, it was as if perhaps I had been testing myself, letting my body decide whether it would allow the creation of a child that could be all mine.

This was something I could not, must not, consider. I knew I was being selfish, that I had nothing to offer a new life.

'*Cosa é successo?*'

I looked up to see a group of women a few years older than myself. The one who had asked the question stood close to me, while her friends waited behind her. 'What has happened?'

'*Vuoi venire con noi?*' she asked softly when I didn't answer.

For a second I longed to say yes, let me come with you. I imagined being swept up by these caring women and taken for a cup of hot chocolate somewhere warm where they would listen to my story. I wanted to be looked after. I craved it.

'*No, no grazie,*' I said hesitantly.

'*Sei sicura?*'

Yes, I was sure. How could they possibly help me?

'*Ma stai male*? Are you unwell?'

'*No, non e niente.*'

It's nothing at all.

I went into a bar to phone Sarah Quill. Thank God she was in.

'Sarah? I, I … I've discovered I'm pregnant. I don't feel well, I don't know what to do, I feel dizzy all the time.'

'Come over right now.'

She was calm and kind and waved aside my apologies for not being in touch.

'This is not insurmountable,' she said.

Luckily I had arranged to spend Christmas with Ben in England, although I had to go to Florence first. Not wanting to tell Luisa what had happened, I pretended nothing was wrong. For two days I sat in a conference on Renaissance architecture with her, not hearing a word that was being said, thinking about the curled up foetus inside me.

Finally I got to London and as soon as I could I was at the Pregnancy Advisory Service, organizing a termination for the 21st of December.

I phoned the number I had for Mike. He sounded strange and incoherent.

'I'm having an abortion,' I blurted out.

There was a pause, and then he began rambling again. Maybe he had taken drugs?

I telephoned Paul to arrange to see him.

When I got to his house I told him I was pregnant. We were sitting on his bed drinking tea. 'Is it mine?' he asked coldly.

'Of course it's yours, I haven't had a period since I last saw you. Well, not a proper one anyway.'

'You've slept with somebody else, haven't you? I can tell.'

How could he tell? Maybe he was testing me, but I confessed. I tried to explain that my relationship with Mike had developed out of a friendship and wasn't going anywhere . . .

'These things always mean something. What's your new boyfriend like then? Why don't you go rushing off to him?'

'He isn't my boyfriend . . .'

'Well, what else would you call him?

I left quickly, and returned to Ben's flat. I walked into his study and stood by the long oak table where he was working.

'Daddy, I've got to go away tomorrow to see a friend in Brighton, I hope that's OK. I'll stay the night there.'

This time, I didn't want him to know.

'Yes, of course,' he said distractedly, briefly looking up from his books.

The clinic was in Ealing. I had some Christmas money set by, so this time I could pay for it myself. The ward I found myself in after the operation was more like a dormitory, with four of us recovering overnight. I was struck by the pale, intense beauty of the girl in the bed next to mine, a white South African, who recounted a sad tale of rejection by not only her lover but also her family when she informed them she was pregnant. A friend had lent her the money to come over and she had had a long, difficult journey. Later, when the doctor was doing his rounds, he stopped by her bedside and said bluntly, 'You were never pregnant.'

'But how could that be possible?' she whispered.

'There was nothing there.'

'But I did the test . . .' Tears were forming in her eyes.

'I don't know why you're crying,' the doctor said gruffly. 'The fact that you are here means that you took a risk, that it was possible that you *were* pregnant.'

He moved away to reach my bed and looked at his notes. 'I would say you were about three months pregnant. There may be heavy bleeding.'

With that he passed on to the next girl's bed.

'I'm so sorry,' I said to the crying girl, as if apologizing for the doctor as well as for my child. 'How could this have happened to you?'

Instead of answering, she turned her face to the wall. Next morning when I woke she had already gone.

At the beginning of January, just before returning to Italy, I received two letters. The first was from Paul.

Dear Nessa

By the time you read this I'll be long gone. I don't want you to telephone while you are still in England. The time for words is long past and I don't want to see you again.

You're a hard woman in places Vanessa and most of the time, you're acting out scenes and feeling feelings you assume are the 'correct ones' under each circumstance. What are you with your new haircut and boots? Trendy student? Woman of the world? Femme fatale? Or what? With me you know you can exorcize your hang-ups – you can have migraines and moan. But I refuse to be a comfort station to anybody. My chauvinist ego can't stand it. Besides I want to be loved.

There will always be a guy who has had a nervous breakdown or something and who'll identify with you. That's probably what happened in Venice. A kindred spirit who said the same things I said.

Goodbye

'Why doesn't he care about the baby?' I wanted to shout.

Dear Vanessa,

Sorry to appear apparent but I'm sorry we haven't been in touché with each other since the epic phone call where I was raped. I have been carted off to a Loony Binny which is heavy. Do come and see me: Long Grove Hospital, Epsom, Surrey.

I hope that you are not feeling anything after the abortion contact. I have been drawing and reading prolifically.

Be peaceful and careful

Take care

Mike had been diagnosed with schizophrenia. Should I have guessed? To me there had been no sign. I knew in my heart that I should go to visit him, but I could not face it. Instead I wrote back saying I was sorry he was ill, and wished him better soon. Then I returned to Venice with a bag full of contraceptive pills I wouldn't need.

Luisa put me in touch with a girl called Alessandra who had worked for Christie's and had a room to rent in an apartment by the Rialto Bridge. The flat was cheap and well located; it was also chilly and damp but better than going back to Cici.

Alessandra had Italian friends, so my circle widened. One of these, Filippo, worked at the 'Soprintendenza', the equivalent of the Arts Council. I told him about the dissertation I was researching on Medardo Rosso, a late nineteenth-century Italian sculptor. Rosso's heirs had inherited a large body of work, including drawings and photographs, which were housed in a museum near Milan. But Italian bureaucracy was making it impossible to get in. Within a month or so,

Walking on the Lido, Venice, January 1978.

not only had Filippo managed to gain access for me, but the descendants had offered me lunch, called me 'Professoressa' and given me free rein to look at the piles of original photographs and archive material stored there. This was the power in Italy of having the 'right' contacts. Nothing could get done without them.

I still met with Sarah Quill and the smart English-speaking set of Venice. One evening Philip Rylands, a Cambridge academic, invited me to dinner and sat me next to Peggy Guggenheim. He introduced me with the words: 'Vanessa is the daughter of Ben Nicolson.'

'Oh really,' she drawled, 'I knew him well in the nineteen-forties ...'

I smiled but realized she had made the usual mistake.

'You are probably thinking of the *artist* Ben Nicholson,' I explained. 'But my father is an art historian. Our surname doesn't have an "h" in it.'

'Oh really?' She sniffed, turned the other way and didn't speak to me for the rest of the evening.

I recounted this story to Ben. In my letters I liked amusing him with anecdotes about the English elite. 'It's such an insular society that you can't go anywhere to dinner without all the others being there, even if most of them dislike each other intensely!'

He began writing to me more often, informing me when a Rosso sculpture was coming up for sale, or suggesting books I should read. I responded with pleasure, rising up to his higher opinion of me, sensing that I had something to contribute to our conversations. In April he wrote that he was planning to visit some exhibitions in Florence. Could I come and stay with Luisa so that we might see each other?

I sent him a postcard of a Titian painting. 'Dear Daddy, Can't wait to see you! I'll come down by train. Could you bring some Marmite?'

It was like the cards I used to send him from boarding school.

We arrived in Florence on the same evening. He stayed in Luisa's apartment, just as she was often his guest at his flat in London. Luisa was always pragmatic in these arrangements.

Over breakfast he suggested, 'Let's go to Prato for the day.'

That afternoon we sat in a square in the spring sunshine, drinking coffee and talking about my dissertation. I explained my research – I wanted to establish what were casts and what were variants, and how the different materials Rosso used for the same subject informed the work. I became animated as I spoke and he listened carefully. My confidence in what I was saying grew as I sensed he was taking me seriously.

'It sounds interesting,' he said, I hope proudly. 'I look forward to reading it.'

The following day he returned to England and from London sent Luisa a postcard.

9 May [1978] All perfectly lovely. I look back on my stay with such nostalgia. Vanessa looking more delightful than ever. Had to

Ben on his last visit to Florence, May 1978.

wait 3¼ hours at Pisa airport but found a friend on board. Thanks for a wonderful three days.

Ben

I took the train to Venice, but was back in Florence ten days later. Luisa had planned a trip to London and I decided I would take advantage of her empty apartment to focus on finishing the dissertation. One afternoon as I was working on it, the telephone rang.

'Vanessa, it's Francesca.'

My heart sank. She was the daughter of Luisa's friend Professor Masciotta, and it was she and her brother Eligio who had introduced me to Nico, my first boyfriend. I hadn't kept my promise to let her know when I was next in Florence.

'Hi, I'm so sorry I haven't been in touch!' I felt guilty. 'I'm just trying to finish writing my dissertation, I've come to Florence for some peace and quiet. I should have phoned you, I know, I ...' Excuses were tumbling out of my mouth. God, how the hell did she know I was here?

'Don't worry,' she interrupted in a flat voice. 'Look, I need to talk to you urgently.'

'What about?'

'Can you come over?'

'I'm just in the middle of typing up some footnotes, could I come later?'

'You need to come right now. Please, just come.'

Francesca buzzed me into the building and opened the door to their apartment. This was the first time I hadn't been met with a smile. I followed her into a dark sitting room, still burbling my excuses, sensing that something was up. The shutters were closed and in the gloom I didn't instantly spot her father. He slowly pulled himself out of the armchair in the corner of the room. I hadn't seen him for a few years and was struck by how much he had aged.

'Come, sit down.'

Something felt unreal, stilted, unsettling, as if I'd walked into a bad play. His eyes would not meet mine. We both looked at Francesca.

'Francesca, will you make us some coffee?' She nodded at her father and walked out of the room towards the kitchen. I sat in the chair he offered me and he finally looked at my face. And then down again, into his lap.

A pause. He cleared his throat.

'The thing is ... well, it's about your father.' He was examining his hands, the front and the backs of them and then the sides. I looked at them too, gnarled and old, peppered with brown spots.

'Has he had an accident?' I sensed I needed to help him out.

'Well, yes ... no, not exactly.' His brow furrowed some more.

'Well, is he all right?'

Professor Masciotta started crying, tears streaming down his red cheeks. I'd never seen a man of his age cry. We sat in silence for a moment until he blew his nose with a big handkerchief. And then he muttered, 'He was younger than me.'

I tried to swallow.

Francesca was coming back with our coffee. I smiled stiffly but she wouldn't meet my gaze as she poured the black liquid into the little coffee cups. Something terrible was dawning on me. I almost felt sorry for them as they struggled to articulate the thing they had no wish to say.

And so I asked, very slowly, '*É morto?*'

Professor Masciotta wiped his teary eyes and nodded, almost imperceptibly. 'Your mother asked me to tell you.'

'*Ma ... non è possible,*' I whispered. The Professor was saying something about it being very sudden, Ben had collapsed in an underground station after an evening out, 'It was a blood clot apparently that had gone to his heart ...'

'I'm sorry, I have to go.' I shot up before he could add anything else. Rounding the corner into my mother's street, I bumped straight into Eligio, Professor Masciotta's son.

'Where are you going in such a hurry?' he asked jovially as he leant in to kiss me hello. I watched his face coming towards me as if in slow motion. *He doesn't know, the world – my world – has completely changed and he is still smiling under that stupid moustache.*

'Ask your father!' I answered as I pushed past him and away.

I unlocked the door to my mother's empty flat. It was horribly quiet. I wondered what I should do as I sat immobile on Luisa's sofa, as if in a waiting room.

The telephone rang again. Nicoletta, a journalist friend of Luisa's, was telling me that I was to take a flight back to London the next day and that Luisa was going to meet me at the airport – the *Burlington Magazine* (which Ben edited) had paid for her to fly to Pisa and bring me back with her. But why hadn't *she* phoned? Why all the passing of messages through others?

An anxious evening and sleepless night was made bearable only by the companionship of my friend Clare who came over to stay with me. The following morning I took the bus to the airport. When I saw Luisa coming through Arrivals and went to embrace her, she didn't return my hug. She seemed hesitant and uncertain what to do. Maybe she was trying to keep her emotions in check. 'We have a lot of things to sort out,' was the first thing she said to me.

On the plane she began telling me what had happened.

'I arrived at your father's flat as arranged but nobody answered the door, so I went round the corner to the Pounceys and they gave me a bed for the night. And the next day we phoned the *Burlington* but Sally said he hadn't come in the day before, and there was nothing written in his diary, and then Mrs O'Neill told the Pounceys that he hadn't left her the key on a string through the letter box as he normally did for her to get in to clean and . . .'

I could hardly hear her. I just stared at the clouds floating past the aeroplane window and tried to shut everything out.

We took a taxi from the airport directly to Ben's flat. His secretary Sally was waiting to let us in with a spare key. She had telephoned Notting Hill police station to report him missing and had been told that Ben's body was in a mortuary.

'We sent an officer round to his address but no one answered the door,' the officer had said, 'so we were waiting for someone to contact us.'

The familiar smell of stale tobacco hit me as soon as we opened the front door. I wandered from room to room in a daze, noticing the breakfast debris and the morning post still sitting on the kitchen table next to the ashtray. Another overflowing ashtray and empty glass were on his desk. The bottle of whisky on the drinks tray was almost finished. Luisa was talking about giving away his clothes to charity, and all the other jobs that needed doing. 'We must remember to check whether anything was left at the dry cleaners. And these books from the London Library need to be returned.'

But I was thinking about other things. About how he had seemed only two weeks ago. Remembering the way his laughter kept merging into a racking cough. He had been smoking a packet or two of untipped Players cigarettes a day for about fifty years. When I had shown concern for his health, he had confessed that his doctor had pressed him to cut down.

'Is it worth it?' he had said. 'It's too difficult at my age. I've tried before and it's absolutely impossible. What's the point?'

His words echoed in my head as I stood in the doorway of his messy bedroom.

What's the point? The point is that you shouldn't have died, not now, not at sixty-three . . . I need you here. Why are you always leaving me?

My mind filled with Nonna, and how she had gone too, without an explanation. I felt nine years old again, trying not to cry for fear that I wouldn't be able to stop, feeling a buzzing in my ears and pounding dread in my heart.

It was the socks that broke me in the end. There they were, discarded and threadbare, one on his chair, the other on the floor. They looked so vulnerable, so intimate. I couldn't bear to touch them. And then I crumpled onto his bed and cried like I had never cried before, from somewhere deep within. Luisa left me to it and returned to the Pounceys. I don't think she could bear to see my distress: to witness how much I loved this man whom she felt had let her down.

My friend Jenny came over and was kind, staying in the bed I usually slept in, while I went into his. But I could not sleep. I thrashed around, holding onto the sides of the mattress as if drunk, to stop the spinning. I sobbed until I was too weak to cry any longer, clasping his pillow to my mouth to breathe in his smell, clutching at the small comfort it offered me.

The next morning Luisa returned and we set off in a taxi to Golders Green crematorium. We sat next to each other in silence. I was holding some flowers I had bought in Holland Park Avenue earlier that morning. At the crematorium we met Nigel, my cousin Juliet, her husband James, and Ben's friend Ginette whom I knew my mother did not like. We all embraced awkwardly. Nigel took my flowers to place them on the coffin along with a beautiful bunch he had picked from the garden at Sissinghurst before leaving for London. My wilting bunch looked inadequate by comparison, but I consoled myself that Ben had always been rather indifferent to flowers, so he wouldn't have minded.

I muttered something about coming to see the coffin too, maybe to have a last look at my father, but Nigel said it was better for me not to see him dead, and the coffin was probably closed by now. I squashed the thought, *But I need to see him*. During the brief service I tried to imagine Ben's long body lying inside it, and wondered if he was still wearing his pinstriped suit.

Everything felt wrong and unreal.

*

```
From:-    Mr E.J.Jeffery                          MIDDLESEX HOSPITAL.
          Head Night Porter                              W.1.
To:-      Mr D.P.Lyons                          TELEPHONE: 01-636 8333
          Deceased Persons Officer                  EXTENSION:
```

Date 23.5.78

Personal effects of mr Benedict Nicholson B.I.D. 23.5.78 (just after midnight)

Witnessed by Police:

1 Brown brief case
1x£5.00 note Serial No AZ79 9724 74
4x£1 notes   ""   ""   L40 427503: L40 427504: H41 807550:H67 27908:.
14p in coins, 2 Biros, Pkt containing 8 cigarettes, bunch of 7 (seven) keys,
pay advice note and correspondence, Photographs two small and one large,

another pkt of cigarettes containing 3 cigarettes;Driving licence:Spectacle case,

Barclay Visa Card No 4929 760 189 171: american Express Card No 3742 348 960 6100

T.P.L.membership card. National trust membership card,Times newspaper cafeteria
Pass, Britis h museum reading room pass, British museum print room pass,
National health cardNo D.J.C.320 9614:

1 Seko Wrist Watch with leather strap: 8 Calling cards: Annual ticket for
Sissinghurst Castle ,Kent, 1978 Diary: 1 brown wallet: Sainsbury Centre for

visual Arts book:..

Plur Clothing... .....

The Memorandum to Mr D.P. Lyons (Deceased Persons Officer) typed by a Mr E.J. Jeffery, Head Night Porter at Middlesex Hospital, where Ben was 'B.I.D.' (I presume this means 'Brought In Dead') lists his possessions, found in his briefcase, as the following:

Personal effects of mr Benedict Nicholson [*sic*] B.I.D. 23.5.78 (just after midnight) Witnessed by Police:

1 Brown briefcase
1 × £5.00 note
4 × £1 notes
14p in coins, 2 Biros, Pkt containing 8 cigarettes, bunch of 7 (seven) keys, pay advice note and correspondence, Photographs two small and one large, another pkt of cigarettes containing 3 cigarettes; Driving licence: Spectacle case,
Barclays Visa Card; American Express Card
T.P.L. membership card. National trust membership card, Times newspaper cafeteria Pass, British museum reading room pass, British museum print room pass, National health card

1 Seko watch with leather strap: 8 Calling cards: Annual ticket for Sissinghurst Castle, Kent, 1978 Diary: 1 brown wallet: Sainsbury Centre for visual Arts book ...
Plus clothing ...

Nigel made an official complaint to the Metropolitan Police that despite all this identification thirty-six hours had passed before anyone was notified, and then only because Ben's secretary had telephoned to report him missing. A brief apology was received a few days later.
Did we wish to take it further?
Nigel declined.

To his friends he will be irreplaceable. By turns kind and tactless, wily and innocent, taciturn and garrulous, humorous and solemn, he was always loveable and always unclassifiable – appropriately so, for he hated classifying others.

('Ben Nicolson', Obituary, *The Times*, 26 May 1978)

In July a memorial service was held in St James', the beautiful Wren church in Piccadilly. It was very formal. I wore the maroon skirt and blouse I had on that last day we spent together in Prato. The fact that Ben had said how much he liked the outfit had lodged in my mind, because he never normally commented on what I wore. The church was packed with over 500 people. Sir Kenneth Clark gave the eulogy, speaking of Ben's reputation for scholarship and his stature in the world of art history and connoisseurship. Nigel gave me a copy of the speech.

'Power was certainly the last thing he sought,' Sir Kenneth said. 'He was the gentlest and most modest of men, who often expressed his opinions in a diffident manner. But his devotion to a standard of intellectual truth gave him a strength, which his acquaintances did not always recognize.'

Later, Sir Kenneth shook my hand, muttering that he was sorry for my loss. I remember feeling detached, and noticing how his eyes looked like little slits cutting across his face. At the gathering afterwards, Nigel came up to me to compliment me on how I had handled being 'chief mourner'.

'You walked down the aisle with dignity,' he said, 'like a bride.'

Luisa stayed for a while with me at Ben's flat. She was hard and remote, and seemed bitter and envious at the attention Ben was receiving. One morning as she washed up, simmering over another obituary or letter of condolence that she thought hadn't fully understood Ben's real character, she exploded.

'No one has any idea how cruel he was to me! They say he was a wonderful father. Huh? He never loved you! He left us, he only cared about you because I forced him to!'

Sitting behind her at the kitchen table, I stopped slicing the bread. Before I fully realized what I was doing, my right hand began moving the knife up and down over my other hand until it drew blood, the physical pain giving me relief from the bottled-up fury I felt inside. I couldn't bear her telling me he had been a bad father, that I hadn't been loved. I wanted to tell her she was wrong, but all I felt was pain, the pain was winning. I wanted to gouge it out, like pulling a splinter from an infected finger. If only I could get it out, the wound might begin to heal.

Later I held Ben's battered photo of me sitting on my tricycle, by the house where we lived before my parents divorced. I came across the picture nestled in a fold of brown leather in the wallet returned to me by the police. It was such a comfort to find it there.

He must have cared about me a bit, I thought, *to keep it there for so long.*

I never cut myself again.

Luisa was right. After Ben died there was much to sort out. In fact so much, it took years. There was probate and the requests made by Ben in his will: 'Any art books that they may require to the Department of Art History, Oxford University.'

How many would they require?

'I request my daughter to keep as heirlooms and not sell the Rodin sculptures which Rodin gave her great-grandmother.'

I love those sculptures, I would never sell them.

'To the National Gallery, London, one picture to be chosen by them.'

Which one would they choose?

His art collection, bought freely and wisely when prices were low, required huge amounts of tax to be paid as their market value had escalated. So much had to be sold. Some items were bequeathed to friends; the small Saraceni painted on copper was chosen by the National Gallery; the three Rodins and a Dutch sixteenth-century painting went on long loan to the Fitzwilliam Museum in Cambridge; two pictures were sold to a museum in America. The painting I loved most, a Caravaggesque study of three richly costumed figures playing draughts which had hung above Ben's writing desk, went to the Ashmolean Museum in Oxford. I go there sometimes to look at it still.

A year after Ben's death, a Select Committee was set up to look into the taxation of works of art. Ben's friend, the art historian Denis Mahon, was campaigning for incentives for individuals to offer impor-tant works of art to the nation in lieu of tax, and he introduced me to the Conservative MP heading the Committee.

I made several trips to Westminster to meet and discuss my case with the MP. On one occasion, after giving me dinner in the House of Commons restaurant, he drove me home.

'So when are you going to show me this collection then?' he said as we sat in his car outside the flat.

'Oh of course, would you like to see it?'

As soon as we sat down in front of one of Ben's paintings, he put his hand on my knee. I was appalled. I remember looking at his hand and thinking, *How strange, what is he doing?* I was half his age, and a grieving daughter. He was jowly, bespectacled and to me so old – nearly forty – and on top of it all, married with children. I was wearing a woollen jersey dress over thick woollen tights and flat shoes. I had not been provocative in any way. What gave him the right?

'What I like about you, Vanessa,' he said as he leant into my side of the sofa, 'is that you seem a discreet young lady.'

I edged away from his hand and coldly asked him to leave.

So much to sort out. Solicitors, valuers, forms to fill in. Ben's property and land in Kent: Horserace House and over 150 acres of woods and lakes around the Castle itself. I gave most of the land to the National Trust in lieu of tax. By then I was working at the Tate Gallery and the *Evening Standard* came to take a photograph. 'Vanessa gives her slice of Sissinghurst' ran the headline in the Londoner's Diary. I thought the photograph awful, but the piece did provoke a fan letter in wobbly handwriting, asking for my autograph. I signed a card wishing the old chap many happy visits to the castle and its grounds.

Then came the truth about my father's life.

I had been sensitive to the barbed remarks made by Luisa, and aware of magazines he kept, featuring beautiful naked boys perched in provocative poses. But I didn't have actual proof of Ben's homosexuality until I found part of a journal hidden amongst his socks, a handful of paper torn out of a larger book, separated from the other papers and notebooks on his desk. I stood rooted to the spot until I had finished reading it.

Ben's voice permeates the lines of his inky, often illegible handwriting. As well as references to lonely evenings alone, there are accounts of drunken late nights with good friends, of conversations and jokes shared. For all his seriousness and melancholy, Ben liked having fun. He loved new word games and playing with hypothetical situations. 'What five things would you least like to have said about you behind your back?' 'If you had two days left to live what would you do?'

The journal is in the main a confessional account of his love for Simon, a boy he met at an exhibition in Bologna in the summer of 1968. It also records a social world peopled by writers, artists and intellectuals, combined with forays into the seedier side of homosexual London.

LONDONER'S DIARY

Vanessa gives her slice of Sissinghurst

THE SPLENDID domain of Sissinghurst Castle is now almost complete. Thirteen years after the monument and its enchanting gardens were made over to the National Trust by Nigel Nicolson, his niece Vanessa has transferred the remaining 167 acres of the famous estate that once belonged to Harold Nicolson and Vita Sackville-West to the public good.

The deal has been struck in settlement of the duties on the property of her now valued by the Exchequer at £27,000 which has been made over by his only daughter.

"I've kept a cottage and garden on the estate," Miss Nicolson, 24, an art historian currently doing voluntary research work in the Tate Gallery archives, tells me, "I'm glad to retain some sort of connection with Sissinghurst and equally glad that the National Trust will keep it up."

Fittingly the Castle's new summer season has just begun and for the first time the public will be able to roam across all the acres that can be seen from its great tower.

VANESSA NICOLSON

father Ben, for 30 years the distinguished editor of the Burlington magazine, who died in 1978. When the original National Trust transaction was made for the castle and its surrounds of 285 acres, he kept the other patch of Kent country —mainly scenic woodlands and orchards. It is this

Ben had told me the story of his meeting with Simon, how he had been in the main room of the exhibition peering at a picture, when he had become aware of a tentative English voice behind him.

'Sorry to bother you, but would you mind if I shared your catalogue? They seem to have sold out,' the voice had said.

Ben had looked around and observed a handsome young man in his early twenties.

'Of course,' Ben had replied, 'but how did you guess I was English?'

I could imagine Simon's eyes sparkling with amusement at the sight of this stooped middle-aged man, glasses perched on large nose, crumpled shirt flapping over creased linen trousers, looking exactly like the eccentric English gentleman he unequivocally was.

'As if he couldn't tell!' I would say at this point, and Ben would laugh his rasping smoker's laugh before continuing, 'I passed him the catalogue, and we went around the rest of the exhibition together.'

Back in London, they began seeing each other regularly. Simon blossomed under the attention, finding in Ben a caring father figure and mentor. Ben, blinded by his infatuation, respected the fact that Simon was not gay and introduced him to his influential friends and acquaintances without expecting anything from him apart from company. But he found it a struggle. In his journal he wrote:

> Tonight he was almost more than I can bear in beauty. And that smile! I find myself hesitating to make a good joke, so as to be spared that captivating smile. I wish he could occasionally fail me as a human being. But he never does. I am terrified of his perfection.

3 December 1968

> I told him (by letter, being easier) I had no lustful feelings towards him. I did not deliberately deceive him. I wrote it with all sincerity. But of course I realize this is an act of self-preservation. If I fail to persuade myself of this (and I do) his presence would be intolerable. I feel the tension most when I rouse him in the morning and find him naked in bed in a lascivious posture – a whole arm outstretched

and dangling. Or when his eyes light up and his whole face crinkles in gaiety.

The journal records their ups and downs, flirts and tiffs – reading at times like that of a teenage girl suffering from unrequited love, joy one minute, doubt and despair the next.

13 March '69

The time will come when he will leave me. He will love and be loved. A woman who didn't love him in return for his love would be a monster or a lesbian. How shall I behave then? I am hoping that I shall behave like the second fiddle in an orchestra: who, when the first violinist falls ill with pneumonia, takes his place at the head of the violins, while knowing all along that when the pneumonia is over, he has to step back to his lowly place. I shall not meanwhile get any folie de grandeur.

S. lived with me for a fortnight, but it was a strain on him. One evening late he murmured the words, miserably 'such intensity of feeling'. This made me realize how casual I must always appear. He cannot realize that I love him in every way, and so, as soon as I become conscious of his oppressive resistance to my love, in order to still hold on to him, I must minimize it.

A photograph of Simon smoking a cigarette appeared on Ben's kitchen cupboard. Aged twelve I fancied him myself, and wished that I could take the photograph for my dormitory wall. At that time Simon was often around when I saw Ben. He came with him to collect me at the end of terms, he joined us for meals and theatre outings in London. I liked him because we shared jokes and teased Ben together. Instead of his photograph

I was able to take to school a little brass rubbing he gave me. I still own it; in fact it hangs, framed, above my desk.

Ben was writing a book on Courbet. At proof stage, and without telling him, he added a dedication, 'For Simon'. He placed an early copy in a big brown envelope and sent it to him. For weeks he heard nothing back. He told me about this as we sat in his cramped kitchen eating breakfast. By then I was about fourteen and had long moved on from my little crush, and felt for my father because I could see how bewildered he was by Simon's silence. He simply could not understand it.

Although Simon got back in touch after a month or so, something had shifted in the relationship. He was distant and was no longer interested in accompanying Ben to art world gatherings. He wanted to stand on his own feet.

Joanne, a 'hippy chick' from California who came to work for Ben via George Melly, had got to know Simon in those years. 'Simon can only be described as being "on another trip",' she wrote to Ben once she had returned to America, trying to cheer him up. 'I feel he has consciously and deliberately cut himself off from his former friends and his former life to devote himself to a more politicized existence. He's now working in a nursery school taking care of small children in a deprived neighbourhood, spurning the privileges that his education and his middle-class childhood gave him, living on a tiny wage, and I think it seemed necessary to him to cut himself off from all temptations into worldliness and privilege. Sadly (and ironically, since you are perhaps the least worldly person I know), this meant breaking off his friendship with you.'

Ben was deeply hurt. So he did what he always did in times of trouble: he withdrew into the safety of his work at the *Burlington* and found another book to write, with more research to occupy him in his spare time. His journal reveals that every so often he would go out to a 'queer pub' and find himself in conversation with a young man, 'not at all attractive to me, knowing that at any moment I would be offered sexual services'. But his heart wasn't in it. He writes that as soon as an offer was made he would give the boy a ten-bob note and leave hastily for home.

In fact he had been frightened by a nasty experience recounted to me in the aftermath of his death by Gordon, an openly gay colleague who had worked in the advertising department at the *Burlington*. Gordon had come round to help me sort out Ben's books and while we were looking through them I told him that I had evidence that Ben was gay. Gordon laughed at my naivety.

'We used to talk about it,' he said. 'There was the time when Ben brought two boys back and they held him to ransom, threatening to slash his paintings. Did he ever tell you?'

No, of course he hadn't.

I shuddered at the thought of my terrified father being taken hostage in his own flat, wondering whether they were going to go through with their threats before possibly turning their violence towards their victim. It was around this time (early 1970s) that the writer James Pope-Hennessey, ex-lover of Ben's father Harold and brother of art historian John, had been brutally murdered by three young men he had met in a bar.

'What happened?' I asked Gordon, horrified.

'Oh, it was all right, he managed to pay them off in the end.'

From Ben's journal:

10 June 1970

Last night I nearly took a boy home. He was rather beautiful and tattooed all over his arms. These tattoos excited me. But I didn't invite him to leave with me. There was an ill-concealed twist of his mouth which I interpreted as delinquency. He might have threatened me with his fists, once the door of my flat was closed. It would not have mattered if he had got away with all the money in my pocket – a paltry £7 – but he would never have believed that there was not more to be had, and nothing that I could have said would have persuaded him that my possessions were unsaleable. Sleeping with boys in 1970 is much more difficult than it was when the act was illegal, because nowadays boys who invite these practices are also crooks.

The 'Simon' journal held further secrets. Ben had anguished over revealing some information to 'a man from the Ministry of Defence' who made contact in October 1969 to clarify some 'research' about the time Ben had spent in Paris in the mid-1930s with his friends, Anthony Blunt and Guy Burgess, and a third man, 'a Marxist'.

'I recalled the episode perfectly – without knowing his name I remembered the Marxist who seemed to me most unpleasant, aloof, supercilious.'

He then notes that he had checked his diary from that time and found a mention of the Marxist, a man called Klugman. 'This I transmitted to the researcher but having done so, I am left a little anxious. What if he comes back for more information (knowing now that my documentation is valuable)? How do I know he is not gunning for Anthony, and that in all innocence I shall reveal some fact that will prove of use? Supposing Anthony is arrested as a Soviet spy? What shall be the reaction and behaviour of all of us? The idea is romantic and absurd. And highly seductive.'

Further on: 'Stuart [Stuart Hampshire, Professor of Philosophy at Stanford University, a friend of Ben's from Oxford] writes from Princeton that there is nothing sinister about giving information about Communists in the '30s to the Ministry of Defence. I trust his judgment and will therefore go on doing so. The researcher has indeed applied to me for more facts. Stuart rightly and sympathetically says, "I must admit also that I love recalling details of the past." I had suppressed this to myself, and it took his letter to show me I thought so too.'

He doesn't mention what 'further facts' they needed to know, but they clearly thought Ben was a valuable source. When, shortly after his death, the story broke of Blunt being a Russian spy, the telephone in Ben's flat rang incessantly. After the fourth request from a male voice asking to speak to Ben Nicolson I didn't immediately answer that he was no longer with us, but asked, 'Who wants him?'

'I'm calling from the *Daily Mail*.'

'I'm sorry, he died six months ago.'

The journalist hung up without another word.

By my early twenties I was an expert in inheritance law, such were the intricacies of what my father left. Sometimes I longed to be left alone to carry on being a student without these worries. Inevitably, concentration on my studies fluctuated. I was awarded a First for my dissertation on Rosso and for the Italian exams I took at the beginning of the academic year, but I seriously messed up another exam the following summer. I sat desperately trying to recall historical facts and none would come to me. I stared hopelessly at the paper, trying to pull myself together, until finally I walked out, having written one or two paragraphs of gibberish. It felt as if I had thrown away four years at university in half an hour.

I found myself walking through the campus in a daze, in the direction of the health centre. I walked in and asked to see the university psychiatrist who had supported me through various depressive episodes. He found me in the waiting room, shaking uncontrollably.

'I've messed everything up!' I cried.

'Calm down, Vanessa,' said Dr Ryle in his soothing voice.

'But you don't understand! I've failed, I just went blank, how will I ever face my mother?'

Dr Ryle admitted me to the health centre that afternoon and I spent the next day sleeping. The day after, the 'Modern European Mind' exam paper was delivered to my room and I scribbled furiously on Nietzsche and the alienation of modern man, helped enormously by the ranting of a student next door who was having a breakdown and thought he was God.

I was awarded a 2.1. On the day the results were released, I queued up for the telephone behind other students telling their parents the news of their degrees.

'I got an upper second!' I shouted down the telephone to Luisa.

'You have what?'

'A two-one, it's my degree, an upper second!'

'I do not understand, what is this?' Luisa sounded confused.

'It's quite good really, considering . . .' I said, my confidence ebbing away.

There was a pause and then she asked, 'What did Minky get?'

My heart sank. Minky had been one of only two students awarded a First in Art History that year. I knew my achievement would be deemed inadequate by comparison.

'Umm, she got a First.'

'I see.'

I put the phone down with a deflated shrug.

It wasn't mentioned again. When Luisa came to the graduation ceremony, she gave Minky a big hug. 'Congratulations, well done!' she said. I turned away, and for the only time in our relationship felt a surge of volcanic envy for my closest friend, not for her well-deserved grade but for that maternal pride denied me.

I had no idea what to do when I left university. Minky moved into Ben's bedroom in the London flat, paying me half the rent and hoping that the landlady would not cotton on as I was not supposed to sublet. While Minky studied for an MA, I rather half-heartedly went along with Luisa's suggestion to do a course in connoisseurship at Christie's in South Kensington. Having felt too 'posh' and privileged at Sussex, I now experienced the other extreme. One American woman invited me to dinner and I spent five minutes trying to make conversation with the unresponsive man who had answered the door and taken my coat, only to realize that he was her butler, not her husband.

When the course ended I decided I wanted to work in an art gallery or museum. I knew that the recently appointed Director of the Tate Gallery had been external examiner for my dissertation and he had awarded me a First for that piece of work, so I hoped he would respond. I wrote to him explaining that I had spent the summer after graduation doing voluntary work at Brighton Museum and very much wanted to do the same at the Tate. His secretary telephoned me within a couple of days to tell me that Mr Bowness was inviting me in 'for a chat'.

I was shown up to his light-filled office at the top of what is now Tate Britain. 'I enjoyed reading your dissertation,' said Alan Bowness. I relaxed. He then told me that he had shared a long-running joke with my father, because when he married the artist Ben Nicholson's daughter, the newspapers had reported that he had married Ben Nicolson's daughter, i.e. myself – a baby at the time.

The following week I began helping out in the Tate archives under the formidably efficient Sarah Fox Pitt, and when a permanent position was freed up a few months later, I got the job.

1981

Spring 1981. I was going to Florence to see Luisa for Easter, but I decided to break my journey and stop off in Paris for a day or two to call on a university friend. Steve was living there and working in an advertising agency. I had met him towards the end of my time at Sussex, and we had become friends. Brought up in north London, he was impulsive, gregarious and self-deprecating. He had also been sending me regular postcards from Paris, recounting the trials and tribulations of his work and love affairs.

Dear Vanessa,
    Am still pounding the streets of Paris, various apartments and love affairs have passed me by, but work is good. I had a part in a Yellow Pages ad as barman. My right arm is now a star. Why don't you come to Paris?
    Love Steve xx

I arrived in Paris in the morning, and we spent the day walking through parks and art galleries, sitting in cafes, and talking incessantly about books, film, music, art. We laughed over his disastrous love life – his latest passion was for a girl from Capri who lived on a barge. 'We drink vodka and Guinness but as soon as I get lustful, she starts off on another long conversation. I'm giving up!'

With Steve the day after arriving in Paris, April 1981.

That evening I shared his bed. I felt so comfortable with him that it seemed the natural thing to do.

'I want you,' he whispered.

'I want you too,' I answered. And after he kissed me and mumbled, 'We should be careful, shouldn't we?' I realized that, despite all the experiences I had had, at that moment I was beyond being careful. Warmed by wine and Paris and his company, I did not want to wait.

A couple of days later I set off for Florence. Steve skived off work to see me off. As the train pulled out of the station he shouted, 'I'll try to come and see you!'

Once in Florence, I missed him badly. How was I going to get through the next week and then return to London, with no arrangement in place to see him again? I felt miserable, imagining that he would soon forget me and be back on that barge with the girl from Capri ...

On my third morning in Florence as I was about to go out for a walk, the doorbell rang. I picked up the intercom. '*Si?*' I said in a distracted tone, expecting it to be the postman.

'Delivery from Paris,' a familiar voice replied.

I gasped. 'My God! Is it really you?'

I pressed the buzzer and ran down the stairs to meet him. He looked exhausted. I embraced him, speechless.

'I had to stand in a corridor on the train all the way here,' he sighed.

Florence suddenly seemed a great place to be. He teased me about being a 'posh' art historian, 'Whereas I'm just a boy from Edmonton.' In the afternoons we sat on my mother's sunny terrace next to the studio flat where Luisa let him sleep. He was so different from Paul – light-hearted, curious, fun to be with. I could tell even Luisa was charmed. 'A young Jewish boy (*un giovane ebreo*)' she wrote in her appointment diary, 'came to see Vanessa by train from Paris. He stood up all the way.'

After Easter we had to return, he to Paris, I to London. The regular postcards were replaced by love letters, telling me he missed me and that he would try and move back to England as soon as it was possible.

I knew it was going to happen. It was my punishment for being reckless. But this time I didn't indulge in fantasies about having the baby, not immediately. I knew what arrangements needed to be made and I made them quickly, informing Steve what had happened and what I was going to do about it.

The clinic was somewhere near Oxford Street. This time I was given a room of my own after the operation, though I would have preferred the distraction of a ward. Steve came to London to visit me and was clearly upset. I felt withdrawn and unresponsive as he sat by my bed trying to talk to me. 'Steve visits but I feel in a bubble,' I wrote in my diary. In the middle of the night and unable to sleep, I wrote more.

The distance between men and women is frightening. I despised you for it being me lying in that cold, soulless room, waiting to have my child (your child) ripped out of me, being wheeled on a trolley like a lump of meat through empty corridors and swinging doors, white masked men telling me to open my legs, pulling my arm, syringe poised, lights above glaring, waking to half-formed images of a bloody foetus lying somewhere in a bucket, its remains discarded like in a butcher's shop. I hated you for being male, for being separate, for not experiencing the pain and the humiliation, even though I know it was my decision. I was happy when you were upset, happy to see that it had touched you to be a father, even if only for a few weeks.

I'm crying, feeling the cramps and the clots of blood and thinking of a brown-eyed child. Why am I feeling this now? I didn't want to be a mother, I marched all those times shouting 'A woman's right to choose'. I can't be a mother, not yet, and I don't want to be a victim and I don't want to let this affect me, but it has.

Never again. No more killing. One day I shall give life and I shall love that child more than any mother could possibly love.

Two months later, Steve was back in Paris, and an invitation to Sissinghurst arrived from Nigel. The other guests were Bridget and Hugh Sackville-West. Hugh had been my grandmother Vita's first cousin and his wife Bridget was friendly. When, come Christmastime, she invited me to come and visit them on Boxing Day, I was tempted. I hadn't been to Knole, the vast stately home and family seat of my grandmother Vita, for years.

'Do come,' Bridget had said. 'I think Robert, Mary and Lib will be here.' These were three of their five children. 'You must meet them. It's astonishing that you don't know your second cousins. They are about your age, after all.'

I accepted. Just before she put the phone down she said, 'And do bring your boyfriend, won't you?'

'Yes, of course.'

Steve seemed intrigued by the invitation but I was apprehensive. I imagined my cousins would be 'Sloane Rangers' in the mould of Princess Diana. I was convinced I would feel out of place, ever the mongrel, and that they would be snobbish in their stately home with its towers and courtyards, and corridors framed by ancestral portraits.

I imagined that Steve would see it all and despise me somehow or at the very least be intimidated.

We drove through Sevenoaks.

'Is this it?' Steve was indicating the gatehouse next to the National Trust sign that says 'Knole'.

'Er, no, it's through there though.'

We swept through the gates up the endless drive that cuts through the rolling parkland, past the grazing deer and ancient oaks, round the corner and the enormous house stretched into view, looking like an entire Elizabethan town in a film set.

'Bloody hell ...!' For once Steve was speechless.

I parked opposite the monumental door and rang the bell, feeling jittery. We waited for five minutes, and eventually I heard the sound of steps walking across the stone courtyard.

I turned to Steve: 'You know, this may be awful. Bridget and Huffo are lovely, but I don't know what their kids are like ...'

Before Steve had a chance to reply, the door creaked open to reveal a slim, attractive, cool young girl dressed in jeans.

'Hi! I'm Lib,' she grinned.

Steve was a great success. I watched him from across the large table in the dining room. He sat between Lib and her lively sister Mary, laughing and bantering throughout the whole meal. Bridget saw me looking at him and leant over towards me.

'Steve seems nice,' she smiled.

'Yes, he is,' I nodded gratefully, realizing that both Steve and I could be liked and accepted for what we were. That was enough.

In the early 1980s I was working on an art magazine called *Apollo*. I could not believe my luck when I sent in a review of an exhibition I had seen in Italy and the editor, Denys Sutton, published it and offered me a job as his assistant. When I started at *Apollo*, the editorial team consisted of three people: the editor, the designer David Grey and myself. Grey had in his youth been a ballet dancer, and even in his sixties managed to maintain his slimness despite the constant consumption of digestive biscuits. I dreaded him coming to discuss the layouts because he exuded a wheaty smell that made me nauseous. Every so often he had loud disagreements with Sutton. I would hear Grey's door being slammed shut, then Sutton would vent his frustration. A long pole propped in the corner (possibly for opening the window), regularly flew across the room.

I came to understand that most of the time it wasn't David Grey's fault. Sutton could be a tyrant. He had had radical cancer surgery on his throat and had relearnt to speak through a voice box, but this did not inhibit him from venting his prodigious temper. He was exacting and autocratic and would fly into a rage if things were not going his way. If he stayed at home to work, he called every fifteen minutes to give conflicting instructions on the order in which things needed to be done, expecting tasks to be completed in half the time available. He worked on multiple projects at the same time so as well as editing the magazine he wrote books and introductions for catalogues, curated exhibitions, reorganized his library at home – and I was expected to assist him in everything. It was interesting to have such varied work, and I enjoyed the writing and researching, but a lot of the tasks he required me to do were pretty mundane. I soon developed back problems from lugging piles of heavy catalogues and art books backwards and forwards from the West End office to his home in Chelsea, and then on to the London Library.

The worst part was his unpredictability. 'Leave that!' he would snap over the phone when I had finally found a moment to write the monthly 'News from the World of Art'. 'I need you here to put my books back into the bookshelves!'

The next morning it would be, 'Haven't you written "News from the World of Art" yet? What's wrong with you?'

Fortunately he had good days when he would arrive with a smile and could be amusing, even flirtatious, entertaining me with stories of his early female conquests. He was particularly proud of his success with a dental assistant he had seduced. 'Her breasts would come towards me as I sat in the dentist's chair, I couldn't resist . . .' he would chuckle. Or he would offer to buy me a good lunch, or arrange a private view. I loved

Working in the Apollo office, 1984.

the evening visit just for the two of us to the busy 'Genius of Venice' exhibition at the Royal Academy, after all the crowds had gone. I was nervous of accompanying him, but he encouraged my tentative remarks on the paintings and then left me to enjoy the exhibition alone. It almost felt like being with my father again.

He could also be complimentary. 'You look smart today! Who is your tailor?' he once asked me, and when I told him truthfully that I had picked up the 1960s suit in a charity shop he looked genuinely confused. 'A shop? For charity?' He had never heard of such a thing.

Sadly, his good days became increasingly rare. The little confidence I had in myself was ebbing away. In my head, the times Sutton was pleased with my work counted for nothing, whereas his criticisms gained momentum and affected me out of all proportion. If he mislaid a document that I could not find for him I would feel culpable. Everything seemed like my fault.

Then a silly mistake became the catalyst for my collapse.

Sutton was snobbish – he acknowledged it himself, seeing nothing wrong with elitism. When the Queen of Denmark responded to an issue he had dedicated to the Danish Royal collections, he was overjoyed – until he came to the part of her letter that pointed out an error: two captions in one of the articles had been transposed. The mistake had been made during the layout, but we ought to have picked it up on the page proof.

I thought he was going to have a heart attack.

'Vanessa!' he croaked as he banged his stick several times against his desk. I rushed in to see what had happened and he passed me the letter from the Queen.

'You stupid, stupid girl!' he rasped, as I took in the contents.

'How *could* you get this wrong? You have humiliated me in front of the Danish Royal family! The whole of Denmark will be laughing at me!' His face was crimson.

'I'm ... I'm sorry ...' I stammered, feeling quite sick.

I saw no point in blaming Mr Grey, who had designed the page, but I wish now that I had said, 'If you remember, Mr Sutton, you did check the proof as well as myself, and *you* didn't notice the mistake. How am I supposed to tell one Danish castle from another?'

'Well?' Mr Sutton looked furious.

'I'm so sorry,' I said, yet again.

'Is that all you have to say for yourself?'

I stared at a fixed point on the floor.

'You may well blush!' he spluttered. 'I simply can't have these mistakes being made. Now I shall have to write to the Queen personally to explain that I have an idiot for an assistant ...'

'Yes, of course ...'

'Just go home now,' Mr Sutton dismissed me with a wave.

An hour later Steve found me in the bathroom, gingerly stepping into a hot bath.

'You all right? Back home early?' he asked cheerfully.

I didn't meet his eyes. 'Sutton found a mistake in the latest issue, and was really angry,' I muttered. 'Two of the captions got mixed up, and the Queen of Denmark complained ...'

'The Queen of Denmark?'

'Oh, it doesn't matter ...'

'You sound hopeless,' he laughed, and left the bathroom.

I dragged myself to work the following day. No mention of the episode was made, but I didn't feel any better. My sense of failure worsened until I became so anxious about messing up again that I began trying too hard, checking and rechecking things. Weekends were spent recovering, either in bed with a migraine, or feeling wrung out. My stomach was constantly in knots, as were my neck and shoulders. This went on for weeks, months even.

Things hadn't been great with Steve either. He had come back from Paris to live with me in Ben's flat but we had separated for a while after he had slept with someone I had thought a friend. Then we had got back together and moved to the house in North London I had bought with Luisa. Now I felt he was only staying there because he had nowhere else to go.

I could feel that awful, familiar despair growing inside me, more Hissing Serpent than Black Dog, venomous when prodded into life. I tried to kick it away, but there it always was, slithering around after me. I dreaded every day that lay ahead and every sleepless night.

I waited until a weekend when Steve was due to go out for the day to finish a job he was doing. Once he had gone, I tidied and cleaned up. In the previous days I had made sure that all the bills had been paid and that my files were in order. There was nothing left for me to do. One last wipe of the kitchen surfaces.

Then I wrote a note for Steve to find: 'Not exactly Marilyn Monroe, am I?'

I felt so tired, so unglamorous. What I had decided to do had no tragedy about it, it just needed to be done, and then I would be released from dragging myself through yet another day.

I propped up my note by the window of the spotless kitchen. I brought a jug of water and a glass to my bed. I calmly locked our bedroom door. On my bedside table I had the Valium prescribed by my doctor, some migraine medication and a bottle of painkillers. I got into bed.

I'm not sure whether I was fully dressed or still in my nightclothes. I can't even recall the time of day; morning, I think. But I remember sitting up in bed and reaching for the pills. I swallowed a handful of Valium, then all the migraine pills, then a handful of paracetamol, about forty pills in all, maybe less, maybe more. I curled down under the duvet to wait for oblivion, to surrender to sleep. I wanted to feel peaceful. But I was beginning to feel anxious. My heart was racing.

Let's hope this works soon. Get on with it, pills.
I closed my eyes.

I don't know how much time passed but I could hear my name being called from far away.

'Vanessa? Vanessa, can you hear me?'

It was a man's voice, an unfamiliar one. Then another voice, also male. It sounded unhappy. I was drifting in and out of consciousness, but vaguely aware of being carried down the stairs of my house, then the sound of a siren. Then nothing.

I wake, spluttering. Something is in my mouth, a tube. It hurts. I am lying on a table with very bright lights above me. Around me doctors and nurses are shouting, two of them holding my shoulders down as if I might sit up and jump off the bed. My first thoughts are, *What the hell are you doing? Don't rescue me!* But the sounds I want to make will not come out. It is like being in a nightmare that won't let you speak.

Finally the pain and the noise abate. I am wheeled on a trolley to a ward and then helped into a bed. It is a general ward, with a couple of free beds. Opposite is an old lady with closed eyes. She looks dead, her sheets draped over her like a shroud. In the next bed an enormous woman is sitting up staring at me, with an equally large man sitting in the chair beside her. I look away.

A doctor is telling me I am a very lucky young woman.

'We have pumped out your stomach,' he is saying. 'If your boyfriend hadn't come home and raised the alarm, you could easily have died.' He looks very severe.

That was the idea, you brainless man. Am I supposed to be grateful?
I feel very weak. My throat is sore.

'The ambulance men found the empty pill bottles by your bed. Can you remember how many paracetamol you took?'

I shake my head.

'Miss . . .' he pauses to check my name on his notes. 'Nicolson. You do understand that the number of pills you consumed could have caused major organ failure?'

I nod slowly. He doesn't seem to understand. *I want to die.*

'Well,' he sighs. 'Try and rest. Tomorrow morning the psychiatrist on duty will need to speak to you before you are discharged.'

With that, he leaves. Behind him, Steve is hovering, waiting to sit beside me. He looks upset. 'You silly thing,' he says with a sad smile, perching on my bed. He says it with such tenderness that I want to cry.

'I'm sorry,' I whisper.

'I had to kick the bedroom door in. I'd only come home because I'd forgotten something.' On such thin string we hang.

He sits still for a while longer but neither of us speaks. 'I'll see you tomorrow,' I say, turning over. Steve kisses the back of my head and is gone.

Christ, I can't even kill myself properly.

Two pretty nurses on night duty are giggling and whispering about their boyfriends. When I manage to catch their attention to ask for water, they look annoyed. I can sense their scorn as they raise their eyes to each other as if to say, look at her, time waster, now she wants water!

The next morning I am told I will be discharged, but not before meeting with the hospital psychiatrist. I wait for hours. Steve arrives.

'Shall we just leave before he comes? No one will notice,' I say, fed up with hanging around.

'Better not,' says Steve.

Finally the psychiatrist appears, looking flustered.

'May I sit down?' He pulls up a chair without waiting for the answer.

'I need to ask you some questions.'

I nod again.

'I'm doing research into whether suicide runs in families. Has anyone in your family ever taken or attempted to take their own life?'

I pause for a moment. 'There was my mother's first cousin Anna,' I say flatly. 'She killed herself a few years back with an overdose of pills.' I pause while he writes something down.

'Or is that too distant a relative?' As ever, wanting to please.

'No, no,' he seems satisfied with the answer. 'Anyone else?'

'No, nobody else.' I think of my mother telling me she wanted to throw herself off Battersea Bridge when she was unhappily married: 'The only thing stopping me from throwing me off that bridge was you.'

'Not that I know of, anyway.'

It seems the depressive tendency runs in families like a curse, weaving its long thread of despair through the generations. Once one member has broken the taboo of naming it, it makes it more acceptable that other family members will follow suit.

Nori and my mother Luisa grew up in a beautiful villa in Fiesole, just outside Florence, with their extended family: parents, younger brother Gino, their aunt and uncle and four cousins, Maria, Anna, Vannozza and Elena. Luisa felt closest to Anna, born exactly a month before her in November 1920. Gentle, beautiful Anna became a poet, married a dashing and adventurous man, gave birth to two sons and seemed to have everything anyone would wish for. But her life was marked by melancholy. This was attributed to the grief Anna's mother Andreina had suffered while pregnant – Andreina's only son had succumbed to the Spanish flu, the epidemic that spread across Europe after the end of the First World War, and died, aged one year old in 1919.

Anna's depression deepened as she grew older and by her late fifties it was clear that she needed help. She was admitted to a clinic but it was too late. She had decided to commit suicide. The staff did not realize that she was hiding the sleeping pills she was given before bedtime and one night she swallowed them all at once. When I was told this sad news, it did not surprise me. The last time I had seen her was the summer that Minky and I had worked on the stretch of beach she and her husband owned. She had spent the days dressed in black, hiding from the sun, withdrawn from life. 'It was born inside her,' Luisa used to say about Anna, 'this strange longing not to be alive.'

*

Luisa with sister Nori and Anna's son Andrea in the foreground.
'Antecchia', Anna's home near Arezzo, April 1955.

'Mary phoned last night,' Steve said as he drove me home. 'She was very upset when I told her what had happened. She's at Knole and she has invited us for lunch tomorrow.'

Since the Boxing Day trip when I had introduced Steve to my relatives, Mary had become a good friend. But I didn't feel like seeing anyone.

'No, Steve, I can't . . .'

'Come on, it will do you good. She understands, and it's only us. It'll take your mind off things.'

And so the following day, a Bank Holiday Monday, we drove to Knole. I'm not sure what Mary had told her parents, but nobody asked any questions. I felt detached and walled-in, but also peaceful and resigned. No one seemed to mind that I was quiet.

When I returned to work on the Tuesday, Sutton was in a reasonable mood.

'Good morning, Vanessa. I trust you have had a restful weekend?' he said as he came in. He stopped by my desk. 'You look rather pale. Are you feeling unwell?'

'I'm fine, thank you.'

'Ready for work then?'

'Yes, Mr Sutton, of course.'

'Jolly good. Bring me those page proofs that arrived on Friday, will you? And get Mr Grey to make some tea.' He turned on his heels and walked into his office.

2008

I don't want to write the next bit. It's the bit I know best, the bit I have gone over and over in my head. It's like a horror film I don't want to see but one that seems to constantly rewind itself back to the beginning.

So this is it.

It is Monday morning and it's hot and sunny. I walk our dog Dotty with my friend Mary; I go round to my neighbour Victoria to collect the new sunglasses I had left at her house the day before. I come back to find a messy kitchen.

'Can't you *ever* clear up after yourself?' I ask, but Rosa pushes past, muttering something about me being 'stressy'.

She walks out of the kitchen, in a bad mood because Adam went back to his holiday job yesterday afternoon and she is missing him already. As I clean up, I hear her stomping up the stairs and into her room. I am resentfully washing up her cereal bowl when she passes me again dressed in her bikini and flip-flops, a swimming towel over her arm. I look up through the glass above the sink. She has stopped to search for some goggles amongst the detritus on the table by the back door. As she throws everything around, I feel even more exasperated. And then she finds the goggles buried under some scarves and off she goes.

I finish clearing up and then I walk to my study, sit at the desk and write '21 July 2008' on the top of a blank piece of paper. I'm feeling guilty about not having written to Luisa for a while. My glasses are

grubby and I remember that I have a new cleaner spray that I was persuaded to buy when I picked out my sunglasses. I go upstairs to the
bedroom to get it. Before leaving the room, I straighten up the duvet
and open a window.

A girl raises her arms to dive into a swimming pool.

I look out to the garden, struck by the beauty of the day. A cloud-
less blue sky, birds chirruping. A day that promises warmth and
relaxation. I shan't go to London, I think. Normally I leave the gardening to Andrew but I decide that today I shall prune some roses. We
are having a delayed family party on Saturday to celebrate Ellie's
twenty-first birthday. I want the garden to look good before she gets
back from holiday in a few days' time.

As I turn away from the window, the stillness is broken by a terrible sound.

Andrew is shouting, hysterical, stumbling into the house.

'Get an ambulance! Quick! Rosa's had a seizure!'

Something in his voice makes me pick up the telephone without
asking why it's so urgent this time. I dial 999.

'Police? Ambulance?' the voice answers.

'Ambulance.'

The woman on the other end of the phone is asking questions.
Address, postcode, name.

'It's my daughter Rosa.' My voice is surprisingly calm.

'How old is she?'

'Nineteen.'

'What has happened?'

I pause. Some creeping dread makes me feel I don't want to know.
Andrew has disappeared.

'Um, I'm not sure. I'm just going to see . . .'

I run out of the house with the cordless phone, across the garden.

'She must have had a seizure while swimming in our pool,' I say
into the telephone as I'm running. Andrew wouldn't be in such a
panic otherwise.

I go through the gate to the pool and see Rosa laid out on the warm York stone. Andrew is kneeling next to her, looking bewildered. I realize he must have lifted her out of the water, as she is wet. And unconscious.

'My husband found her.' I tell the operator this quite calmly, with no emotion. 'Yes, he has got her out, she is lying by the side.

'Unconscious, yes.'

She asks me something else but the sound is breaking up.

'I can't hear you!' Now I realize I'm shouting.

The woman's voice is unruffled but concerned.

'Do you have a mobile? I can phone you right back.'

Why didn't I think of phoning from my mobile?

I give her the number and race indoors to get it.

I'm back at the pool and Andrew is still sitting there with a blank stare on his face. I look at him, and think, *You fix things. You're supposed to fix this.* His sad, defeated eyes say, I can't, not this time. For a second I realize he knows what I don't want to know, so I push the thought away.

The operator has called me back. 'The paramedics are coming. Don't panic.'

I'm not panicking.

'Now listen to me very carefully. Hold her chin up and pinch her nose, then breath into her mouth. Alternate that with pumping her chest.'

I swallow hard. Got to get it right. I drop the phone and Andrew picks it up as if it weighs a ton. Rosa feels slithery, like a fish. Cold and wet. So pale. Taste of chlorine. Pump her chest, got to get it right. Thirty times, one hundred times. Pump, pump. Pump. Please, please splutter and breathe.

Please, please, please.

I hear a car. I leave Rosa and Andrew and rush out to it, feeling relief that someone more competent than I will be able to take over, someone who knows what they are doing. I see a female paramedic getting medical paraphernalia out of the boot and relax slightly. But she looks so young, and no one else is with her . . .

And now a police car is arriving, followed by an ambulance. Everyone rushes to the pool.

'Move aside, please.'

A policewoman leads Andrew and me away from the pool but I keep trying to peek around the wall of people around my girl. I can't see anything.

'Is that the mother?' I overhear one of the ambulance men asking the paramedic, and she says yes.

'Yes! I'm the mother! She's my daughter!'

'Please, madam, we are doing all we can but you must leave us, could you wait somewhere else?'

It's their turn to pump her chest. Pump, pump, pump.

Andrew and I sit next to each other on a garden bench around the corner from the pool and wait in silence. I don't know what to do. I go back to the house and move from room to room, staring out of the windows, willing time to move backwards so I could be at the point of watching her look for the goggles and say, 'Don't go for a swim, not today, give it a miss . . .'

Why didn't I follow her? Rosa would never allow us to watch her constantly, though we always tried to check, discreetly. Why hadn't I this time?

The silence is broken by a juddering noise overhead and I rush outside again. An air ambulance is landing in the field opposite the house and Rosa is being carried across the garden on a stretcher, wrapped up in the blue towel that an hour ago she was holding in her hand. We are not allowed to travel in the helicopter.

'Do you think you are able to drive to Maidstone hospital?' asks a middle-aged policewoman.

'I feel a bit wobbly,' I answer.

Actually I feel very sick and strange.

Another police officer offers to drive us and we sit in the back of the police car still not speaking, stunned and anxious. When we arrive, we follow the police officer into Accident and Emergency. I notice that he has a gun hanging from a belt around his hips.

The police officer's walkie-talkie keeps crackling but he ignores it.

He is mumbling something to the nurse at reception and she looks past him, straight at us.

'Rosa Davidson's parents?'

We nod. She gives me a look of such compassion that my heart aches.

'Come this way, please.'

The policeman shakes our hands and says goodbye. I thank him for the lift.

'Good luck,' he says.

The nurse leads us to a windowless room with comfy chairs and a telephone.

'Do make any telephone calls you need to.'

Suddenly I don't want to be shown this kindness and consideration. I want to be treated dismissively as if our being there is for nothing particularly important. I have been in this hospital so many times, after Rosa's had bad seizures, and usually we wait for hours in a room full of people trying to get attention. Now I don't want to be separated from the noise and bustle of that waiting room. The silence here is deafening.

Andrew and I move around the room awkwardly, still not speaking to each other.

I stare at the telephone.

'Maybe we should let people know? Ellie? Adam? Your sisters?'

'I'll phone from my mobile.'

And he leaves the room, desperate to escape its oppressive sadness.

I sit down and wonder what to do. My breathing is shallow. There is nothing in my head, just a sort of frozen calm. It's lunchtime. I look in my bag and see one of those energy bars that I keep there in case I should feel suddenly hungry. I open the bar and mechanically munch half of it. I put the half-eaten bar back in my bag and notice tea, instant coffee and water provided on a little tray on the table next to me. I'm staring at the water jug thinking, *And now I must drink*, when there is a knock on the door.

It's the nurse.

'I can take you up to the intensive care unit now, if you'd like to follow me. Oh, where is your husband?'

We walk out the door to look for him, and Andrew is coming towards us, switching his phone off. 'I've left messages for a few people,' he says as he approaches.

We follow the nurse into a lift and then down a corridor. She presses bells, keys in numbers. We are shown another room with a single bed, an armchair, a table with coffee-making paraphernalia. It feels like a bedroom in a cheap bed and breakfast. We are visitors without suitcases.

The nurse says, 'Make yourself comfortable. Someone will be with you shortly,' and she disappears.

Andrew and I still do not speak. It feels to me that should we speak, this nightmare will become real, and I want it to remain a nightmare that we will wake up from.

Another nurse puts her head around the door. She has a jolly, round face.

She comes in, introduces herself. 'Would you like to see Rosa now?'

We wait as she presses the panel to let us into intensive care. We are given a plastic apron and told to wash our hands. We find ourselves in a dimly lit room, a twilight world between life and death. The only sound is of monitors beeping and whirring. There are two patients, an ancient woman to the left, and Rosa, about seventy-five years younger, attached to ventilators and cardiac monitors. Every tube, drip and pump imaginable is attached to her body, helping her to breathe and feed mechanically.

'You can come and see her whenever you like,' the nurse is whispering. 'But if you could go to your room now, I think the doctor wants to speak to you.'

We wait, sitting on the bed. The doctor comes in and pulls a chair up to sit facing us.

'I'm afraid Rosa is very, very ill.'

He has a kind, gentle face but his eyes look tired. He speaks about Rosa's injuries, the water in her lungs and something about her brain and lack of oxygen, and I look at Andrew, who is staring at the doctor with great concentration.

The doctor glances at me and slowly I find my thoughts forming into sentences.

'I'm so sorry, I can't take this in. I just feel like I'm in a dream. I'm going to wake up in a minute.' I try and stifle a nervous, inappropriate giggle.

The doctor says something back but I can't grasp the meaning; it's as if I am watching his mouth open and close with the sound turned down. But I do hear him say, 'We shall have to see what happens overnight. Rosa may make the decision for us. It's up to her now.'

Well that's OK then. Because Rosa is strong, and Rosa wants to live, so Rosa you will fight this, and rally and recover.

Adam arrives, having been driven from his home in Rugby by his brother. We show him the routine: press the buttons, gel on the hands, apron on. My heart lurches as I watch him slump into the chair next to his girlfriend's bed, taking her limp hand in his, whispering words of love and encouragement.

Andrew's sisters appear looking anxious and concerned. I am thankful for their familiar faces in this strange, unfamiliar place. Andrew has managed to reach Ellie who is on holiday in Croatia, and she has booked the next flight home.

Later I persuade all the visitors to go back to our house. I want to stay at the hospital. Andrew hesitates but there isn't room for so many of us in our temporary bedroom. When they leave, I feel a twinge of regret that they have gone and left me alone, but this is replaced by a strange, resigned calm.

I go back to Rosa and sit by her bed. I talk to her softly, saying repeatedly, 'Sorry. Sorry I couldn't save you. Forgive me, I'm sorry. Forgive me.'

She is motionless.

'I love you. We all love you, you can't die. *You must not die.*'

I stroke her arm as I mumble these useless words. I even start praying.

'God, I know you don't really exist, but please if you do, make her well. I'll do anything, anything. I might even start believing in you.'

And then I think, *And if my child does not live, I will know you definitely don't exist.*

At some point I must have fallen asleep. I wake, my head slumped into my arms, leaning on the corner of Rosa's bed. The nurse is checking a drip on the other side.

She sees me stir: 'You all right?'

It takes me a second to remember.

'Oh yes, thank you.'

I have pins and needles in my left arm.

'So what does your daughter do?' says the nurse in her mock-cheerful voice.

Do?

I look miserably at her lifeless body.

'Um, well, she's a student.'

'My neighbour's daughter is a student, she's going to university in September. Really excited by it,' the nurse says chirpily.

'Lovely,' I say automatically, feeling anger flicker in my heart. *Why am I being polite? Why should I care about your stupid neighbour's daughter when mine is lying here?*

The nurse is saying, 'I think you should try and get some rest, I can call you if anything changes.'

I go back to the 'relatives' room' and I climb into the bed, still wearing my clothes. My body feels leaden but my mind is racing, and I lie with my eyes wide open staring into the dark room. I put the bedside light back on and glance at my watch. It's two a.m. I try to eat the other half of that energy bar. I drink water. A maternal voice in my head is telling me to take care of myself so that I can cope, so I can be strong. I must try and sleep a bit, but I keep thinking of Rosa lying on her own, around the corner. I should still be at her side, encouraging her to stay alive. I must get up again.

I'm not sure how long I lie there, half awake, half asleep, thinking I am about to get up, but it's still dark and there is someone knocking at the door. It's the nurse and she is saying, 'I'm sorry, Rosa has taken a turn for the worse, I think maybe you should call your husband.'

I phone Andrew, waking him, telling him to come back immediately. Then I go back to Rosa. She looks the same but the monitors seem to be making more desperate noises, bleep bleep bleep, drrrr.

There are doctors and nurses all around her bed; electrodes are placed on her heart; 'defibrillation', I think it is called.

I stand back, watching, feeling helpless, holding my breath. I'm talking to my daughter in my head. *I gave you life, Rosa, I felt you growing and moving inside me, and now, look at me, I can't do anything, but some miracle has to happen, it just has to, please* . . . I'm grinding my teeth and sending a telepathic order to her heart, *Come alive, come on, beat, come alive, breathe . . . COME ON!*

What happens next? Trying to recall the half hour that follows feels impossible, like attempting to make sense of a missing piece in an otherwise vivid dream. The room, the doctor, the nurses, are all out of focus. I can't see Rosa any longer, she is a shape in a bed surrounded by people. I've lost her. Rosa, come back to me.

I think we are asked to wait next door. We are like obedient children, doing what we're told. Time passes. The door opens and the doctor comes in and sits down on a chair.

Our daughter isn't going to recover. The doctor is saying so. I can see that clearly now. He is so sorry, they did everything they could.

'If she lived she would be severely brain damaged.'

I try and bat away an image of Rosa, so bright, so proud, so tall, so vain, as a broken body slumped in a wheelchair.

We agree to the life support machine that is keeping her artificially alive being turned off. Is that all it is, a switch between life and death? And then – surely it must be later – the doctor is talking about using parts of Rosa's body to help others and I'm saying yes, well at least some good could come of this, while Andrew shakes his head, and we have a little bicker about that.

'I can't deal with this,' he says.

'But it may help someone else?'

His eyes say, 'Why should I care about someone else?', and I almost agree with him.

The doctor leaves and when he returns he tells us that Rosa's heart and lungs and kidneys are too damaged, either because of the water in the lungs or the epilepsy medication in her system. But her eyes may be useable. Andrew winces. I am taken to a telephone to speak to a woman about the removal of the eyes. She keeps explaining the process but I can't concentrate, and really I don't want to know the details.

Just take her eyes and leave us alone.

'I'm so sorry for your loss, Mrs Davidson, but we have to put you through this; it's my duty to make you understand the procedure.'

The conversation is interminable. I feel dizzy. When she has finished at last I put the telephone down and go to the bathroom. I retch and retch, but nothing comes but bile.

Ellie has landed at Gatwick. She arrives a couple of hours later and I watch Andrew from a distance, walking towards her in the hospital car park and giving her a big hug. I see her legs buckling under her and she is virtually dragged towards me, held up by her boyfriend Oli and her father. I embrace her but her body is limp and unresponsive. She is ashen and can't meet my eyes. We manage to get her upstairs to the bedroom by the intensive care unit and we huddle there, as people come and go. All the official things need to be done: papers to be signed, permissions granted, phone calls to be made. Rosa's god-mother Kate arrives at the hospital looking stricken.

And then the nurse with the round face comes in to tell me it is necessary to identify her body.

I have just returned from the 'chapel of rest' where you are laid out. I left you there and I shall never see you again, but I can't let myself stay with that thought, not yet. From now on you will be treated as a body to be disposed of and that is too unbearable to contemplate. The life support machine was switched off exactly five hours ago with our permission. Our permission? I can't believe we gave permission for you to die as if we were agreeing to you going on a school trip.

And then they moved you to that strange place.

I agreed to formally identify you, somebody had to. I go with Ellie and Kate. Andrew remains upstairs in the little room next to intensive care that has been our home for the last twenty-four hours. He says he cannot come. He covers his face with his hands as he says that.

A middle-aged woman, possibly a nurse or someone official, leads the way into a small, claustrophobic room. In the centre is a screen with a kind of window covered by a curtain. For a second my mind wanders to the thought of those bits of cloth covering plaques in new buildings before they are declared open. I am invited to draw back the curtain and as I do so you appear framed like a three-dimensional hologram set against a dark background.

The woman says, 'I'm sorry to have to ask, but can you confirm that this is your daughter?'

And I nod, 'Yes, yes, it is,' although the nod comes out like a shaking of the head, because I want to say no, no it isn't.

Ellie, Kate and I stare at this bizarre vision. 'Could I see her properly?' I ask. It is as if you belong to the hospital now.

'Yes, of course.' And the woman leads us around the corner into the ante-room where you are laid out with a purple satin drape covering you from the neck down. It looks slightly grotesque. I am thinking, What are you doing here, Rosa, in this sepulchral scene? What have they done to you? Laid out like a twenty-first-century version of a Renaissance tomb, your features are carved in a bad imitation of marble. It is you and not you; you are there but you are not there.

There is a slight ringing in my ears like I used to get as a child when I was going to faint. Then the nausea is back, and the tightness in my chest. I have to move. I go right up to your body in slow motion, as if wading through a swamp. Up very close. I am trying to fix this image in my memory, for despite the feeling of unreality, I am only too aware that this will be the last time I shall see you in real, human form and not conjured up in ghostly dreams.

Your hair is brown and matted, like the dry but unwashed hair of a swimmer. Your eyes are closed, a purple hue around the eyelids. Your skin is sallow, a slightly yellow-grey complexion. Most striking are the very white lips, a bluish tinge to the outline.

I imagine a portrait painter mixing the colours, trying to fix this likeness on to a blank canvas. I think of your teenage experiments with make-up, when you would choose strange colours for your lips and eyes. I scrutinize every detail of your face as I did when I had just given birth and was getting to know my new child. I try to remember the feel of you, the smell of you, as you were last week, as you were as a baby, as a little girl. But at the same

time I hold back, remaining an observer; I cannot afford to let myself sense
anything with my heart, for if I do I will collapse.

It is time to leave.

So I lean down and gently kiss you on the forehead for the last time.
Strangely, I feel self-conscious, as if I have seen an actor do this in a film. Struck
by the coldness of your skin, the coldness of stone against my lips, I say goodbye.

Three months after Rosa's death I went to Florence. Luisa had said
she didn't feel up to coming to the cremation or even to the memorial service we held six weeks later. I knew that Luisa didn't 'do'
funerals; she has avoided them since her own mother's as she finds
them too distressing. I had anticipated her decision, and met it with
some relief. We planned a service that reflected Rosa's age and interests and I didn't want to have to worry about Luisa's disapproval of the
way we chose to celebrate her life. Ellie put together a sequence of
photographs of her sister to some music, and Adam and Rosa's university friends did the same, adding grainy film of her having fun. 'It's
what we used to play to get us into the mood to go out,' Adam said to
explain the energetic soundtrack. I was touched by this. But I was sure
Luisa would have considered the music 'inappropriate' for a church
service and might upset us by making her dissatisfaction clear. Most of
all, I could not face having to take care of her – it was hard enough
having to look after myself, and present a front of dignified grief. As
with Ben's death, I felt that if I allowed myself to feel too much, I
would disintegrate, and the loss of control would be awkward for me
and everyone else.

I arrived at Luisa's flat and she made no mention of recent events.
I slept in my old bedroom, the one my girls used to stay in when we
visited their grandmother. The single bed felt small and lonely, and I
began wondering why I had come.

The next morning Luisa joined me in the kitchen while I was finishing breakfast. She sat down opposite me and suddenly announced,
'I'm not going to be able to come and stay with you in England this
Christmas, I am too frail for the journey. I hope the four of you will
come and stay here instead.'

Four of us? How could she have forgotten? I looked at her with horror.

'The *four* of us? Rosa is *dead*!' I shouted, tears pricking my eyes.

Neither of us budged from our seats. I began sobbing into my hands. After a minute Luisa began to tell me about the time she had been in London after the war and was having tea at the Ritz.

'What are you talking about?' I wanted to scream through my tears.

'... and I saw this young man at the next table. He was handsome and well dressed, and suddenly he made a terrible noise and fell off his chair ...' She paused.

Oh no, I see what you are getting to. He must have been having a seizure.

'... and he lay on the ground making strange movements and noises and everyone looked embarrassed and ignored him and then I left.' Again she paused, as I continued crying. 'So you see, although it's terrible for those who are left behind, it would have been much worse for Rosa as she got older and people didn't understand.'

No, it's you, Mummy, who doesn't understand.

But I didn't say that. I wiped my eyes with the back of my hand and said, 'I'm going out.'

I didn't know where I was heading. I walked through the centre of Florence, pushing through groups of tourists, young people nattering into their mobile phones, workers on their way to their mid-morning espresso break, young mums holding their children's hands. Girls who reminded me of Rosa were everywhere, and as I walked I tried to recall Rosamond Lehmann's words written after the death of her own daughter, words that had struck me so powerfully: 'I had to learn, and relearn, and learn again day after day, week after week, month after month, that I was truly left behind to crawl on and on the best I could, in external exile, through the stone streets full of other people's daughters.'*

I walked across the city, past the Cathedral and the smart shops of the Via Tornabuoni, over the Ponte Vecchio and to the wide square of Piazza Pitti. I was near the main entrance of the Boboli Gardens,

---

* Rosamond Lehmann, *The Swan in the Evening: Fragments of an Inner Life*, Virago, 1982.

where I used to play as a child. At the ticket booth for the Pitti Palace, I said in Italian that I wanted to go into Boboli.

'Ten Euro,' the young woman answered in a bad English accent, not looking up from her magazine.

'*Dieci Euro?*' I retorted in my best Florentine voice, and continued in Italian, '*Ma non voglio visitare il Palazzo, voglio solo stare nei giardini per mezz'ora.*'

The girl swivelled her eyes away from the magazine to give me a withering look.

I tried again. 'I only want to pop into the gardens and I'm not interested in going into the Pitti Palace. As a child I used to live opposite the other garden entrance and went in every day for free!'

'How long ago was *that*?' she answered, as if I were more ancient than the garden itself.

I held her gaze for a few seconds, then turned and walked down across the square and into the Via Romana, past the antique shops and bars, past the high wall with the line that indicates where the 1966 flood reached. *How much smarter this area is now*, I thought, *compared to the 1960s when I lived here*. Number 34 still had the '*Pensione Annalena*' sign attached to the wall, but the battered front door had been replaced by a shiny new mahogany one. I noticed it was ajar and I sneaked in to have a look. I walked across the tiled floor, through the vestibule and the glass doors, into the main hall with the stone stairs that once took us up to our daily visits to the dining room of the Pensione.

My God, that smell of damp and plaster. I felt eight years old again.

An old man was coming down the stairs and I nodded, '*Buongiorno*', and quickly left, back into Via Romana. Then I noticed the cafe I used to go to with Nonna to buy ice cream, the one owned by an old man who piled the cone with extra chocolate because he knew how much I loved it.

I went in. A group of middle-aged men were sitting at a table discussing football. They don't sell ice cream there any more.

'*Un cappucino per favore,*' I asked the young man behind the bar, and when he turned back from the Gaggia machine to place the cup on its saucer in front of me, I found myself saying something chatty along the lines of how strange it was for me to be here, as I grew up in this street in the 1960s, and how my Nonna would bring me here for ice cream, my *cioccolato e limone*. The young man did not respond. Not a smile, not a polite 'oh really?' Not an 'Mmm' of acknowledgement. He did not even bother to look up at me.

The familiar surge of pain and rage was welling up, from chest to throat. Tears spilled from my eyes like water from a split pipe. I gulped down the coffee and threw some change onto the counter, ran out of the bar and up the road and into the first church I could see, ironically called San Felice ('Saint Happiness'), where I slumped into a pew and wept in the darkness, unnoticed (or perhaps ignored) by the two old women busy replacing the dead flowers with new blooms.

By the time I arrived back at Horserace, autumn was established. Floundering, not knowing how to be, in my silent, sad house, I searched for help wherever I could find it – Reiki, massage, therapy – but I could not hold on to any peace. I even went to a psychic, who told me that Rosa was angry with me for taking her eyes. I shivered. How could this woman know about her eyes? Then she said Rosa was standing behind me with her hand on my shoulder. I turned around quickly, trying to catch hold of her before she disappeared.

I decided to join a support group for bereaved mothers. The host had lost her eighteen-year-old daughter in a car accident that had killed both the girl and the teenage boy travelling with her. I was the first to arrive, clutching a wilting posy of flowers. What a wretched bunch we were, drinking tea or was it wine, telling each other the stories of our losses: a suicide by hanging, a murder by a stalker, a car accident, a misdiagnosed illness. One large woman said nothing at all but slowly munched through the box of chocolates placed in front of her. Overwhelmed by the torment and anger in that room, I sobbed and ranted all the way home in the privacy of my car.

I went to collect Rosa's ashes with my friend Julia. In front of the funeral parlour, Julia put her hand on my arm protectively.

'Are you sure you're ready for this?'

'Yes, of course, it needs to be done.'

I had written a list of errands that morning, before setting off to the local town: Milk, Bread, Eggs, Vegetables, Pay newspaper bill, Collect Rosa's ashes.

'Maybe you should come here with Andrew?'

'It's fine,' I said decisively as we walked through the door.

'Hello, I've come to collect Rosa's ashes,' I greeted the woman who came forward to help us.

She asked us to wait and reappeared five minutes later with a large, maroon carrier bag. I smiled stiffly as she handed it to me.

'It's surprisingly heavy, must be the lead in the casket,' I said lightly and then as I turned to walk through the door that Julia had opened for me, I felt my legs becoming unsteady.

I leant against a wall in the street, trying to catch my breath, but it would not come. My hands were tingling, my chest was tight, I could not breathe. Help! My breath seemed to be stuck in my throat and unable to reach my lungs. It made me feel strange, and the stranger I felt, the more I panicked. I managed to tell Julia that another friend lived close by, and we staggered over there and Pip wrapped me in a blanket and brought me tea as I lay on her sofa and slowly recovered. An hour later I was strapping the casket into the back seat of the car, laughing hysterically because it reminded me of strapping Rosa in when she was a toddler.

I don't know why I found this funny.

We buried your ashes yesterday. A small group of those who loved you most set off from home. Dad wanted to walk the wicker casket down through the orchard. You told me once that you would like to do that walk to the church on your wedding day, in a procession through the apple blossom. But rather than in a wedding dress, you were in a casket, and the procession was subdued instead of celebratory. Dad was so shaky, he clung on to the casket as if it were giving him support.

When we got to the cemetery, climbing through the gap in the orchard hedge, we met the vicar all dressed in his robes. He passed around the 'order of service' and I noticed the mistake immediately – your date of death was given as 2009 rather than 2008. When I pointed this out, the poor Reverend looked as if he wanted the ground to swallow him up, he was so mortified. But I tried to reassure him that at this point it really didn't matter.

We stood around the hole in the ground, a tearful group of people who miss you. When it came to putting the casket into the earth, Dad looked so distraught that I took it gently out of his arms. I knelt onto the grass, placing it deep into the earthy space. I didn't feel anything except a numb ache that almost seemed to belong to somebody else. It was if the real me had floated off somewhere to watch myself.

The others have all gone back to their lives now, to their families and their jobs. Today I walked to the cemetery by myself. The lovely flowers everyone brought were still there and the parish warden had put up a temporary plaque to mark the spot.

ROSA ILARIA NICOLSON DAVIDSON
Died 22 July 2008
Aged 19 years

It was the '19 years' that hit me, the reality of how young you were, in this place surrounded by memorials to people so old. What would you have been like at thirty? Fifty? Seventy? Ninety? How dare fate rob you of all those years, your future? Our future?

The afternoon was balmy and still. I lay down on the ground next to the grave, as if on a bed next to you. All I wanted was to go to sleep and sink down through the freshly dug lid of grass, down to where you are. And stay there. I rolled over so that I was lying face down, right over the place that had been open twenty-four hours before. I could smell the grass and feel the mud in my nose and in my mouth, and then I sat up and the howl came, like the howl of an animal, deep from within. I let it resonate around the tombstones. I didn't care if anyone heard me, I just wanted you to hear me, calling through that layer of earth, calling down, trying to reach you.

It's Christmas and I can't bear it – the rituals, the box under the stairs with the tree decorations and Rosa's stocking. I sit on the floor holding the pretty label I had decorated, saved from last year – 'To Rosa, all my love Mum' – until my tears smudge the ink. Two distant acquaintances, unaware of what has happened, send cards addressed to all four of us, but it is strangely comforting that as far as they are concerned Rosa still exists.

I try and create the Christmas she loved, the tree and the turkey, the crackers and paper hats and the games after lunch. Andrew's sister Caroline and her family are with us and we all make an effort, but the joy has gone. We can pretend it's fun, but it isn't, at least not for me.

As soon as the festivities are over I take a plane to a retreat in Kerala. I go to yoga and meditation sessions. I cry a great deal in a bedroom with a large fan and a fluorescent strip of light across the ceiling. A strange-looking creature – I think it's a gecko – keeps me company. One day I walk the length of a beach and sit down on the sand. I want to walk into the sea and not come out, to let the current swallow me and take me away from this pain. I sit there for a long time, transfixed by the waves reaching out towards me and then retreating, calling me into the sea, then leaving me be. I remain so long in the same position that my legs go numb.

I have little sense of time, but as the hours pass I remember Ben. For years I found it hard to walk past his favourite Italian restaurant in Notting Hill Gate. It was a dark and cavernous place with large raffia-covered Chianti bottles that served as candleholders and fading prints of Naples on the walls. Whenever he went there, the owner would welcome him at the door with outstretched arms, '*Ah, Mista Neecolson!*' and lead him to the same table every time, facing the window.

We had an arrangement whereby I could turn up at one o'clock if I happened to be around on a Sunday and have lunch with him.

'Signorina, come in, your father he will be so 'appy to see you!' the waiter would say as he pointed to the figure hidden behind a large Sunday newspaper.

The newspaper would be lowered as I approached.

'Hello, Vaness. Steak?'

And I would take a seat opposite, smiling.

'Yes, please.'

2014

Six years have passed since Rosa's death and in many ways it feels like a long time, dragging on and on; in another sense it seems hardly any time at all. The loss of her still regularly catches me off guard and every single morning when I wake I crave her return.

I may not appear changed, but I know I am. I see old friends, and very occasionally make a connection with someone new. I follow Ellie's life with love and admiration. She has many good friends and is settled in London with an interesting job in the art world. On the third of May she sends me texts saying 'Happy Birthday to Rosa'. She is great company and I applaud her determination to grasp what life has to offer, to live every day to the full. That is how it should be but it can't always be easy for her. She carries the same little tattoo once worn by Rosa – a rose motif designed by Adam. We carved it on to our girl's tombstone, and Ellie and Andrew had it copied on to themselves.

Maybe it is my age, but I find it hard to look forward – to 'move on' – that infuriating phrase intended to comfort the bereaved. What am I supposed to move on to? How best distract myself? Why be social when I don't want to be? Large gatherings are hard work, so I tend to avoid them. I have always found them difficult. The standing around, the not knowing what to wear, the self-consciousness of what do I say, how do I belong. The dread of being bored or boring.

It's much worse now. 'What do you do?' people ask. What do I do

305

now? I've just written a memoir. What is it about? It's about loss and motherhood, and if they press me I might add, it's about coming from an unusual, privileged background but craving an ordinary family life, and how this was sabotaged by my daughter's death. I don't normally say that, of course, unless the person seems particularly sympathetic. No, instead I say, 'I used to be an art historian. What do you do?'

Then there is the question about children. That's the one that always seems to come up, sometimes even before 'Where do you live?' and 'What do you do?'

I am practised at that one. 'I have a daughter called Ellie,' I say, 'who lives and works in London.' Do I leave it there, denying Rosa's existence? I have never been able to do that. 'I also had a younger daughter,' I continue, 'but she died a few years ago.' And then I witness the intake of breath, the mumbled 'I'm sorry', or the quick change of subject, 'Oh dear ... um, and where do you live?' Or the revelation, given slightly too quickly, that they too have suffered a tragedy – 'my brother died', 'my friend/sister/husband has just been diagnosed with cancer ...' – and we nod sympathetically at one another until they remember they 'must just say hello to James over there', and I am left alone, the spectre at the feast.

So it was with some trepidation that last summer I accepted an invitation from my cousin Robert, now Lord Sackville, and his wife Jane, to a mid-summer party at Knole. But I said to Andrew – who is as bad as I am – 'We can't keep hiding away.'

Everything was going well. I found myself sitting between Robert and a friendly and intelligent vicar, in the beautiful Colonnade room. I only found out later that my fellow guest was a man of God. 'I'm not going to tell you what I do,' he said at the beginning of the evening, 'not yet.' We talked about his love of Florence, and he did ask me about my children. When I said the line about 'my younger daughter', he didn't change the subject. 'Tell me about her,' he said gently. And I described her quirky character, her lithe beauty, the challenges she overcame, the sadness of losing her. He listened with attention, and I was grateful for the space he gave me to bring her alive.

We finished our meal. People began moving around to talk to

others. The vicar got up, and I smiled at the woman now seated closest to me. Blonde, middle-aged, wearing pearls and a floral dress. She seemed rather drunk. We exchanged the usual pleasantries. How did I know Robert, where did I live?

'So do you have children?' she slurred, leaning over, and I gave my usual response, quickly trying to change the subject as soon as I had made my revelation. I didn't want to talk about Rosa to her.

She mumbled something else that I could not hear.

'Sorry?' I asked.

She repeated whatever it was. The room was filled with the noise of laughter and conversation.

'Sorry, I still didn't catch that,' I repeated.

Again, she said something.

Not wishing to say 'Sorry?' for a third time, I simply smiled and looked away.

'I don't think you heard what I said ...' she insisted.

'You're right, I'm sorry ...'

'I said,' and now she was shouting, *'you seem remarkably unaffected by grief.'*

For a second I looked at her in disbelief. And then I laughed, bitterly.

So Rosa, that's the end of our story.

Here I am still at Horserace, the house I both love and hate, where you were conceived and where you died. The place continues to fall apart, soaking up whatever money we throw at it, endlessly repairing its rotting windows, micey attic, damp walls. But if you came home today you would find little changed. You might wonder why Dotty wasn't welcoming you with her wagging tail and miss Dipstick slinking past your legs. But everything else is much the same. The photo of you and Ellie cuddling Dad on a rainy holiday in Le Touquet is there, stuck on the pinboard by the fridge; the one of us walking along the breezy beach sits framed in the sitting room.

We are always talking about leaving, but I am sure we shall be here for a very long time.

Rosa walking ahead.

ACKNOWLEDGEMENTS

I am hugely indebted to Sigrid Rausing for her belief in this book, for her unwavering support and her transformational editing suggestions. I would also like to give special thanks to copy-editor Sarah Bance, as well as Christine Lo, Sarah Wasley, Ka Bradley, Aidan O'Neill and Sara D'Arcy at Granta; my agent Andrew Lownie, and to David Waller for introducing me to him; to Lennie Goodings, Jemima Hunt, Shelley Weiner and Caroline Natzler for editorial suggestions; to those in the writing groups I attended, particularly Jane Metter and Ian Pert who heard me read early versions, listened with attention and would not let me give up. Thank you all for your contributions.

Thanks to Adam Nicolson for lending me family correspondence, to Juliet Nicolson for her positive encouragement over this project, and apologies to Rebecca Nicolson for writing more about the family! I am thankful to Mary Sackville-West and her mother Bridget for their warm support over the years and grateful to Francesco Vertova and Malù Vertova for discussions about the Italian side of my family; thanks too go to my sisters-in-law Diana Tettmar and Caroline Freedman and their children.

I am grateful to Catherine Fox for helping me to make sense of it all and also thanks to Chrissy Richman.

I am so lucky to have and to have had some good friends who have listened to my worries about this project over half a decade, or simply been there for me at one time or another. I would like to thank my second family, Briony Fer (Minky), her husband Adrian Forty and their daughters Cesca and Lil; Alison Turnbull, Alister Warman, Ed Gilbert, Sarah and Jeremy Aynsley, Caroline Barrie, Mary and Trevor Kain, Hilary Wilce, Alison Waters, Ian Ruffin, Corinne Corbett-Thompson, Dee Sheldrake, Ian and Victoria Hislop, Chris and Cathy Hughes, Andrea Collett, Shaun McDonagh, Julia Eisner, Steve Brown, Kate and Charlie Boxer, Sue Saunders, Helen Jones, Paul Corcoran, Pat Brown, Liz Irwin, Julia Warr, Martin Brierley, Sara Scott, Rufus Olins, Clare Reynolds, Selma and John Pickup, Kathy and Matthew Wolfman, Linde Wotton, Pip Gill, Kate and Clive Crook, Victoria Bathurst, Sue Brooks, Alkarim Jivani, Debbie Rix, Debbie Doole, Ginny McIntyre, Sylvie Herold, Kathy Fox, Julie and Roland Comet, Janet Alden-Smith, Jeremy and Shirley Nelson, Clare and David Hindmarsh, Lee Rankin, Siobhan Atherley, Julie Simpson, Jenny Boswell, Tessa Chisholm, Julian and Anne-Marie Berger, Kerena Mond, Mary Rose Thompson, Joanna Terry, Elsbeth and Ged Edmondsen, Vanessa Herringshaw, Emily Best-Shaw, Nick and Sarah Fer, Jane Howard. I would like to remember Joanne Sonn, my father's assistant in the 1970s, who sadly died on 4 May 2014.

Thank you to the bereaved and courageous mothers who offered me friendship and were willing to share their stories with me: Anne Coombe-Jones, Jenny Shepherd, Honey Denny, Alison Donelan, Margaret Firminger and my old school friend Lydia Biggie.

Thank you to Rosa's friends too: to Adam Brazier for giving her so much happiness in the last ten months of her life, to Sarah Sheldrake for singing her beautiful song at the funeral, to Sophie Wotton, Stephanie Rankin, Agnes Reeve and Jenny Gerard-Pearse (and their mothers), to Stephanie Lucas for sticking up for her at primary school, to Owen Stanfield, Joe Rantor and Laura Hall for friendship at university. And to Rosa's au pair Anja Kunz, who keeps in touch.

I owe more than I can say to my husband Andrew, who has helped me enormously with his insightful reading of this memoir and his editing skills. Thanks for sticking by me. And a big thank you to our daughter Ellie for allowing me to write about her sister and their childhood.

There is another important person I need to acknowledge. I have asked myself many times, 'To whom am I addressing this memoir, what am I writing it for?' At first I thought it was for Rosa, the daughter who would never be able to hear my story. But as I conclude, the truth comes to me with more clarity. This book has been written for another significant person who cannot hear: for my niney-four-year-old mother, who was unaware of me writing it. Why didn't I tell her? For fear of upsetting her, and for not wishing to dredge up painful memories she would rather forget. Because of her insistence on her own truth and her anger at anyone who contradicts it; for the shame I feel in treacherously revealing our family's 'dirty linen' to illustrate my story. But I needed to give words to the things she will not speak about.

I don't know, Luisa, if you will ever read these lines. I don't have the courage to tell you about them. But if you come across the book and reach the end of it, please believe that in spite of our past arguments and misunderstandings, I care about you and do not want to cause you unnecessary distress. My hope is that this book will enable you to better understand me and your granddaughter Rosa in our good and bad, our sad and mad entirety, even if you may not find it in your heart to forgive us. Ti voglio bene.